THE HISTORY THIEVES

IAN COBAIN was born in Liverpool in 1960. He has been a journalist since the early 1980s and is currently an investigative reporter with the *Guardian*. He has won a number of awards for his journalism, including the Martha Gellhorn Prize and the Paul Foot Award. He has also won several Amnesty International media awards. His first book, *Cruel Britannia* (Portobello, 2012), won the Paddy Power Total Politics Award for Debut Political Book of the Year.

'An enjoyable account of Britain's obsession with official secrecy' Chris Mullin, 'Books of the Year', *Observer*

'Meticulously researched and immensely readable' *Irish Times*

'Important and highly readable . . . Our only weapon against those Orwell used to call "the striped-trousered ones who rule" is to expose and deride them – a job Ian Cobain does most effectively' Geoffrey Robertson QC

'Cobain's excellent book teaches us both the history of [the government's] secretive snooping, and how it imperils us all today' Clive Stafford Smith

'This is a very important book. Essential reading' Mark Curtis, author of *Secret Affairs: Britain's Collusion with Radical Islam*

'Cobain's chilling book [is] more vital now than ever . . . [it] deserves to change the way we see our recent past' *Daily Mail*

'Cobain's easy prose turns potentially dry subject matter into an intriguing set of stories . . . If so much of their history is concealed, the British are not who they think they are' *New Internationalist*

Also by Ian Cobain

Cruel Britannia: A Secret History of Torture

Ian Cobain

The History Thieves

Secrets, Lies and the Shaping
of a Modern Nation

Portobello
BOOKS

First published in Great Britain by Portobello Books 2016
This paperback edition published by Portobello Books 2017

Portobello Books
12 Addison Avenue
London
W11 4QR

A CIP catalogue record is available from the British Library

9 8 7 6 5 4 3 2 1

ISBN 978 1 84627 585 2 (paperback)
ISBN 978 1 84627 584 5 (ebook)

Typeset in Bembo by Avon DataSet, Bidford on Avon, Warwickshire

Printed and bound by CPI Group (UK) Ltd, Croydon, CR0 4YY

In memory of Peggy Cobain

Contents

Acronyms and Abbreviations

CID	Criminal Investigation Department
CMP	Closed Material Procedure
FCO	Foreign and Colonial Office
FOI	Freedom of Information
FRU	Force Research Unit
GC&CS	Government Code and Cypher School
GCHQ	Government Communications Headquarters
HET	Historical Enquiries Team
IRA	Irish Republican Army
IPT	Investigatory Powers Tribunal
IWM	Imperial War Museum
JIC	Joint Intelligence Committee
MI5	Directorate of Military Intelligence, Section 5
MI6	Directorate of Military Intelligence, Section 6
MOD	Ministry of Defence
MRF	Military Reaction Force
NSA	National Security Agency
PDRY	The People's Democratic Republic of Yemen
PII	Public Interest Immunity
PIRA	Provisional Irish Republican Army
RAF	Royal Air Force
RUC	Royal Ulster Constabulary
SIAC	Special Immigration Appeals Commission
Sigint	Signals Intelligence
TNA	The National Archives
UDA	Ulster Defence Association
UDR	Ulster Defence Regiment
UVF	Ulster Volunteer Force

Introduction

One Saturday morning in the summer of 2013, two British government intelligence officials called at the offices of the *Guardian* in London to oversee the destruction of several of the news organisation's computers.

The hard drives of those computers held a mass of documents from the UK signals intelligence agency, the Government Communications Headquarters, and its US partner, the National Security Agency. There were thousands of documents, many thousands, and they detailed the way in which the two agencies had attempted – and largely succeeded – in their ingenious attempts to capture the details of every digital communication that was being sent or received by anyone, anywhere, at any time.

Before that morning's visit the *Guardian* had been under threat: if the two government officials were not permitted to witness the complete destruction of the hard drives, senior journalists could face prosecution under the Official Secrets Act, or an injunction, or both.

It appeared to be an extraordinarily pointless gesture. The *Guardian* had already told the government's most senior official, the Cabinet Secretary, that there were copies of the documents in the United States, and that he would be unable to prevent American news organisations from reporting on their contents.

But the visitors were not to be deterred. One had arrived

with a rucksack from which he took a machine resembling a microwave oven. It was a degausser, he said, a device that destroyed magnetic fields. Once the hard drives had been drilled and hacked with angle-grinders, the broken pieces were fed into it.

The machine was switched on, and after a few moments, much to the satisfaction of the two watching intelligence officials, it made a loud pop.

It is sometimes argued that government secrecy and democracy are incompatible: that access to information must be granted in order to hold governments to account. Access is said to be associated with knowledge and the freedom of ideas; it is hailed as a way of making sure that political leaders represent the interests of those they lead. Secrecy, meanwhile, is said to be deployed to preserve exclusivity and mystique, and in order to conceal blunders.

Many of those engaged in the day-to-day business of government dismiss this as bunkum. According to those who actually govern, good government will always, from time to time, be closed government.

And no doubt they are correct. It is not difficult to see that a degree of secrecy is required by government. A high degree must always surround questions of the state's military capabilities, for example, both during war and at times of peace. And those who are responsible for preserving collective security at times of terrorist threat expect, understandably, to be able go about their business without fear that their effectiveness will be undermined through disclosure.

Some confidential space must also exist within which policy may be formulated: civil servants and other policy advisors expect to be able to give good and robust advice without fear of embarrassment or censure as a result of the publication of that advice.

But where should the limits be drawn? For example, is it legitimate for a democracy to go to war without the public being consulted, or informed? Is it acceptable for a government to covertly gather and store data on its citizens, and to share that data with foreign powers? And how should we ensure that the limits are observed? Should the secret state be publicly accountable? Or should the mechanisms of political oversight of the security and intelligence agencies, as well as their operations, be hidden from public view? How is the balance between accountability of government and the frankness of discussion within government to be weighed? Should policy-makers and advisors be accountable to the present, or to history? And how much of the remaining, everyday business of government actually needs to be concealed from the public?

These are questions with which every government has to contend. In 1946, for example, Sir Edward Bridges, who had served as Cabinet Secretary throughout the Second World War, offered a succinct view of that which governments might properly wish to keep from the public. In May that year, Bridges advised the Prime Minister, Clement Attlee, on the restrictions that might be imposed on wartime ministers who wished to publish their memoirs. 'In the international sphere,' he wrote, restrictions ought to be placed on 'information whose disclosure would be injurious to us in our relations with other nations, including information which would be of value to a potential enemy.' Within the UK, Bridges suggested that restrictions should be placed on disclosures that would be 'destructive' of the confidential relationships between government ministers, and between ministers and their advisors.

Fifty years later, Tony Blair attempted – briefly – to set New Labour apart from governments that had come before by arguing for transparency within Whitehall, and putting into motion the legislation that should have created one of the world's most progressive freedom of information regimes.

In spite of Bridges' admonitions and Blair's campaign pledges, the application of official secrecy in Britain has, for the past couple of centuries at least, gone far beyond that which is required for the safe and secure business of government. Official secrecy is not merely rooted in the preferences and practices of those in government. It is integral to public life. Britain is not a nation where official information is merely kept closed on occasion and handled with care: it is a nation where a culture of secrecy runs wide and deep.

One close observer of the British state, Peter Hennessy, has described secrecy as being as much a part of Britain's landscape as the Cotswolds: 'It goes with the grain of our society. Its curtailment, not its continuity, would be aberrational.'

Another, the former Cabinet minister Richard Crossman, observed in 1971 that 'secretiveness is the real English disease and in particular the chronic ailment of British government'. Responsibility for this, Crossman suggested, lay in Whitehall's tendency to resent the prying eyes of journalists, the historian's hunger for knowledge, and even the curiosity of the public. 'One result of this secrecy is to make the British electorate feel it is being deliberately kept in the dark and increasingly to suspect the very worst of its rulers; another is to ensure that the House of Commons is the worst informed legislature in the world.'

Whether one sees the phenomenon in terms of topography, like Hennessy, or pathology, like Crossman, there can be no argument that it is characteristic of Britain; that it is a pervasive feature of British political life and the wider culture of the nation. And that it has consequences – for our perceptions of the world around us, and for our understanding of ourselves.

Any questions about ourselves, our communities or our nations invariably lead at some point to the past.

It is for this reason that genealogy has enjoyed great popularity in recent years: anyone who has looked into the history of his or her own family – through the examination of birth, death and marriage certificates, by unearthing census and electoral records, by reading letters consigned for years to lofts and bottom drawers, or through gentle conversations with older relatives – is attempting to uncover new truths about who they are and where they have come from.

Some of those truths may be comforting; others perhaps will be disturbing. The inquirer is likely to discover that their family, like any other, is a group of people who tell each other stories, and that sometimes those stories are not entirely true. The family can be a place of secrets and lies, as well as truths, and a clearer understanding of the facts of family can be unsettling: it can shake an individual's sense of identity.

In much the same way, our sense of who we are as a nation appears at times to rest largely upon the stories that we tell ourselves, one generation passing on the folk's lore to the next. And yet, as long as public administration in Britain remains such a private affair, hidden carefully from view, we may misunderstand such fundamental matters as our reasons for going to war, our relationship with foreign states and peoples, and the way that justice has been pursued at home and abroad. As long as official secrecy can be deployed in a manner that may create an information vacuum, such a space may be filled with myths and falsehoods. And as long as a culture of secrecy prevails, and so much of our history is concealed, it may be that we are not quite who we think we are.

This book explores the way in which Britain's culture of secrecy has been more than 200 years in the making. In the early nineteenth century it rested upon the supposedly gentlemanly virtues of 'discretion', or 'reserve' or 'reticence' – all euphemisms for secrecy. Later that century it was reinforced through statute as a consequence of a period of growth of government and a rapid expansion of the clerical classes. For the most part, these newly recruited clerks were poorly paid young men who did not share ties of family, schooling and class with their political and civil service masters, and all too frequently they were tempted by the rewards to be made from transactions with a burgeoning newspaper industry that lived and breathed through disclosure.

The culture of secrecy has been buttressed by five Official Secrets Acts. As a consequence of Section 2 of the 1911 Act, for most of the last century Britain was a place where the unauthorised disclosure of any official information, no matter how trivial, was an offence punishable by up to two years' imprisonment. It is a law that weighed heavily on successive generations of public servants, and it still informs some of the thinking of the civil service, more than a quarter of a century after its repeal.

In addition to the Official Secrets Acts there are, according to some estimates, around a hundred other statutes that forbid the disclosure of information. There are extensive controls in the United Kingdom over the disclosure of information about government business, over historical documents, over military affairs and over the work of the courts. There is no constitutional right to free speech, as in the United States, although there is a degree of protection in domestic and European law. Challenges to such secrecy are rare, partly because, as Peter Hennessy says, we are so accustomed to it – it goes with the grain of our society – and partly because there is frequently a double confidentiality at work, whereby nothing is more carefully concealed than the extent to which concealment is being practised.

An examination of the secrecy that has been applied during military operations over the past seventy years leads to the conclusion that it is the British public as much as the enemy that has been confused, misled and, sometimes, kept in complete ignorance as the country has fought one small war after another.

Who now, for example, recalls the role that the British played in 1945 in starting the war against the Việt Minh in Vietnam – on behalf of the French – by flying an entire division of troops to the country, and by then rearming Japanese prisoners of war and compelling them to fight the Vietnamese while under British command? Or the four-year war that the British led against Indonesia in the 1960s, very often on Indonesian territory? Or the eleven-year Cold War counter-insurgency operation in Oman in the '60s and '70s, a war so secret that it remained unreported for more than six years, with many in the British military even unaware that it was being fought?

How many British people are aware that not a year has passed since at least 1914 when their forces have not been fighting somewhere or other around the world, and that the British are unique in this regard?

It is said that those who cannot remember the past are condemned to repeat it. But what is to be the fate of those who cannot forget their nation's recent military history because they never knew it in the first place? How are they to make sense of Britain's role within the world, and its relationships to allies and foes? How are they to begin to judge whether military adventures being proposed today or tomorrow are to be supported or condemned?

And how are we to judge the final days of Empire when we now know they were accompanied by an extraordinarily ambitious act of history theft, one that spanned the globe, with countless colonial papers being incinerated or dumped at sea? This conflagration became known – to those in the know – as Operation Legacy, and it was intended to erase all trace of the darker deeds of Britain's colonial enterprise. Thousands more files were spirited away from the colonies and hidden for decades in a high-security intelligence facility in the south-east of England. The British state of the late twentieth and early twenty-first century was attempting to protect the reputation of the British state of generations earlier, concealing and manipulating history – sculpting an official narrative – in a manner more associated with a dictatorship than with a mature and confident democracy.

This culture of concealment and retention was not confined to the colonies. Nor was it only during the dying days of Empire that records have been withheld or disclosed in a manner that has little to do with transparency and accountability, but which is more concerned with selectivity and censorship. Despite a statutory framework that allows historical government papers to be withheld for decades, and freedom of information legislation that contains dozens of exemptions, some valuable files are routinely destroyed, while the application of official secrecy during the declassification of other files has resulted in millions of 'public' documents being concealed from the public, quite unlawfully.

For decades, closed government archives have existed in the Home Counties, the Midlands, on the south coast and in Northern Ireland. The latter houses the official record not only of the overt war that Britain fought against the Provisional IRA for three decades, but also of the covert conflict – the so-called dirty war – of extra-judicial killings, subtle state control of death squads, and gun-running. All of this happened, but the evidence remains almost entirely hidden from public view.

It is no surprise that the UK's intelligence agencies do not operate in an open and transparent fashion: it is to be expected that details of operations, the identities of officers and agents, and much else will remain classified. But it is not only current and recent intelligence operations that remain hidden. Historical matters have also been successfully concealed, sometimes in a manner that has allowed an official – and misleading – narrative to flourish.

At the end of the Second World War, for example, a great many stories about the secret intelligence campaigns against Germany were recounted with official blessing, and one volume of official history after another was published. But the most significant story, that of the extraordinary enterprise that was central to the British intelligence war against Germany – the story of Bletchley Park and the cracking of the Enigma ciphers – was very carefully buried. It was not until decades after the war had ended that the public was permitted to learn that many of Germany's strategic intentions had been known and understood by the Allies throughout much of the war, and that an entire dramaturgy of strategic deception had been created as a result.

The work carried out at Bletchley Park was not revealed until 1974. And it was to be a further two years before the public was to discover that the wartime organisation that operated there, the Government Code and Cypher School, was still at work, under a new name: the Government Communications Headquarters, or GCHQ. A magazine journalist's investigation revealed the existence of this extraordinarily large and very well-funded intelligence agency, which was devoted to peacetime signals intelligence and which had, for the previous three decades, been working alongside MI5 and MI6 as well as its American partner, the National Security Agency, or NSA. The individuals who disclosed this were, of course, prosecuted under the Official Secrets Act.

Until the end of the Cold War, the agencies were disavowed – their very existence never officially acknowledged – and the names of their directors were official secrets, even though they were well known to Britain's enemies. GCHQ and its activities were no secret to the Soviet Union, however: the KGB had had a man working on the inside for years. But the British people were shocked by the disclosure of its existence, just as they would be almost forty years later when the documents leaked by Edward Snowden revealed the extent to which they had been the subject of the bulk data-collection operations mounted around the clock by GCHQ alongside the NSA.

Meanwhile, the intelligence agencies continue to exercise complete control over the declassification of their own historical documents, with the result that Britons have less access to the archives and know less of the history of their secret state than Russians do of theirs. While MI5 and GCHQ have declassified a small and carefully selected number of files, in a manner that no doubt sculpts a favourable history, MI6 has not made public a single page of any of the files that it has created since its foundation in 1909.

In the courts, where it is said that justice must not only be done, but be seen to be done, there has been a growing tendency since 9/11 for hearings to be held behind closed doors. In camera procedure has been deployed in the criminal courts in a manner that has concealed from the public evidence of the British authorities' involvement in the torture of defendants. One particular court which is largely concerned with complaints about the intelligence agencies holds secret hearings at which the agencies are permitted to be present, but the complainants are not. This court is so furtive that even its location is an official secret.

Secrecy has also been permitted to spread to civil cases in which the government defends itself against allegations of serious misconduct. There have been a number of allegations that the government had been involved in the kidnap and mistreatment of its own citizens during the so-called rendition programme, and when some of these allegations began to be corroborated, through the disclosure in court of official documents, the government responded by introducing the Orwellian-sounding Justice and Security Act. This piece of legislation ensures that such evidence can now be considered in secret, with even the claimants' lawyers barred from court. This in turn is leading to the creation of a body of secret case law to which only a privileged few government officials and lawyers currently have access.

These are areas that are explored within this book. So too are the artful means by which the British state has successfully secured its many secrets over the years.

But this is not a history book. Nor is it a book about history; it is a book about today.

In setting out to recover some of the episodes from our past that have been concealed from view, it seeks to reveal a truer picture of who we are as a nation. And, in tracing the seam of secrecy from the past to the present, it aims to show how the acts of concealment that are being carried out today will come to shape our future.

1

A Short History of a Very British Disease

The Origins and Rise of Official Secrecy

At the start of the nineteenth century, the British people felt quietly confident that they enjoyed the most open system of government of any of the great European powers. Although the state was growing, along with the power of the state, politicians of every hue proclaimed that they embraced transparency as a defence against the abuse of that power.

In 1836, the government reduced taxation on the sale of newspapers, a step that encouraged the growth of a free press. Two years later, the government imposed upon itself a legal obligation to preserve and make available its own documentation, by passing the Public Record Office Act. Such documents, which had been called 'Muniments of the Kingdom', were renamed the 'People's Evidence'. The Act provided for a single repository of government papers, which was completed in 1858, and its reading rooms opened in Chancery Lane in central London eight years later.

It was the accepted wisdom that transparency, or 'publicity', as it was called, was the only means by which to promote political and social wholesomeness and truth, and few were prepared to disagree. The philosopher Jeremy Bentham, for example, wrote in 'Of Publicity', a chapter in his 1790 'Essay on Political Tactics': 'Secrecy, being an instrument of conspiracy, it ought not, therefore, to be the system of regular government.' As the right to vote was extended, Bentham warned, publicity, regular elections and a free press were needed to protect the public from the 'bullies, blackguards and buffoons' who might be returned to power. Secrecy suggested something corrupt: 'Without publicity, no good is permanent; under the auspices of publicity, no evil can continue.'[1]

Lord Acton, the Victorian historian who observed that absolute power corrupts absolutely, was similarly damning of secrecy. 'Every thing secret degenerates, even the administration of justice,' he wrote. 'Nothing is safe that does not show how it can bear discussion and publicity.' The philosopher John Stuart Mill believed that mankind, 'in all periods of tolerably enlightened morality', would condemn concealment, while Josephine Butler, the feminist, went further, suggesting that if Britain had a fully free and effective press, it would no longer need a police force.

To the most enlightened minds of the day, transparency was a sure sign of British social and political progress. Secrecy, on the other hand, was not merely illiberal and unhealthy, it was, as Acton wrote, a 'foreign' trait.

This went to the heart of a peculiarly British problem: if secrecy was anathema, then when it was deployed by government, it must itself be kept secret. In the event, it took an Italian to reveal to the Victorian public what the establishment had managed to conceal for more than a century.

Giuseppe Mazzini was a charismatic Italian lawyer and politician whose campaign for the unification and independence of his country had in 1837 resulted in him being forced to seek exile in London where, from his drawing room, he continued to plot revolutionary change in his homeland.

One morning in the spring of 1844, a messenger called at his house in north London with some dreadful news. Two of his fellow plotters had been arrested shortly after landing in Naples, and executed. It was a grave blow and Mazzini was bewildered at the manner in which the Neapolitan authorities had been able so quickly to apprehend his friends. Puzzling over this, he began to wonder whether the British government had been opening his mail and divulging its contents to Naples. He arranged for his correspondents to place poppy seeds, strands of hair and grains of sand in their letters, all of which were sealed with wax before being sent to him. Each letter arrived without its tell-tale enclosures.

Mazzini enlisted the assistance of a Radical MP, Thomas Duncombe, who presented a petition to the House of Commons on behalf of the exiled Italian and three of his associates. He protested at the introduction of 'the spy system of foreign states', which he asserted was 'repugnant to every principle of the British constitution'.

In reply, the Home Secretary, Sir James Graham, disclosed that the government had enjoyed the power to 'open and detain letters' since the reign of Queen Anne. He also admitted that he had indeed ordered the opening of the mail of one of the petitioners, but was not prepared to say which of the four was the target, as 'it was not for the public good to pry or inquire into the particular causes which called for the exercise'.[2]

Duncombe responded with a furious denunciation. The Home Secretary, he said, had 'sheltered himself under a sort of mystery and silence', while the government as a whole appeared to be believe it was 'justified in screening and sheltering behind this official secrecy'.[3]

The country shared Duncombe's outrage. The revelation that the government was opening citizens' private mail caused what Graham's biographer described as a 'paroxysm of national anger'. It was the greatest political scandal of the day. 'No man's correspondence is safe,' declared *The Times*. 'No man's confidence can be deemed secure; the secrets of no family, of no individual, can be guaranteed from reaching the ear of a Cabinet Minister.'[4] MPs feared their own correspondence was being intercepted.

Under pressure from Duncombe, Parliament, the public and the press, the Prime Minister Sir Robert Peel agreed to establish a select committee to investigate the affair.

The committee met in secret. Nevertheless, it eventually became clear that Sir James Graham was right and the government had acquired the power to intercept correspondence as a consequence of long usage. As early as 1657, the government authorisation that had established a regular Post Office had stated that the opening of mail was 'the best Means to discover and prevent any dangerous and wicked Designs against the Commonwealth'.[5] In 1703, a year into Queen Anne's reign, a 'Decyphering Branch' of the Post Office,* which opened mail and attempted to break codes, had been established under the control of an Oxford don, Edward Willes. He had turned the organisation into a family enterprise, with the role handed down to successive generations. More than 140 years later, what was by then known as the Secret Department was run by Edward's descendant Francis Willes.[6]

One key to the success of the Secret Department was the skill with which it made copies of the wax seals that it intended to break. It had no legal power to do this: technically it was an act of forgery, which was an offence punishable by transportation.[7] In the wake of the Mazzini investigation, the Secret Department was closed down and Willes and his assistant, another member of the family, were quietly pensioned off with money from a secret government fund.

The Post Office espionage scandal demonstrated not only that successive British governments of every complexion had been opening their opponents' letters; it also showed that they were capable of conducting significant elements of their business

---

* Jonathan Swift appears to have been one of the few people in eighteenth-century Britain who was aware of the Decyphering Branch, writing in *Gulliver's Travels* of a government department which secures plotters' letters, and then 'can discover a close-stool to signify a privy-council; a flock of geese, a senate; a lame dog, an invader . . .'

in complete secrecy. Moreover, the reaction to the disclosures suggested that the British public had little understanding of the manner in which such secrecy had been preserved, for generations, by traditions of discretion and a respect for silence among the country's ruling elite.

Members of the Cabinet were – and still are – committed to secrecy by the oath of the Privy Council, an institution which dates back more than 700 years and whose name means, quite literally, secret committee.

Those taking the oath pledge to be true and faithful servants of the monarch, and utter a vow of secrecy, unchanged since 1250: 'You will, in all things to be moved, treated, and debated in Council, faithfully and truly declare your Mind and Opinion, according to your Heart and Conscience; and will keep secret all Matters committed and revealed unto you, or that shall be treated of secretly in Council. And if any of the said Treaties or Counsels shall touch any of the Counsellors, you will not reveal it unto him, but will keep the same until such time as, by the Consent of Her Majesty, or of the Council, Publication shall be made thereof . . . so help you God.'

The oath is Britain's oldest secrecy measure. It was intended originally to offer council members a degree of protection from interference by the monarch: disagreements were kept private, and the council as a whole could stand behind the decisions that were eventually taken. This would evolve into the modern doctrine known as Cabinet collective responsibility. In the nineteenth century, it was thought to be a grave and mysterious affair: even to disclose its wording would be considered an act of treason.

During the first half of that century, when the oath was protecting the work of the Willes family and other official secrets, the British civil service was a relatively small body. Positions were granted on the basis of parentage, schooling and social status rather than academic achievement or experience. It was an age when it was thought that a well-bred man should know what to say and when not to say it; that the ability to keep a secret was one of the defining characteristics of the gentleman. So it was perhaps inevitable that a culture of 'honourable secrecy' should be prevalent within that service.[8] Among the politicians and civil servants who emerged from the same social elite, there was an informal understanding that public administration was best conducted as a private affair.

Although there was a permanent civil service by the 1830s, there was no security of employment for its members, but rather a system of patronage, and any civil servant who was thought to have betrayed the confidences of his patron would face dismissal. In time, this bond between the unelected official and the government minister would develop into the doctrine that is the twin of Cabinet collective responsibility, and which is today known as ministerial responsibility – the convention that officials are under an obligation to keep confidences, while ministers are accountable for the actions of their departments. With a minister's authority, departments may release some information in order to explain and defend those actions.

The s-word would rarely be uttered, civil servants preferring such terms as 'discretion' or 'self-possession', 'reticence' or 'reserve'. Moreover, failure to observe the code of conduct that those terms describe was considered by some in government to be not only vulgar and dishonourable, but sinful. In a letter to his wife in 1841, Sir James Stephen, Under-Secretary of State for the Colonies, wrote: 'There is a Christian virtue to which I never heard an allusion from the pulpit, and of which I have scarcely witnessed the practice in any circle in which I have mixed, although all Roman Catholic books are full of it. I mean the duty of silence. Unless I am much mistaken, frivolity of discourse, mere talk for talk's sake, is one of the most besetting sins of our generation.'

As far as Sir James and the other Whitehall mandarins of his day were concerned, the dissemination of official information could only be governed by what one historian describes as 'the gentlemanly distaste for unnecessary noise of any sort'.[9]

This discretion extended even to records of debates within the Cabinet: there weren't any. The taking of minutes was strictly forbidden.* The decisions that the Cabinet made were regarded as private advice to the monarch. Any minister who wished to publicly disagree with the Cabinet was expected to resign, and would then be obliged to ask for the monarch's permission before making his reasons public.

When Lord Rosebery, the former Prime Minister, was researching his biography of Robert Peel, he knew that no record would exist of the debates within Cabinet about the Mazzini affair, or indeed of any of the other major events of the day. Rosebery had misgivings about the degree of secrecy that surrounded the Cabinet, which he attempted to see as an outsider might. 'To the inquiring foreigner,' he wrote, 'nothing can seem more extraordinary, in a country with so much democracy about it, than the spectacle of a secret council, on the Vatican model, and sworn to absolute silence, conducting the business of a nation which insists on publicity for everything less important.' Putting aside the question of whether or not Cabinet government is efficient, he added, of all the odd systems of government in the English-speaking world, 'the strangest is the government of the British Empire by a secret committee'.

If the Mazzini affair of 1844 was a moment when honourable secrecy – and the practices that it concealed – came briefly to be challenged by the British public, the tradition came under more protracted strain during the second half of the century,

---

* No records of Cabinet meetings were kept until David Lloyd George became Prime Minister in 1916 and established the Cabinet Secretariat.

when it faced two pressures arising from the rapid development of British society.

An increase in government business meant that more civil servants needed to be recruited. The growth in paperwork, in particular, was prodigious. In 1800, for example, the number of documents created at the Treasury each year averaged 4,800; by 1849, it was 30,000. New methods of filing, indexing and registering needed to be created.[10] And the new recruits who carried out this menial and poorly paid work were not 'gentlemen' – they were young men of an entirely different social order. Group loyalty began to evaporate.

Meanwhile, the government's decision to ease taxation on newspapers, along with improvements in general education and the growing railway network, assisted the burgeoning newspaper industry. This was an industry that lived on disclosure, and it was prepared to pay handsomely for some of the government documents that were being copied, laboriously, by hand.

Before long, secrets that had for generations been protected by traditions of 'discretion' and 'reserve' would be regarded by some of these new clerical workers as commodities to be acquired and sold. New measures would be required to dissuade them. Official secrecy was about to become an integral part of the infrastructure of the state, and – as with so many other characteristics of British life – its foundations are rooted deep in the English class system.

Initially, the government attempted to rely on the civil law on the occasions when it became aware of official papers being offered for sale; in 1833, for example, the Foreign Office obtained an injunction to prevent the sale of papers relating to late-eighteenth-century diplomatic relations with Bavaria, Austria and Prussia, on the grounds that they were the property of the state.

But success was never certain in the civil courts, as in 1837, when the Foreign Office failed in an attempt to prevent the sale of papers that had belonged to Lord Wellesley, the British ambassador to Spain.

So, in 1858, the government tried for the first time to use the criminal law to deal with a leak. In November that year William Gladstone was sent to investigate the situation in the Ionian Islands, then a British protectorate, whose inhabitants were demanding union with Greece. Before he arrived, the *Daily News* published two dispatches from a British official on the islands which appeared to prejudge the outcome of the mission. The leak was traced to William Guernsey, who had been turned down for a position at the Colonial Office, and who had exacted his revenge by copying the dispatches while visiting a friend who worked at the department's library.

Guernsey was charged under the Larceny Act and, to underline the gravity of the case, the Attorney General, Sir Fitzroy Kelly, was wheeled out to conduct the prosecution at the Old Bailey. It was, Kelly told the jury, impossible to overstate the potential dangers of such disclosures: they could plunge the country into war and result in enormous sacrifices in blood and treasure.[11] Guernsey was well defended, however, and the judge was clearly unimpressed by the government's attempts to deploy the common law in the cause of official secrecy. He directed the jury that the *Daily News* had acted quite properly in publishing the contents of the dispatches, and pointed out that for Guernsey to be found guilty of the crime of larceny, the prosecution would need to show that he had intended permanently to deprive the Colonial Office of the documents. The jury took fifteen minutes to acquit.

As a consequence, fresh attempts were made to impress upon civil servants the need for discretion. Sir Ralph Lingen, the Permanent Secretary to the Treasury, issued a minute entitled 'Premature Disclosure of Official Documents', in which he declared that breaches of official confidence were 'offences of the gravest character' to which most the honourable civil servant would never stoop. Moreover, he said: 'The unauthorised use of official information is the worst fault a civil servant can commit. It is on the same footing as cowardice by a soldier. It is unprofessional.'

In spite of the warnings, minor breaches of the code of secrecy continued, and in 1878 the government found itself back at the criminal courts to prosecute a serious leak. This time the target was Charles Marvin, a twenty-three-year-old former warehouseman who had been hired as a temporary clerk at the Foreign Office on a wage of ten pence an hour.

In May 1878 the private secretary of Lord Salisbury, the Foreign Secretary, had asked Marvin to copy out the text of a secret agreement that Salisbury had struck with his Russian counterpart, Count Schouvaloff, in advance of a congress of the European Great Powers and the Ottoman Empire. Marvin was told that Salisbury required it for a statement in Parliament, and that it would be reported in *The Times*.

Marvin decided that if the document was to be made public, he should seize the opportunity to supplement his meagre income. He memorised the entire treaty, dashed to the offices of the *Globe and Traveller*, a newspaper that he occasionally supplied with titbits of information, and quickly wrote down a summary. He was rewarded with forty guineas. The newspaper rushed out a special late-night edition, with its report headlined 'The Berlin Congress Decided Upon! Terms of agreement between England and Russia'.

Arriving at his office the following morning, Marvin discovered that none of his superiors were aware of the leak: they were not the sort of people who would read the *Globe and Traveller*. It was to be several hours before the storm broke, and when it did, blame immediately fell upon poor Count Schouvaloff.

That might have been the end of the affair, had Salisbury not decided to tell a brazen lie about it. Asked in the House of Lords whether the newspaper's report was accurate, the Foreign

Secretary replied: 'The statement to which the noble Lord refers and other statements I have seen are wholly unauthentic and not deserving of the confidence of your Lordship's House.'

Marvin was outraged. Not only was Parliament being misled, the Foreign Secretary was also casting doubt upon his credibility as an unofficial source of official secrets. He wrote confidential letters to several newspapers, confirming that as a Foreign Office clerk he was aware of the authenticity of the report. For good measure, he wrote a verbatim copy of the first 11 clauses of the treaty and sent that to the *Globe and Traveller*. Salisbury's lie was nailed.

But the editor of the *Morning Advertiser*, one Captain Hamber, no doubt aggrieved that Marvin had not leaked the contents of the treaty to his own newspaper, handed the letter he had received from Marvin over to the police. The young clerk was promptly arrested and charged under the Larceny Act with removing the document and stealing the notepaper upon which he had written the summary.

Fortunately for Marvin, the magistrate before whom he was brought took a charitable view of his conduct, saying it was 'not unnatural' that he would leak the document to a newspaper with which he already had a relationship, having been told that the information would be made public in Parliament and in *The Times*. Under cross-examination, the head of the Foreign Office's Treaty Department admitted that there was nothing within its rules to prevent staff writing to the press. Marvin was also able to prove that the notepaper on which he had written his summary was his own, and not the property of the Foreign Office. The charges were dismissed.

Marvin lost his job, and the Permanent Secretary to the Foreign Office condemned his conduct as typical of the 'cheap and untrustworthy class of people' that the department was obliged to employ. *The Times* also lamented the fact that secrets of state were being entrusted to people whom it described as 'cheap irregulars of the Foreign Office', adding that in an age when information was as marketable as cotton, Whitehall should 'not in future seek to buy difficult reticence for ten pence an hour'.[12]

Marvin went on to become a celebrated and well-paid author, and in his bestselling memoirs he too pointed out the folly of paying clerks such a pittance to make copies of the greatest secrets of the day. 'I was so disgusted,' he wrote, 'that I resolved to place upon the market every piece of information that chance threw my way.' He dedicated the book to 'my benefactor Captain Hamber, editor of the *Morning Advertiser* and Discloser of the Discloser . . . with sentiments of gratitude and esteem'.

In the wake of the Marvin trial, warnings were once more circulated around Whitehall, appealing to the better instincts of civil servants and threatening disciplinary action against those who breached confidences, regardless of the degree of harm caused. This time, the government went further and redrafted the civil service rules, making it clear that the need for secrecy was not confined to matters still under discussion, but included matters already decided upon. This remains in force to this day: all official information is to be regarded as confidential, unless it is decided otherwise.

The new rules seem to have had little impact, however, and the flow of unauthorised disclosures to the press continued. The *Globe and Traveller*'s editor, Captain Armstrong, was overheard 'boasting at the Clubs' that there was 'no confidential paper which he cannot buy', while one newspaper, the *Echo*, openly advertised its rates: £5 for minor news and up to £100 on receipt of 'great secrets'.[13]

In 1887, the government concluded that firmer measures were required after a draughtsman at Chatham dockyard was found to have sold secret warship designs to a foreign power, probably the French. He was dismissed from his post, but in the wake of the failed prosecution of Marvin there was thought to be insufficient evidence to bring criminal charges. In Parliament, furious

MPs demanded to know whether the draughtsman had been 'made to take an oath of secrecy and fidelity' on receiving his job at the dockyard, and there were fresh calls for the government to introduce a new law 'to deal with public offences of this nature, as in other countries.'[14] Their demands for reform fell on sympathetic ears, as the Prime Minister by this time was Lord Salisbury, who had been so humiliated when Charles Marvin had exposed his lies to Parliament.

The Admiralty immediately began drafting new legislation that would make it an offence to disclose official information without authority. The draft was initially entitled the Breach of Official Trust Bill, and then renamed the Public Documents Bill.[15] These names indicated the initial purpose of the law: the criminalisation of unauthorised disclosures. Measures to deal with espionage were added later at the insistence of the Foreign Office, and by the time it reached Parliament in 1889, it was known as the Official Secrets Bill.

The Bill contained separate clauses to deal with espionage by foreign powers and leaks by British civil servants. When the government brought it to Parliament it highlighted the former, emphasising the threat posed by 'the Queen's enemies', in the hope that little attention would be paid to the measures that were being taken to criminalise disclosures from within its own ranks.

The Bill sailed through Parliament. It received its second reading at the Commons late at night on 28 March 1889, in between lengthy debates on bankruptcy in Scotland and a Weights and Measures Bill. The reading took less than two minutes. The Attorney General, Sir Richard Webster, uttered only sixty-eight words to introduce it: 'I wish to say just a word or two with regard to this Bill. It has been prepared under the direction of the Secretary of State for War and the First Lord of the Admiralty, in order to punish the offence of obtaining information, and communicating it, against the interests of the State. The Bill is an exceedingly simple one, and I beg to move its Second Reading.'

Just one MP, Charles Tanner, the member for Mid Cork, raised any objection to the cursory nature of the presentation, accusing the Attorney General of 'trifling with this House in introducing a measure of this importance with such brief explanation. I earnestly protest against the method and manner in which measures of this sort are brought in at this hour of the night.'[16]

Tanner secured a second debate the following month, at which only two MPs spoke. One pointed out that the clause which prohibited any disclosure that was 'contrary to the interests of the state' could have the effect of criminalising legitimate criticism. The second complained that the new law did not go far enough. 'Until the Government deals with the press,' he said, 'nothing in connection with this matter will be satisfactory. Instead of attacking the poor clerk, the government should go further and attack the real offenders – the people who obtain secrets and publish them for profit. I look upon the Bill as a farce.'[17]

The Bill was approved and then moved to the House of Lords, where just one peer made a brief comment, 'that in some of its details it goes too far'.[18] Again, the Bill was approved. Britain's first Official Secrets Act had passed through both Houses after three debates that lasted a total of nine minutes.

Inevitably, given the speed with which the Bill was passed, it contained several flaws. The most obvious was that it provided for the prosecution of foreign spies only during times of war; peacetime espionage would go unpunished. Another failing was that it did nothing to prevent memoir writers from divulging past secrets.

Almost before the ink was dry on the Act, some in government had wanted to introduce new legislation to deal with these omissions. But Sir Henry Campbell-Bannerman, then the Secretary of State for War, advised in 1895: 'Let this sleeping dog lie. If we find burglars pass him, we may stir him up.'[19] The following year the Attorney General proposed a Bill that would have shifted the burden of proof away from the prosecution and onto the defendant in Official Secrets cases, but in the face of protests from an opposition MP, the proposal was dropped.

Fresh consideration was given to new legislation during the Boer War of 1899 to 1902, at a time when a number of journalists were considered to be making considerable nuisances of themselves. The *Manchester Guardian*, for example, had angered both the government and members of the public by reporting on the conditions in which Boer civilians were being held in what were freely described as concentration camps. In 1901 the pioneering investigative journalist William Thomas Stead published a pamphlet entitled *Methods of Barbarism* which revealed that British troops were raping, looting and engaging in needless destruction of property. Stead, a man who advocated what he described as 'government by journalism', was being kept extraordinarily well informed by a small group of close friends, but he could not be prosecuted under the 1889 act as he was the recipient, rather than the source, of the unauthorised disclosures.

In 1908, in order to close this loophole, the government brought forward a Bill that proposed to criminalise the unauthorised publication of official information by journalists like Stead, and to extend the law beyond civil servants and government contractors, to any member of the public. The Lord Chancellor acknowledged that there could be difficulties in reconciling free speech and official secrecy, but assured the House of Lords that 'anyone in the press conducting his duties honourably would be quite safe'.[20] Fleet Street clearly differed with the government over the meaning of honourable journalism, however, and was alarmed to see that journalists were being bracketed with spies.

The Times continued to regard attempts to exercise legal control over information as an essentially foreign vice, condemning the Bill as a bid to 'graft upon British law some of the worst features of Continental bureaucracy', while the Institute of Journalists warned of a 'too wide and indefinite menace to the freedom of the press'.

In the face of such strident public opposition, the Bill was quietly withdrawn. And the 1889 Act may have remained on the statute books, unamended, were it not for the efforts of one of the bestselling novelists of the day, William Le Queux. It all started with a publicity stunt.

One morning in March 1906, people making their way to work along Oxford Street in central London were alarmed to see a number of well-built men wearing Prussian army uniforms and spiked Pickelhaube helmets prowling up and down the pavement and bellowing warnings at passers-by: warnings that a large army of their countrymen had landed on the east coast of England and was, at that very moment, sweeping westwards, towards the capital.

This was a moment when the British Empire was feeling surprisingly vulnerable, and many of those on Oxford Street would have regarded an invasion by the Hun as a real and terrifying possibility. No doubt it would have been something of a relief to see that some of the men in uniform were handing out leaflets bearing the words *The Invasion of 1910* – the title of a new novel that was being serialised in that morning's *Daily Mail*. This may just have been a way of whipping up public interest, but it was a stunt – and a novel – that spoke directly to a mood of fear that was starting to grip Edwardian Britain.

'The object of this book,' the author, William Le Queux, wrote in the preface, 'is to illustrate our utter unpreparedness for a war from a military standpoint; to show how, under conditions which may easily occur, England can be successfully invaded by Germany.'

The Boer War had ended just four years earlier in 1902, and the hard-won victory had left the country questioning why it had taken almost three years of bitter fighting by an army of

450,000 men to overcome a rebellion by a few thousand farmers. One of the reasons was the poor physical state of the average British Tommy. The War Office had been alarmed by the sight of the men, drawn largely from the urbanised and under-nourished poor, who had presented themselves at recruiting offices on the outbreak of war. One in three had been rejected on medical grounds; in some towns the rejection rate was nine out of ten. Even after selecting only the fittest to fight, there was still an appreciable difference in height between the officers and the men facing the Boers on the battlefield.

At the end of the war, the government had established a Committee of Physical Deterioration to ensure that the British soldiery of the future would be fit to fight for King and country. There was a new awareness that the country's armed forces had become overstretched as they attempted to police a dominion that extended around the globe and was home to 235 million people. Every year without fail, in one corner or another of that enormous Empire, an armed insurrection could be expected. But the security of the Empire was not the only concern. Britain's small professional army was often compared unfavourably with the large conscript armies of continental Europe. Meanwhile, the great naval arms race between Britain and Germany was gathering pace, and there was a growing nervousness that the Royal Navy might not win.

Although Le Queux had no direct military experience to draw upon for his novel, he worked closely with the Boer War hero Earl Roberts, a former field marshal, who helped him to identify the likely invasion beaches and plot the line of German attack. Roberts also wrote a preface, recommending the book 'to the perusal of everyone who has the welfare of the British Empire at heart'.

In Le Queux's original version of the manuscript, the Germans had landed at Yarmouth and Lowestoft, before moving swiftly on to the capital, but for the purposes of serialisation this was considered highly unsatisfactory by Lord Northcliffe, the *Mail*'s proprietor. Northcliffe was a man with an absolute abhorrence for all things Teutonic (his final will, written shortly before his death in 1922, included the claim that German agents were poisoning his ice cream) and a genius for building higher circulation. On his orders, the manuscript was rewritten, with a shadow army of 'advance German spies' destroying bridges and railway lines ahead of an invasion force that swept through the country, attacking one town a day. The location of each day's action was always a place where Northcliffe calculated that he could gain new readers, and every morning the paper would publish a map of that afternoon's battlefield. The chapters bore titles such as 'British Abandon Colchester', 'Fierce Fighting at Chelmsford' and 'Battle of Epping'. One German army swung north-west and captured Birmingham and Manchester, while the main body of troops moved north-east, before launching their climactic, catastrophic assault on the capital, to capture the very heart of the British Empire.

Over the course of the serialisation, the *Mail* saw a huge increase in its circulation figures and the book brought Le Queux worldwide fame, as it was translated into twenty-seven languages and became a bestseller around the world. It even sold 130,000 copies in Germany, but only, to Le Queux's horror, after it was rewritten to remove the eventual German defeat. Although the scale of Le Queux's success was exceptional, his novel was one in a long line of invasion novels that had been gripping the reading public for years. The first such book, *The Battle of Dorking*, had been written by a British army officer and initially published anonymously as early as 1871, shortly after the Prussian victory in the Franco-Prussian war. During the first decade of the century alone, around 300 invasion novels were published in Britain, including the most famous of them all, *The Riddle of the Sands*. Written by another Boer War veteran, Erskine Childers, and published in 1903, *The Riddle of the Sands* is a yarn about two gentlemen yachtsmen, Carruthers of the Foreign Office and his friend Davies, stumbling across a German invasion plot while sailing along Germany's Baltic coast. Its epilogue warned that Britain faced an enemy with 'a peculiar genius for organisation', that its navy was understrength, and that 'we have no North Sea naval base, no North Sea Fleet, no North Sea policy'. It was a publishing sensation, immediately selling thousands of copies. So popular was the genre that P. G. Wodehouse was unable to resist lampooning it: in his 1909 comic novel *The Swoop! or How Clarence Saved England*, the country was invaded by several armies. 'England was not merely beneath the heel of the invader. It was beneath the heels of nine invaders. There was barely standing-room.'

It made no difference that *The Times* dismissed the alarm that these books were provoking as not 'worthy of the serious notice of a great nation',[21] nor that Prime Minister Henry Campbell-Bannerman denounced Le Queux in the Commons as a 'pernicious scaremonger'. The British public, it seemed, rather enjoyed being scared. It was a trait with potential for both political and commercial exploitation. Elsewhere in Fleet Street, editors were not slow to notice that invasion scare stories sold newspapers, and their reporters were expected to satisfy that demand.

By 1908, many members of the British public were genuinely fearful that German spies were living among them, waiting for the signal to act. One newspaper, the *Weekly News*, offered rewards to readers who could spot them. Another, the *Quarterly Review*, warned that there were 50,000 German waiters and publicans working in Britain, and claimed that they were at the heart of the Kaiser's perfidious intelligence network.[22]

Newspapermen and novelists were giving voice to the fears of their readers, but this blurring of the boundaries between fact and fiction began to have a bewildering influence on public life. Lord Rosebery, a former Prime Minister, on meeting Erskine

Childers at the House of Commons, enquired how much of his book was true. Before long, MPs with east-coast constituencies were dispatching panicky letters to the Admiralty, which ordered an inquiry.[23]

Without doubt, the most influential of the literary scaremongers was Le Queux, who didn't just spark public panic through his fiction, but who genuinely believed that invasion was imminent and pressed his case in person too. Eventually his diatribes would have their desired effect: a series of measures would be taken to deal with the possibility that 'German advance spies' might indeed be at large in the country.

Extraordinarily, given that the invasion scare was being fuelled by fiction, these measures would include a piece of legislation that not only would counter the threat of espionage, but would criminalise both the communication and the receipt, without authority, of *any* piece of information generated by the government. It would be a draconian anti-transparency law, one that would be condemned in the American press as 'a legal monstrosity', but which would neatly codify Whitehall's growing penchant for closed government, with the result that the United Kingdom would become one of the world's most secretive democracies. While few today still read Le Queux's fiction, he made a lasting contribution to Britain's secret state.

After the remarkable success of *The Invasion of 1910*, Le Queux had become one of the country's most prolific and best-paid writers, and his work was known to be much admired by Queen Alexandra. He was now able to command twelve guineas per 1,000 words, the same rate as H. G. Wells and Thomas Hardy, and he was soon churning out an average of five novels a year.

Le Queux travelled around Europe, establishing a reputation as a highly clubbable raconteur, and dropping hints wherever he went that he lived half his life within the shadowy world of international espionage. He also continued to warn of threats to the defence of the realm, particularly from the 'German advance spies' whom he claimed to bump into on the south coast of England. And he continued to enjoy the confidence and support of Lord Northcliffe, the proprietor of the *Mail* who by 1909 also controlled the *Observer* and *The Times*, both of which published a series of articles highlighting the supposed spy menace.

Eager to capitalise on the success of *The Invasion of 1910*, in May of the same year Le Queux published another scaremongering bestseller, *Spies of the Kaiser: Plotting the Downfall of England*. In it, he wrote: 'I have no desire to create undue alarm. I am an Englishman* and, I hope, a patriot. What I have written in this present volume in the form of fiction is based upon serious facts within my own personal knowledge. During the last twelve months, aided by a well known detective officer, I have made personal inquiry into the presence and work of these spies, an inquiry which has entailed a great amount of travelling, much watchfulness and often considerable discomfort.'

The book depicted Britain's political leadership as supine and 'the advance guard of our enemy' as devious, disciplined and omnipresent. Berlin was controlling an espionage network that employed many of the Germans who were working in Britain at that time as barbers, publicans and waiters: only the dachshunds appeared to be above Le Queux's suspicions. To reinforce his claims, he named specific bars and clubs in London that he alleged were frequented by agents of the Kaiser.

Members of the public began to write to Le Queux describing their own encounters with German tradesmen or labourers whom they suspected of being spies, and Le Queux would forward this correspondence to his good friend Lieutenant Colonel James Edmonds, head of counterintelligence at the War Office. Edmonds was delighted to be receiving these letters as he was struggling with a small budget and frustrated by Secretary of

---

* Le Queux had been born in London to an English mother and a French father.

State for War Richard Haldane, who had been educated in Germany and was fond of the country, and who refused to take seriously the German spy menace. Armed with a batch of Le Queux's letters and a number of cuttings from the *Mail*, the *Observer* and *The Times*, Edmonds finally succeeded in persuading Haldane to set up a sub-committee of the Committee of Imperial Defence which would examine 'the nature and extent of the foreign espionage that is at present taking place within this country and the danger to which it may expose us'.

Haldane chaired the new sub-committee, and other members included the First Lord of the Admiralty, the Home Secretary and the Commissioner of Scotland Yard, along with the influential political fixer Lord Esher. Edmonds told them that five reports of suspected spies had been received in 1907, forty-seven in 1908, and twenty-four in the first three months of 1909. There was evidence, he went on, that these agents were not only gathering intelligence, but preparing to sabotage docks, bridges, ammunition stores and telegraph lines.

It was clear that many of these reports amounted to little more than local rumours. A Norfolk innkeeper, for example, reported 'two foreigners, stoutish, well set-up men' who were seen in a pub; and a Lincolnshire magistrate reported that 'a foreigner, who gave the name of Colonel Gibson and said he was a retired officer, with a German woman and a boy, neither of whom could speak English, stayed at Sutton-on-Sea, Lincolnshire, for several months in the summer of 1908. He took much interest in the coast and was known locally as "the German spy".'

Sir Edward Henry, the Commissioner of Scotland Yard, volunteered the information that five years earlier he had been obliged to send an officer to Weymouth, where 'a foreign-looking man was seen with a camera in a position to take the rear side of Nothe Fort . . . the man said he was a missionary from East Africa'.

A number of pieces of evidence considered by the

sub-committee came from Le Queux himself, although he is identified only as a 'well-known author'. 'Informant, while motoring last summer in an unfrequented lane between Portsmouth and Chichester, nearly ran over a cyclist who was looking at a map and making notes. The man swore in German, and on informant getting out of his car to apologise, explained in fair English, in the course of conversation, that he was studying at Oxford for the Church, and swore in German to ease his conscience. He was obviously a foreigner. Informant's suspicions being aroused, he returned to the neighbourhood on several subsequent days, and found the cyclist and companions still engaged in exploring tracks and lanes.' On another occasion, a 'well-known author' reported that a German barber in Southsea had been 'discovered by accident to wear a wig over his own thick head of hair' and was interested in gossip about the Royal Navy. And yet another 'well-known author' reported: 'A series of Germans come and go at 173 Powerscourt Road, North End, Portsmouth. They receive many registered letters from Germany.'

It is now known that Germany was preoccupied with Russia and France during this period and it had no spy network to speak of in pre-war Britain. Although a handful of agents were operating in the UK under the direction of Gustav Steinhauer, who had once worked with the Pinkerton Detective Agency in Chicago, they were so incompetent and poorly resourced that they were largely ineffective. One established himself in a houseboat near Plymouth, hoisted a German flag from the stern and threw a series of parties at which he attempted to turn the conversation to naval matters. He was arrested, charged under the 1889 Act and jailed for twenty-one months.[24]

The fact that much of the 'evidence' of an extensive and well-organised spy network came from one man seems not to have been of concern to the sub-committee's members. Nor were they greatly worried that this person had written many of the novels and generated much of the press reporting that had created the spy fever that was gripping the country. The unavoidable explanation for Le Queux's sightings – that he was a preposterous fantasist – appears not to have crossed the minds of the great men tasked with safeguarding the nation. Instead, Le Queux's 'evidence' was instrumental in persuading the sub-committee that urgent action was needed. Even Haldane – while insisting that he did not believe Germany was planning to invade – came to accept that a worrying number of spies were operating around the south-east coast of England, from the Wash to the Isle of Wight.

'The evidence which was produced left no doubt in the minds of the Sub-Committee that an extensive system of German espionage exists in this country, and that we have no organisation for keeping in touch with that espionage and for accurately determining its extent or objectives.'[25]

The sub-committee's warning led directly to the establishment of the Secret Service Bureau, which was broken up within twelve months into two new departments, the Security Service, MI5, and the Secret Intelligence Service, MI6. Le Queux was one of the first to be told about the new secret service organisation, and used the information to defend himself against attacks by those who had seen through him. When the *Manchester Guardian* accused him of propagating a 'German spy myth', for example, he wrote a letter to the editor saying that the 'authorities in London must have been considerably amused by your assurances that German spies do not exist among us,' as a 'Special Government department has recently been formed for the purpose of watching their movements.'[26]

In 2009 an official history published to mark the centenary of MI5 described Le Queux as the 'alarmist-in-chief' of his day. It also acknowledged that he had been a founding inspiration for the agency, as he had contributed many of the 'flimsy and . . . absurd' claims of a German espionage network that led to its creation.[27]

But that was not Le Queux's only lasting contribution to life in Britain. Haldane's sub-committee also emphasised the 'great need' to amend the twenty-year-old Official Secrets Act.

This time, with half the country expecting the Hun to appear over the horizon at any moment, ministers and senior officials were confident they could overcome objections from the press to the extension of the Act.

The secretary of the Committee of Imperial Defence had noted that the sub-committee's terms of reference had extended only to espionage, and that a new Bill need not address 'the publication of documents or information'. Such a clause, he cautioned, would only lead to accusations that the government was 'interfering with the liberties of the press'.

Lord Esher, however, had other ideas and pointed out that only a handful of newspapers had taken exception to the 1908 bill. 'It might be possible to come to an arrangement upon the basis of the Bill with the leading proprietors of newspapers,' he said, adding that such proprietors 'are few in number'. Haldane agreed. 'At the present time,' he said, 'public opinion was more sympathetic towards a Bill of the nature proposed, and this attitude of the public should be taken advantage of.'[28]

Home Office lawyers began work on a new Bill immediately, drawing upon the two failed Bills of 1896 and 1908 as their model, and including measures against both spying and unauthorised disclosure of official secrets in the same piece of legislation.

Section 1 of the Bill covered all forms of foreign espionage. Section 2, on the other hand, was directed at the British people. It was aimed at its civil servants, politicians and police officers and at the information they possessed; at its journalists and historians with their thirst for news and knowledge; and at any ordinary citizen with a sense of curiosity.

Under Section 2, *every* piece of information possessed or generated by the state became an official secret, regardless of its nature, and could be disclosed only in an official statement. Anybody who communicated that information without permission was a criminal.

Section 2 introduced new offences not only for those who communicated such information, but for those who received it. Moreover, the burden of proof was reversed in such cases: defendants were expected to show that the information had been communicated to them against their wishes.

Civil servants would be committing a criminal offence if they went home and discussed with their 'unauthorised' family members any aspect of that day's work *whatsoever*; and those relatives may also have broken the law.

Haldane proposed that the Bill should be introduced by the newly appointed Home Secretary, Winston Churchill. Churchill was enthusiastic about the revised law, having been embarrassed during his first months in office by the unauthorised publication of the memoirs of a former police officer, Sir Robert Anderson, which revealed something of the role the British authorities had played in damaging the reputation of the Irish nationalist leader Charles Stewart Parnell. But Churchill could see that Haldane was in a better position to perform the task: as Secretary of State for War, he could present the new legislation as a pressing national defence issue.

The Prime Minister, Herbert Asquith, appears to have taken very little interest in the Bill. Although he had a long-standing interest in defence – declaring, on entering Downing Street, that national security 'must always hold first place in the thoughts and plans' of those in high office – there is no sign that he thought official secrecy was an essential component of that security. As he is now known to have whiled away his time during some Cabinet meetings writing letters to his mistress Venetia Stanley – letters that gave away a number of official secrets – it may be that he had not taken the subject entirely seriously.

By 1910, the Bill was ready, but the government decided to

bide its time, waiting for the right opportunity. That came in the summer of 1911, when Germany sent a gunboat to the Moroccan port of Agadir in response to the deployment of French troops to the country. Royal Navy battleships sailed from Gibraltar to prevent Germany establishing a Mediterranean base, and for a moment Europe appeared to be on the brink of war.

Sixteen days after the German gunboat appeared off the Moroccan coast, the new Official Secrets Bill was introduced in the Lords. It was to repeal and replace the 1889 act, and when it received its second reading eight days later, Haldane claimed, quite dishonestly, that it did not contain any new restrictions on the flow of official information and was intended only to make the previous Act more effective. A total of just four peers spoke, and all were interested only in Section 1, which dealt with foreign espionage.

There was no debate about the provisions of Section 2, the clause that prohibited the unauthorised disclosure or receipt of *any* official information.[29] In codifying the official obsession with official secrecy, and in criminalising the dissemination and possession of information about the government, Section 2 fundamentally altered the relationship between citizen and state. Yet not one peer said a word about it.

The Bill was passed without amendment and reached the Commons the following month on 18 August. It was a Friday morning and the height of the grouse season, so only 117 of the 670 MPs were in the House. Haldane's junior minister, Colonel Jack Seely, was even more economical with the truth than his Secretary of State had been, maintaining that the vastly enlarged powers the Bill contained were nothing more than procedural matters. 'The actual change in the law is slight,' he said, 'and it is perfectly true to say that none of His Majesty's loyal subjects run the least risk whatever of having their liberties infringed in any degree or particular whatever.'[30]

The Commons was not so much presented with the Bill as

ambushed, such was the government's anxiety that it should become law before anyone at Westminster or in the country as a whole had time to contemplate the effect that Section 2 might have on public life. Seely told the Commons that it was of the utmost importance that the Bill be passed through all its stages that day, but did not explain why, and was not asked. In the event, Section 2 was not mentioned. The first, second and third readings were passed in around forty minutes. Churchill remained silent throughout. Only one MP suggested that there should be more time for debate. Others who attempted to speak out against it were physically manhandled back to their seats.

After lunch that day, a motion that the Bill be reported without amendments was passed by 107 votes to ten. The opponents included the former leader of the Labour Party Keir Hardie, his successor Arthur Henderson, and George Lansbury,* Labour MP for an east London constituency. Four days later the Bill received royal assent.

Seely, a former cavalry officer, subsequently described the extraordinary way in which he drove the Bill through the Commons. It reads like a breathless account of a daring charge upon an enemy redoubt. 'This was the first critical moment; two men got up to speak, but both were forcibly pulled down by their neighbours after they had uttered a few sentences, and the committee stage was passed. The Speaker walked back to his chair and said: "The question is, that I report this Bill without amendment to the House." Again two or three people stood up; again they were pulled down by their neighbours, and the report stage was through. The Speaker turned to me and said: "The third reading, what day?" "Now Sir," I replied. My heart beat fast

---

* Twenty years later, Lansbury's son Edgar would be prosecuted and fined under the Act after his biography of his father was found to be in breach of Section 2. Edgar's daughter Angela Lansbury, the Hollywood and West End actor, later recalled the moment police arrived at the family home: 'We all thought Daddy was going to jail. It was like a Noël Coward comedy.'

as the Speaker said: "The question is that this Bill will be read a third time."

'It was open to any one of all the members of the House of Commons to get up and say that no Bill had ever passed through all its stages in one day without a word of explanation from the Minister in charge. But to the eternal honour of those members, to whom I now offer, on behalf of that and all succeeding governments, my most grateful thanks, not one man seriously opposed.'[31]

Press reaction to the new law and the manner in which it was steamrollered through Parliament was muted. Some journalists, of course, were employed by those proprietors with whom Lord Esher had been confident an arrangement could be reached. No doubt others were misled by the false assurances of Haldane and Seely, and believed that this was merely a procedural affair.

Over the years that followed, there would be ample opportunity for them to see how wrong they had been, and how this new law would utterly transform the relationship between the British citizen and the state.

2

A Psychological Anchor

The Uses and Abuses of the Official Secrets Acts

The 1911 Official Secrets Act marked a turning point in British political history. As a direct consequence of the new law, the British state would become a more private affair, and the actions of successive British governments more mysterious. It would become increasingly difficult for individual members of the British public to decipher exactly how they were being governed, and they would never be quite sure whether their sense of the society in which they lived was entirely accurate.

Within this information vacuum, all manner of myths, falsehoods, official histories and propaganda campaigns would have the opportunity to take root, and in time the press would find that those individuals who possessed information of public interest would frequently be too intimidated to disclose it. A culture of secrecy would become deeply embedded within the official mind, and across wider society.

Encouraged by the feeble initial reaction of the press to the introduction of the new secrecy law, some members of Asquith's Cabinet considered introducing a second Bill that would give the government still further powers of censorship in times of war. At the War Office, Jack Seely took the view that an informal arrangement could be reached, and asked his officials to open discussions with the newspapers' proprietors, rather than with their editors. These discussions resulted in the establishment in August 1912 of the Joint Committee of Official and Press Representatives, made up of newspaper and news agency representatives on the one side, and War Office and Admiralty officials on the other. The committee was to establish a regime of press self-censorship, guided by the government.

Assurances were given by Whitehall that the press would be asked only 'to restrict the publication of news in really important cases where national interests were at stake'.[1] There were mis-understandings from the outset, however, largely because some proprietors failed to tell their editors what was happening. As a result, in November 1912, when the new committee com-municated its first agreed act of censorship – restricting reporting on the construction of submarines – to the *Daily Mirror*, its editor replied: 'On Sunday I received a mysterious letter from you asking me to leave some Admiralty information out of the paper at the request of a mysterious committee. As you did not say which committee you were acting for, I do not know whether it was a committee of the Institute of Journalists, the Press Club, the Cheshire Cheese,* or the Press Association, so that I was compelled to ignore your request.'[2]

Some newspapers, such as the *Manchester Guardian*, objected to requests that they suppress reports on the naval arms race with Germany, which they argued was a matter of great interest and a legitimate subject for reporting and debate. Others objected to the way in which the committee was established and to the fact that it was operating in secret. This was a particular concern to some Irish journalists, and it was not long before letters sent by the committee to Irish newspapers, marked 'Secret' and 'Private and Confidential', began to find their way to newspapers in the United States, where they were published. Despite this, the British press kept its side of the bargain: even the existence of the committee was not acknowledged to the public until 1952.[3]

The letters that the committee sent were given serial numbers,

---

* A Fleet Street pub.

usually with a prefix of B, C or D. In time, all carried the prefix D, and they came to be known as Defence Notices. In this way, Britain's unique and widely misunderstood system of media self-censorship, the D-Notice system, came into being.

During the First World War, the committee operated as the Press Bureau, a more formal unit of the War Office and Admiralty that was concerned with the 'co-ordination and distribution of official news' as well as with the monitoring and censorship of unofficial reports. The language employed in the bureau's notices concerning military matters makes it clear that it regarded them as instructions to be obeyed, rather than as requests to be considered. In December 1914, for example, D-Notice 117 said that reports on a German naval bombardment on the east-coast towns of Scarborough and Hartlepool should not mention the panic of the local people. By Easter 1916, the bureau felt able to insist that no reports of 'disturbances in Ireland' should be made other than imparting information contained in an official communiqué.

Those D-Notices that concerned political affairs were no less demanding. In December 1916, for example, after Woodrow Wilson was re-elected to the US presidency following a campaign that included the slogan 'He Kept Us Out of War', the British press was asked not to publish personal attacks on him. The following March, there was a request that criticism of Russia's internal affairs be muted, and that September, Fleet Street was asked to refrain from using the term 'Yellow Peril' for fear of offending Japan, the Entente Powers' eastern ally.[4]

Despite the relative ease with which the British government persuaded its press to accept a system of voluntary and guided self-censorship, there were still breaches. Following the outbreak of the First World War, one journalist and a small number of civil servants who had received or passed information were prose-cuted under Section 2 of the new Official Secrets Act. A handful of people also found themselves in the dock after disclosing details of government contracts. One of these was a clerk in the War Office, Albert Crisp, who passed on details of army uniform contracts to a tailor, Arthur Homewood, shortly after the war came to an end.

When the magistrate dismissed the case – ruling that something called the Official Secrets Act was intended to apply only to official, rather than commercial, secrets – the government moved quickly to ensure that the true intentions behind Section 2 should not be undermined. The Attorney General brought new charges and the case was heard by a judge at the Old Bailey, who ruled that despite the title of the Act, the law applied to any information, not only matters that might properly be regarded as secret.[5] On hearing this, Crisp and Homewood pleaded guilty and were each fined forty shillings.

By the end of the war, military officials were deploying official secrecy with little restraint, but were anxious that they should not be seen to be doing so. In March 1918, for example, the war artist Christopher Nevinson was informed that he could not show what is now regarded as one of his greatest paintings, *Paths of Glory*, which depicts the corpses of two British soldiers rotting on the Western Front. When Nevinson went ahead and displayed the painting with a strip of brown paper, inscribed with the word 'censored', placed across it, he was reprimanded by the War Office not only for displaying a censored image, but also for making unauthorised use of the word 'censored' in a public space.[6]

Not long after the war finally ended, the government introduced a new Bill that would allow it to retain in peacetime some of the emergency powers that it had enjoyed during the war.

Under the Official Secrets Act 1920 it became a crime to fail to inform the police about the use of an accommodation address, or to retain or fail to return public documents, 'for any . . . purpose prejudicial to the safety or interests of the State'. These new offences were punishable by two years' imprisonment, potentially with hard labour. Section 6 of the new Act created the crime of failing to provide a senior police officer with details of other official secrets offences.

Again, there was precious little debate as the Bill passed through each House. With heavy irony, one peer, Viscount Burnham, the owner of the *Daily Telegraph*, got to his feet and said that he was 'loath to interrupt the silent course of proceedings on this Bill', but he needed to warn the House that parts of it were dangerous. Burnham was aware that many in the country saw the new Bill as a threat to a free press and pointed out that it carried some extraordinarily harsh penalties for journalists going about their duties. 'I do not know a single editor of a national paper who from time to time has not been in possession of official documents which have been brought into his office, very often not at his own request. Is it proposed that any man in that position should be liable to prosecution and be subject to such penalties?'[7]

The Attorney General of the day, Sir Gordon Hewart, made a series of misleading statements about the purpose of the Bill, saying the press had nothing to fear, and that 'no honest or innocent person' need worry about the clause covering accommodation addresses.

One of the few MPs who objected to the Bill was the Liberal Sir Donald Maclean, who said that the government was not genuinely interested in espionage.* Rather, he claimed, the purpose of the Bill was 'to give them war power in peace time to destroy the liberties of the subject . . . It is another attempt to clamp the powers of war on to the liberties of the citizen in peace.'[8] The Bill received royal assent three weeks later and the Official Secrets Act 1920 became law before the end of the year.

---

* Thirty-one years later Sir Donald's son – who was genuinely interested in espionage – was to be the subject of an arrest warrant issued under the Act when he and Guy Burgess defected to Moscow.

*

Given the catch-all nature of Section 2, it was inevitable that a great many offences would be committed every day – whenever, for example, a civil servant came home in the evening and told their spouse what they had done at work that day. Those cases that were brought to trial would appear often to involve trivial offences, and their prosecution would seem vindictive.

In 1926, for example, a retired governor of Pentonville Prison in north London was fined £250 under the Act for revealing the details of the last hours of a convicted murderer. And in 1932 a government clerk was jailed for six weeks for leaking details of three wills a few hours before their official release. The *Daily Mail* reporter who received the information was jailed for two months. The clerk was terminally ill; the Attorney General persuaded the Court of Appeal not to reduce his sentence.[9]

The same year Compton Mackenzie, the writer best known for his comic novel *Whisky Galore*, was planning to publish *Greek Memories*, the third volume of his memoir about his service with military intelligence in the Balkans during the First World War. No objection had been raised to the first two volumes, in which Mackenzie outlined plots to eliminate enemy agents, but this time the Foreign Office intervened to have the book withdrawn on the first day of sale. Shortly afterward Mackenzie was charged under Section 2 of the 1911 Act on the grounds that he had provided his publishers with information that he had obtained while serving as an army officer.

A witness for the prosecution, described in court only as 'Major X', told the court that Mackenzie had revealed that passport control departments of British consulates were used as cover for intelligence work, and that the head of MI6 had been known as 'C' since the time of its first chief, Sir Mansfield Cumming.

The prosecution case was weak, however, and Mackenzie was told that should he plead guilty, the penalty would be no greater than a £500 fine with £500 costs. Mackenzie agreed, but the judge was so angered by the Attorney General's handling of the case that the outcome was a fine of just £100.

The conviction did not prevent Mackenzie from receiving a knighthood twenty years later. But for the next seventy-eight years, anyone wishing to read a copy of *Greek Memories*, deposited at the Bodleian Library at Oxford, was obliged to first apply for Foreign Office permission. It was finally published in 2011.

Three years after Mackenzie's prosecution, a bookmaker called Albert Fulton fell foul of the 1920 Act's clauses covering accommodation addresses. He had given a false address for replies to an advert in the *Daily Telegraph* in which he sought the company of a lady with 'modern ideas, vivid imagination . . . smart, refined and docile'. The magistrate dismissed the charge, but the case was then referred to the Lord Chief Justice. The position of Lord Chief Justice was by then held by Gordon Hewart, who, as Attorney General when the 1920 Act was passing through Parliament, had assured the Commons that this provision would only ever be deployed against spies. Hewart ensured that Fulton was convicted.

Hewart had also promised that the 1920 Act would never be used to target journalists, but on several occasions it was drawn upon to threaten the prosecution of those who refused to disclose their sources. In 1937, two journalists were prosecuted under the Act. Although one was acquitted, the second was fined £5 after refusing to tell police how he had obtained a police message that formed the basis of a story in the Manchester *Daily Despatch*. When the journalist appealed the following year, he too found himself before Hewart, who upheld the conviction.*

---

* In 1985, Lord Devlin, himself a Law Lord, looked back at Hewart's record as Lord Chief Justice and wrote: 'He has been called the worst Chief Justice since Scroggs and Jeffries in the seventeenth century. I do not think that is quite fair. When one considers the enormous improvement in judicial standards between the seventeenth and twentieth centuries, I should say that, comparatively speaking, he was the worst Chief Justice ever.'

As a consequence of the widespread press condemnation of the decision to prosecute the journalist, the Home Secretary, Sir Samuel Hoare, told MPs that in future 'this unusual procedure of Section 6 of the Act will be applied only in cases of the gravest importance to the safety and welfare of the state'.[10] But it was only in June 1938, when a Member of Parliament found himself facing the same predicament as the man from the *Despatch*, that the pressure for reform of the 1920 Act was taken seriously.

Duncan Sandys was a thirty-year-old Conservative MP and Territorial Army officer and, like Winston Churchill – his father-in-law – he occasionally received information about the true state of Britain's military capabilities. When he told the Secretary of State for War, Leslie Hore-Belisha, that he planned to ask a question in Parliament about a shortage of anti-aircraft guns, he was summoned to see the Attorney General, Sir Donald Somervell, who threatened him with prosecution if he did not reveal the name of his source.

An indignant Sandys reported the matter to both the Speaker of the House of Commons and the Commons' Committee of Privileges. The committee – whose members included the Prime Minister, the Leader of the Opposition and Churchill – condemned the threat to prosecute Sandys as a breach of parliamentary privilege. In the wake of the affair, the government finally brought forward the Official Secrets Act 1939, which amended the law so that Section 6 powers could be used only in cases of genuine espionage.

During the Second World War, the voluntary D-Notice Committee system was temporarily replaced with a censorship regime operated by the Ministry of Information. The ministry continued to issue D-Notices, which the chief censor later acknowledged 'covered nearly every conceivable human activity'.[11] Prosecutions under the Official Secrets Acts were rare, however, and anyone accused of disclosing defence information

– or even considered to be guilty of careless talk – was usually brought to court under the Defence of the Realm Regulations. In 1942, for example, a candidate in a by-election at Salisbury was prosecuted under those regulations after he made a remark about the location and condition of a Royal Navy vessel, and was fined £50 with costs of twelve guineas.[12]

Trials of those charged under the Defence of the Realm Regulations were often conducted in complete secrecy, as were the trials of those charged under the 1940 Treachery Act with spying for the enemy. In December 1940, for example, the British public learned of the trial of the first four German spies to be captured in the country when a short statement was issued to the press and the BBC explaining that three had been convicted, and had been hanged at Pentonville Prison a little earlier.[13] This all-embracing secrecy remained in place throughout most of the subsequent wartime Treachery Act trials, and the eighteen executions that resulted from those trials were announced in similar fashion only after they had taken place.

The end of the war did not bring an end to prosecutions under Section 2 of the Act; the Attorney General, Sir Hartley Shawcross, warned that journalists in particular would feel the full force of the law if they were to 'betray the honour of their profession' by soliciting the disclosure of official information.[14] The years that followed saw both Section 1 prosecutions of Cold War spies and traitors, and Section 2 cases brought against the careless, the foolish and the inadequate, as well as journalists and whistle-blowers.

In 1951, two twenty-year-old engineers working at British aerospace enterprises found themselves in the dock for writing to each other about aviation design projects. They were not spies, but aircraft enthusiasts. A third man, aged twenty-two, was also charged because he had posted one of the letters on behalf of his friend. All three were fined £50, and although this was reduced on appeal to £20, all three also lost their jobs.

Five years later, a former civil servant at the War Office who suggested to a former colleague that they should gather evidence of waste in government departments for a newspaper article was fined £50.[15]

A potentially far more serious case concerned the prosecution of two Oxford University undergraduates, William Miller and Paul Thompson, in the summer of 1958. While the pair were carrying out their national service in the Royal Navy, they had caught glimpses of the country's greatest post-war official secret – the existence of large-scale peacetime signals intelligence operations. At Oxford, they wrote about their discovery for the student magazine, *Isis*. The article appeared under the headline 'Frontier Incidents – Exposure', and was accompanied by a photograph captioned 'Mercedes-Benz spy boat'. It described widespread signals interceptions along the Soviet frontier, operations that the pair viewed as dangerously provocative at a time when nuclear war was considered a real possibility.

'All along the frontier between East and West, from Iraq to the Baltic,' they wrote, 'are national servicemen trained in Morse or Russian, avidly recording the last squeak from Russian transmitters – ships, tanks, aeroplanes, troops and control stations. In order to get this information the West has been willing to go to extraordinary lengths of deception. British embassies usually contain monitoring spies . . . messages are sometime provoked . . . the irresponsibility bred and sheltered by the Official Secrets Act is uncontrollable.' Then, in a line that would have triggered serious concern inside the secret state, the student journalists added: 'There is no controlling the appetite of the statistical analysers at Cheltenham.'[16]

Following the article's publication, the *Isis* office was raided and dozens of students questioned, among them the recently appointed editor of the magazine, the future playwright Dennis Potter. The student journalists Miller and Thompson were arrested and charged under the Act. They were committed for trial at the Old

Bailey, where the court was cleared so that the jury could be told a little about the work of 'the statistical analysers at Cheltenham'. When Miller and Thompson changed their pleas to guilty they were each jailed for three months. The Lord Chief Justice, Lord Goddard, said he regarded the defendants as being guilty of little more than 'youthful folly' and added that he would ensure they served their sentences 'in the most favourable circumstances, away from criminals'. Goddard was not known for such leniency when passing sentence on defendants who were not Oxford undergraduates. He then turned to the jury and said: 'I know I can trust you to forget as much as you can about this case.'[17]

The British press also seem to have taken Judge Goddard's advice and soon forgot what the student journalists had disclosed. A D-Notice was also issued, and over the next twenty years there were few further revelations about the activities of the UK's most secret intelligence agency.

The D-Notice system had been revived in the post-war years, and for a while a series of 'DX-Notices' were also issued, covering especially secret matters. It was inevitable, given the garrulous nature of many journalists, that the general public would begin to learn of the existence of the system, and it came to be widely seen as a form of back-door censorship, with people talking about the authorities 'slapping a D-Notice' on stories that could be politically awkward.

As well as the notice issued in the wake of the *Isis* article, others were issued in an attempt to conceal the embarrassment of the intelligence agencies. In 1961, during the trial of the double agent George Blake, the D-Notice Committee asked newspapers and broadcasters not to mention that he was an MI6 officer. Two years later, after *Private Eye* named the heads of MI5 and MI6, the committee's secretary wrote to editors to remind them of a wide ranging D-Notice covering both agencies' operations that had been issued in 1956.[18]

Rear Admiral Sir George Thomson, who was secretary of the D-Notice Committee in the early '60s, explained the system this way: 'The fighting services departments . . . ask me to write a personal letter to the offending editor. This invariably stops further infringements of the particular subject and produces an expression of regret on the part of the editor, which I pass on to the authorities.'[19,*]

When Harold Wilson entered Downing Street in 1964, he was delighted to discover that D-Notices were 'loyally observed, almost without question', by Fleet Street and the BBC, and that most journalists 'were scrupulous in asking for clearance' before publishing anything that might be covered by one of the Notices.[20]

When Sammy Lohan, a retired colonel, succeeded Thomson as secretary, the committee's modus operandi began to involve the cultivation of personal friendships with influential journalists and long lunches funded by a £1,500-a-year MI5 expense account.[21] After lunch, Lohan was expected to pass to MI5 information about the conversations he had with the journalists.[22]

But because the system relied heavily upon individual relationships, it was also susceptible to human error. It came close to collapse in 1967 after a man called Robert Lawson, who had worked as a telegraphist with two cable companies, provided the *Daily Express* reporter Chapman Pincher with a remarkable piece of information. Lawson walked into the *Express*'s offices and informed Pincher that every cable and telegram that entered or left the UK was collected each day by a Ministry of Public Buildings and Works van and taken to an Admiralty building to be examined, before being returned.

Pincher arranged to meet Lohan to discuss the matter at his favourite restaurant, the À l'Ecu de France in London's Jermyn Street. Pincher was a man who would occasionally allow alcohol to oil the wheels of his journalism. On this occasion Lohan

---

* Fifty years later, this could still serve as a description of how the system usually operates.

became a little too well-oiled; he thought he had persuaded Pincher to bury the story, but completely misunderstood the newspaperman's intentions. By the time others in Whitehall woke up to what was happening, the *Express*'s presses were already running. The Foreign Secretary George Brown rang Sir Max Aitken, the newspaper's proprietor, but the confusion was compounded by the fact that these two men were also drunk. Brown was rarely at his best after lunch, while Aitken was at a party with the newspaper's senior management.

The following morning, the eleven million readers of the *Express* read Pincher's scoop, a story which made clear that the cable intercepts were part of a much larger picture involving phone taps and the opening of mail.

Wilson was livid, believing that the *Express* had deliberately ignored a number of D-Notices. He commissioned an inquiry, and was beside himself when he discovered that the inquiry's report would exonerate the newspaper, describe its reporting as accurate, and denounce a number of government statements about the affair as misleading.

What was still not clear to the public – or even perhaps to Pincher – was that the cable and telephone intercepts were the work of a department of government whose existence remained completely secret; nor was it clear to them that this was just one part of the work of the 'statistical analysers at Cheltenham', as *Isis* had put it, or that they were operating in close cooperation with their counterparts in the United States. It would be another decade before these dots would be joined and the full picture would be revealed.

Lohan was sacked, much to the regret of Pincher. 'Sammy had leaked scoop after scoop to me,' the journalist explained in his memoir. There was one final postscript: in the 1990s, Pincher received a telephone call from the owner of the since-closed À l'Ecu de France. This man explained that the back of all the banquette seats in the restaurant had been bugged by MI5 during the Second World War, to capture the conversations of the many foreign diplomats who dined there. The bugs had been upgraded during the Cold War, and were linked to tape recorders in an upstairs room. MI5 had recorded all of the bibulous Lohan's indiscretions.

When the restaurant had closed, MI5 technicians were sent in to remove the bugs, and were horrified to discover that there were two sets of listening devices behind each seat. The restaurant had been wired for sound by a second intelligence agency, possibly from a Warsaw Pact country, working with the assistance of an Ecu employee with Communist sympathies.[23]

Harold Wilson had been elected with the promise that he would transform Britain – 'a nation of Gentlemen in a world of Players', as he called it – and that he would forge a new country with the 'white heat' of scientific and technological revolution.

But many in his party and in the media believed that economic and social progress was being choked by the senior civil servants of the day, the so-called Mandarin class, who were seen as being elitist, amateurish and too remote from the modern world to be entrusted with the administration of the country. Furthermore, by the mid '60s, the secrecy that so completely enveloped the work of these individuals had a slightly absurd air about it.

Wilson asked Lord Fulton, then Vice-Chancellor of Sussex University, to examine the structure and management of the civil service. In 1968, Fulton reported that the doctrine of ministerial responsibility was not tenable in an age when ministers could no longer possess detailed knowledge or control over their departments, and said that much of the secrecy surrounding government was needless. 'We think the public interest would be better served if there were a greater amount of openness,' the report said.[24] The Fulton Report concluded that an inquiry should be established to find ways of sweeping secrecy away.

On reading the report, the head of the Home Civil Service,

Sir William Armstrong, moved quickly, before the notion of an inquiry could gain any momentum. He warned Wilson that an inquiry would be dominated by 'outsiders', many of whom could be expected to be 'biased against secrecy'. The Cabinet Secretary, Burke Trend, added that American officials envied Section 2 and its inhibiting effect on journalism. Trend compared it to the 'cane in the best type of orthodox school'.[25] The idea of a public inquiry was shelved in favour an internal consultation. Perhaps unsurprisingly, the resulting White Paper, published the following year, argued that Section 2 presented no real barrier to transparency: the Act would remain in force.

There may have been many outside government who saw the Act as ludicrous, if not actually malign, but a number of prosecutions ensured that those within the civil service continued to take it seriously. The requirement that they maintain lifelong secrecy about their work was reinforced by the ritual known as 'signing the Act', which all civil servants were expected to perform at the outset and at the end of their careers.

The piece of paper that they signed, Form E74, included the wording of Section 2 of the 1911 Act and extracts from the 1920 Act. The civil servant was expected to read these before signing a declaration that they understood the law, and accepted that they were liable to be prosecuted if they divulged 'any information gained by me as a result of my appointment to any unauthorised person', without prior written approval; and that this prohibition lasted their lifetime.*

The declaration had no force in law – the Acts extended to everyone, regardless of whether they had signed Form E74 or not – but it could be used as proof that an individual was not in ignorance of the code of secrecy.

---

* Various forms of the pledge are still used today. The Ministry of Defence Form 143, for example, includes the declaration: 'I am aware of the Official Secrets Acts and that I am subject to them and that there are serious consequences if I am found to be in breach of them.'

The government may have hoped that its White Paper would draw a line under the debate, but 18 months later, Section 2 was once again under scrutiny. In January 1971, the potential for the abuse of the power that Section 2 gave to the Attorney General of the day had become apparent at the Old Bailey. On trial were the *Sunday Telegraph* and its highly respected sixty-four-year-old editor Brian Roberts, along with Jonathan Aitken, a twenty-eight-year-old journalist and Conservative Party parliamentary candidate, and Colonel Douglas Cairns, a retired soldier who had served as a British government observer of the war in Biafra.

In January 1970, the *Telegraph* had published a report – 'Secret Biafra War Plan Revealed' – which was based upon a confidential study written by the military advisor to the British High Commission in Lagos. This report showed that Wilson's government had covertly been helping the Nigerian federal government to crush the secessionist state of Biafra by supplying consignments of arms, over and above those which ministers had admitted in Parliament.

Cairns had sent a copy of the report to Major General Henry Alexander, who had at one time been his commanding officer. Alexander had in turn supplied it to Aitken, but later insisted he had done so in confidence. Aitken promptly sent the document to his literary agent, who decried its 'breathtaking dullness', but was nevertheless able to persuade the *Sunday Telegraph* to part with £1,200 for a copy.

The decision to bring charges outraged not only British journalists, but journalists across the world, with one *Washington Post* columnist condemning the Official Secrets Act as 'a legal monstrosity, a burlesque of the excellence and fairness of law and judicial procedure on which Britain prides itself'.[26]

The trial opened with the three men – and, in theory, the newspaper – in the dock of Court Number One, but not Alexander, who was lined up to be a prosecution witness. Another of the prosecution witnesses was a Foreign Office security expert who insisted that no civil servant had any right to embarrass the government of the day. He then made a remarkable admission: as far as Whitehall was concerned, 'embarrassment and security are not really two different things'. Later, when asked by the judge, Mr Justice Caulfield, to explain the rules governing the classification of government documents, he replied: 'No, my Lord. I am afraid that those rules are themselves classified.'

In his summing up, Caulfield told the jury that it was impossible to establish a chain of guilt because Alexander had been excluded from the prosecution. All four defendants were acquitted. The judge also warned against attempts to muzzle the press: 'The warning bark is necessary to help maintain a free society. If the press is the watchdog of freedom and its fangs are withdrawn, all that will ensue is a whimper, possibly a whine, but no bite. If the press is muzzled, you may think it becomes no more than a political pawn.'

Prosecutions under the Official Secrets Act could be used as a 'convenient and reasonable substitute' for a political trial, Caulfield said; and with Section 2 approaching its sixtieth birthday, he suggested that it was time it was 'pensioned off'. Pressure for an inquiry into the Act, which had been building since the publication of the Fulton Report, now became irresistible.

The man appointed to chair the inquiry, Lord Franks, a former civil servant and diplomat, invited submissions from Whitehall, the media and the law.

Witnesses who worked in the media said that they believed journalists who received leaked information should no longer face sanctions under the same Act that sought to protect the nation from espionage. Maurice Green, editor of the *Daily Telegraph*, offered the view that Section 2 had been tolerable only when it was not used, and that 'since the *Sunday Telegraph* case . . . the Act has ceased to be tolerable'.

Whitehall's elite was unanimous, however: Section 2 was not only tolerable, it was indispensable. Burke Trend insisted that secrecy must begin with the Cabinet – where he said that any 'unwise disclosure' of discussions was certain to 'engender some degree of stress' – and then spread outwards to embrace every member of the civil service.

Trend acknowledged that, in practice, supposed leaks of Cabinet discussions rarely gave the outside world an accurate picture of what was really happening at the heart of government. The Labour MP Merlyn Rees, who was serving on Franks' committee and who told Trend that he considered himself a 'bit of a connoisseur' of unauthorised disclosures, put it to the Cabinet Secretary that 'the real stuff never leaks'. 'I think that is broadly so,' Trend replied.

Nevertheless, as far as Trend was concerned, Section 2 kept the entire civil service in line. 'You are conscious at the back of everything you say and do all day long there is this tremendous sanction. In a curious way which I cannot easily define it is a psychological anchor. You know where you are. You . . . know that there are certain things which it is very bad indeed to do and that if you do them, then you are going to get much more than a black mark.'

Any 'striptease of government' would end badly, he warned, because civil servants needed to understand that the betrayal – 'and that is the only word one can use' – of anything whatsoever that the government chose to keep secret was a far from trivial offence. 'I agree that there is a distinction between your bad spy and the Section 2 chap, but both are bad people in principle.'

Perhaps the most powerful voice in the inquiry belonged to Sir Martin Furnival Jones, the Director General of the Security Service, MI5. For five years, FJ, as he was known within MI5, had held the post of spy-catcher general at the head of the agency's D Branch. Before that, he had for many years toiled within C Branch, the unglamorous protective security unit concerned with office security and the vetting of civil servants. As a consequence, Section 2 had an indisputable logic for FJ:

everything in government was secret until its disclosure was authorised, and so must be protected as such. After referring to the information that was held within individual civil servants' employment files, he was asked by another committee member, Ian Trethowan, the head of BBC Radio, what this had to do with the Official Secrets Acts.

FJ: 'Every government department, I presume, I am sure, maintains a personal file in respect of its employees.'

Trethowan: 'But is it an official secret?'

FJ: 'It is an official secret if it is in an official file.'

And this remained the case, he added, even when the contents of the official file were common knowledge.

FJ insisted that Section 2 had a wonderful way of concentrating the minds of civil servants: they grew up within a tradition of secrecy, and the repeal of the section would mean that 'the trust that ought to exist will be considerably diminished'. No civil servant should be allowed to escape from its psychological dominion: 'You have got to get at the minds of them all.'

He told the committee that he believed Crown servants were proud of the way in which the criminal law prevented them from talking of their work. 'It is not that they are deterred by the fear of prosecution, but in a sense it is the spur to their intent,' he said.

FJ then said something even more remarkable: 'Most of the information ostensibly relating to the policy of the government or to defence matters, and I can say with absolute assurance that information about my own affairs which appears in the news-papers . . . is 90 per cent inaccurate.'[27]

The head of MI5 was saying that almost everything that anyone read in the newspapers about general government policy was incorrect. The truth never leaked – as a result of the Official Secrets Act – and much of the information that was authorised to be disclosed was false.

Such was the depth and extent of official secrecy, the British people had no real idea how they were being governed. What is more, FJ appeared to relish this state of affairs.

When the Franks Report was published in September 1972, the evidence of Furnival Jones was attributed to the Director General of the Security Service, but his name did not appear: it was an official secret.

In the end, the members of Franks' committee were unconvinced by Whitehall's warriors for the cause of secrecy. 'The present law is unsatisfactory,' they concluded, 'and . . . should be changed so that criminal sanctions are retained only to protect what is of real importance.' They concluded that Section 2 was 'a mess', and that its all-embracing quality was particularly disturbing. 'It catches all official documents and information. It makes no distinction of kind, and no distinction of degree. All information which a Crown servant learns in the course of his duty is "official" for the purposes of section two, whatever its nature, whatever its importance, whatever its original source. A blanket is thrown over everything: nothing escapes . . . the very width of this discretion, and the inevitable selective way in which it is exercised, give rise to considerable unease.'[28]

The report recommended the replacement of Section 1 by an Espionage Act and the replacement of Section 2 by an Official Information Act that would prohibit disclosure of information that might injure 'the security of the nation or the safety of the people'. It also suggested that the receipt of such information be decriminalised.

In spite of the proposed moves to safeguard the freedom of the press, the British media's response to the Franks report was lukewarm, both because it had failed to recommend a new right of legal access to official information, and because the Attorney General would still have the power to decide whom to prosecute. A pledge to sweep away unnecessary secrecy had been included in the Conservatives' manifesto of 1970 when they had fought and won the election. After more than two years in government, however, their appetite for such measures had waned considerably, and when the Cabinet met to discuss Franks' proposals in March 1973 its members were delighted that Fleet Street had shown no great enthusiasm for the proposed reforms.[29] The Labour Party, then in opposition, responded to the Franks Report by promising reform of Section 2, although when Wilson was returned to Downing Street the following year, that pledge would also be quietly forgotten.

In October 1972, a few weeks after the publication of the Franks Report, the government found itself facing another unauthorised and embarrassing disclosure. The contents of a Ministry of Transport document which showed that ministers were quietly considering the closure of 4,600 miles of railway lines – almost half the country's network – appeared in both the *Railway Gazette* and the *Sunday Times*.

After the Director of Public Prosecutions ordered Scotland Yard to identify the source of the leak, police raided and searched the offices of the *Gazette*, claiming they had authority to do so under the Theft Act, and then questioned Harold Evans, the editor of the *Sunday Times*. They went further, threatening to expose one of the *Gazette*'s journalists as being gay if he refused to name the source. Officers had discovered his sexuality by bugging the magazine's telephones, apparently without authorisation.

The government also considered whether the Copyright Act could be brought to bear, prompting one MP to warn: 'If the Government were considering using the Theft Act or the Copyright Act in this way, that would involve some notion that knowledge about the government is government property. That is a very dangerous notion indeed.'[30]

The following year the Attorney General decided that there was insufficient evidence to bring charges against any of the journalists involved, and the government announced that cuts which had been outlined in a 'regrettably mobile document' were no longer being considered. The government never did discover the mole. Only after his death in 2012 at the Swiss assisted-dying clinic, Dignitas, was he identified as Reg Dawson, a senior civil servant and life-long railway buff.[31]

Section 2 continued to exert an influence on British life that was at once preposterous and sinister. Perhaps the best description of its impact was provided by the Liberal MP Clement Freud during a Westminster debate on the clause in 1979. 'If one wants to find out how to look after one's children in a nuclear emergency, one cannot, because it is an official secret; if one wants to know what noxious gases are being emitted from a factory chimney opposite one's house, one cannot, because it is an official secret.

'A man who applied for a job as a gardener at Hampton Court was asked to sign form E74, in case he gave away information about watering begonias. What is worse, if someone is good enough to tell one, then one is an accessory to the crime. My contention is that Section 2 gives the Attorney-General more power than a bad man should have or a good man should need.'[32]

At the same time, Section 2 could be a useful resource for those who genuinely were spies and traitors. In 1955, for example, the former MI6 officer Kim Philby had hidden behind the law when he called a press conference to deny being the double agent known as the Third Man. Asked whether he could shed any light on the disappearance of Burgess and Maclean, he replied: 'No I can't . . . I am debarred by the Official Secrets Act from saying anything which might disclose to unauthorised persons information derived from my position as a former government official.' Eight years later he too defected to Moscow.

In 1979, another former double agent, Anthony Blunt, refused, after he had been exposed, to talk about the role that he had played in recruiting others to the Soviet cause. 'This is, I'm afraid, something where I must take refuge behind the Official Secrets Act.'[33]

From time to time, the British government found itself coming full circle and attempting to deploy the civil law concerning breach of confidence in an attempt to halt unauthorised disclosures, just as it had in the early nineteenth century.

But despite the fiasco of the *Sunday Telegraph* trial and the concerns expressed by Franks, Section 2 continued to be the government's weapon of choice throughout the 1970s and '80s. The habit of secrecy was, it seemed, too ingrained for change to be countenanced – as was the fear of open government, among those who worked within it. Some of the nuts that the hammer cracked were very small indeed.

In 1973, the London bureau chief of *Newsweek* magazine was warned that taking a photograph of an East End employment office, to illustrate a report on unemployment, would be an offence under the Act. The same year, an Essex postman who wrote to his local paper complaining that there were too few counter staff at his local post office received a letter from his employers warning him that he had breached the Act.

In May 1981, a junior Ministry of Defence official was recalled from his post in West Germany to be prosecuted for taking home audio tapes on which he was recording rock music. The charge was withdrawn because the prosecution was never sure what had previously been on the tapes. Two years later a civil servant was fined £500 after his briefcase was stolen on the London Underground. And a few months after that, an accountant employed at the Home Office was charged after passing two documents to a second Home Office employee. The unauthorised and apparently criminal disclosure concerned a plan to manufacture toy typewriters in a prison workshop. Having heard the facts, the judge directed an acquittal.

In March 1984, Sarah Tisdall, a low-ranking Foreign Office official, was jailed for six months after pleading guilty to an offence under Section 2. She had sent to the *Guardian* two documents detailing tactics which the government planned to use in Parliament ahead of the deployment of 160 nuclear-armed US Air Force cruise missiles on UK soil. The sentence was denounced as 'savage' in Parliament, but the judge commented that 'in these days' it was no use claiming that the leaks had done no harm, or had even done some good.[34]

Perhaps emboldened by these remarks, the government decided a few months later to charge Clive Ponting, a senior civil servant at the Ministry of Defence, under Section 2. It was to become the landmark Official Secrets Act case.

Ponting is said to have become disillusioned by civil service life, in part because of the waste and inefficiency he witnessed, and partly because so many senior positions were filled by graduates of Oxford and Cambridge.[35] One of his tasks, ironically, had been to examine breaches of the Official Secrets Act by servicemen and women, and to decide whether they should be prosecuted. In March 1984, he was asked to advise ministers on the answers they should give in response to questions being raised in Parliament about the sinking of the Argentinian heavy cruiser *General Belgrano* during the Falklands War two years earlier.

The *Belgrano* had been torpedoed by the Royal Navy submarine *Conqueror* on 2 May 1982. Of the 1,100 sailors on board, 368 had died and any possibility of a negotiated end to the conflict had died with them. While the British government was satisfied that the action was militarily necessary, it did not want to admit that the *Belgrano* had been outside the 200-mile exclusion zone that it had imposed around the islands when the ship was attacked and sunk; nor that it had been sailing away from, rather than towards, the islands for the previous eleven hours. The government repeatedly maintained the line that the warship had been threatening British lives.

When ministers began providing misleading answers about the attack in response to questions from MPs and a Commons select committee, Ponting was indignant. He copied two official documents that betrayed the true story, placed them in an envelope and posted them to one of the MPs. The document was returned to the Ministry of Defence, and Ponting was quickly identified as the source. Again, the Official Secrets Act prosecution that followed concerned official lies, rather than enemy spies.

The ten-day trial the following February was a highly charged affair: a great deal was at stake. The unauthorised disclosure not only contradicted the official dishonesty surrounding the events that had led to the deaths of so many men, it also made clear that the government had lied to Parliament and misled the public.

Ponting's lawyers mounted a public interest defence, and called as witnesses Merlyn Rees − by then a former Home Secretary − as well as a professor of English law and a leading expert on the British constitution.

During a summing-up described by some observers as extraordinarily biased, the judge made it clear that jurors should accept the prosecution's case. The public interest, he said, was whatever ministers decided it to be. Moreover, he told the jury that they had no discretion in the matter: they must accept his directions. The jurors refused to be browbeaten: they ignored the judge and found Ponting not guilty. It was a decision that was hailed as a vindication of the jury system.

The acquittal of Ponting was a serious embarrassment for the Thatcher government, which had been re-elected amid the euphoria and patriotism that was fomented by the victory in the Falklands. That victory had now been sullied.

Later that year, the government sought an injunction in the Australian courts to halt publication of *Spycatcher*, the memoirs of the renegade former MI5 assistant director Peter Wright, who had retired to Tasmania. It was a move that brought worldwide attention to a book that catalogued illegal MI5 operations, and which confirmed that MI5 officers had plotted against Harold

Wilson when he was Prime Minister. The British government's case was not helped by the Cabinet Secretary, Sir Robert Armstrong, who was flown halfway across the world only to give evidence in which he attracted attention to the Whitehall expression about the need, occasionally, to be 'economical with the truth'. The government's eventual failure to secure an injunction was seen as a humiliating and costly defeat and *Spycatcher* became an international bestseller.

The Ponting verdict indicated that juries were starting to lose patience with Section 2 prosecutions, while the *Spycatcher* fiasco highlighted the limits to the reach of the Official Secrets Act. It was time for Section 2 to be killed off.

In November 1988, exactly eighty years after Asquith's government had first brought forward a Bill to criminalise the unauthorised publication of official information by journalists, the Thatcher government presented a Bill that would sweep away Section 2. Douglas Hurd, the Home Secretary, hailed the 1988 Bill as a 'charter for liberty' and 'an essay in openness which has no parallel in the history of our government since the war.'

It was nothing of the sort. The new law would not result in the disclosure of a scrap of information that was not already available. Rather than granting public access to official information, it was a new secrecy law. In a manner reminiscent of the way in which the 1911 Act was rushed through Parliament, the government introduced a so-called guillotine motion to restrict the amount of time that MPs could debate the proposals.

There were protests from opposition MPs and some Tory backbenchers, including Ted Heath, the former Prime Minister. Heath rightly observed that the provisions of the Bill went 'to the heart of the relationship between the individual and the executive'. British society, he said, suffered from excessive secrecy: 'We are the most secretive western democracy in the world.'[36] The fact that Heath had led the government that had done nothing to implement the Franks Report recommendations rather undermined the force of his argument, however, and on 1 March 1990 the Official Secrets Act 1989 became law.

Section 2 was finally swept away, and its catch-all provision consigned to history. But while the new law clearly defined those categories of information that would trigger prosecution if disclosed – such as defence, international relations and information obtained in confidence from other states – it also removed the right to conduct a public interest defence of the sort that had saved Ponting from conviction and imprisonment.

Furthermore, the new Bill introduced measures that would ensure the disclosure of intelligence information would be an absolute offence: the prosecution would not need to demonstrate that the leak had caused any harm.

For a few years, it appeared that the people most likely to be prosecuted under the 1989 Act were members of the security and intelligence agencies who chose to blow the whistle on their employers' activities.

In 1997, Richard Tomlinson, a disgruntled former MI6 officer, was jailed for a year after he handed a synopsis of a proposed book to a publisher in Australia. That same year David Shayler, a former MI5 officer, was jailed for six months after informing a newspaper that the agency had plotted to kill the Libyan leader Muammar Gaddafi. Unlike Peter Wright, the author of *Spycatcher*, they had not travelled to Australia to make their disclosures; the 1989 Act was shown to have some bite.

Not all prosecutions under the new Act were successful, however. Katharine Gun, a translator working at Government Communications Headquarters at Cheltenham, escaped conviction after she leaked a highly sensitive email shortly before the 2003 invasion of Iraq. The email from a US National Security Agency requested British help with a plan to bug the homes and offices in New York of diplomats from six countries whose support would be vital if Washington and London were to win a United Nations Security Council resolution authorising the invasion of Iraq.

'I thought, "Good God, that's pretty outrageous,"' Gun recalled. She printed out a copy of the email, took it home, and, after stewing about the matter over the weekend, decided to pass it to a friend whom she knew to be in touch with journalists.[37]

After the *Observer* newspaper reported on the secret and potentially illegal spying operation, Gun confessed to her line manager that she was the whistle-blower. She was arrested and charged under the Act.

Before the case came to trial, however, Gun and her lawyers made it clear that she would be relying upon the common law doctrine of necessity, arguing that the pressure of circumstances compelled her to commit a crime. They would say that she had been attempting to prevent the deaths and injuries that would be caused by a war in Iraq that she believed would be illegal. Furthermore, in support of this line of defence, they would be demanding the disclosure of the Attorney General's full legal advice on the lawfulness of the invasion.

The Attorney General, Lord Goldsmith, who had authorised the prosecution of Gun in the first place, was faced with the choice of releasing his advice or seeking a public-interest immunity order to keep it secret, arguably denying Gun a fair trial. Goldsmith announced that the charges were being withdrawn.

But the following year, the government did not hesitate to use the Act to protect details of its top-level dealings with the United States. A civil servant and an MP's assistant were both charged under the Act over the leaking of a sensitive government document. The five-page memorandum contained the minutes of a conversation that had taken place between President George W. Bush and Prime Minister Tony Blair at the height of the US assault on the Iraqi city of Fallujah in April the previous year, during which Tony Blair had expressed concerns about civilian casualties. David Keogh, a civil servant who was working at the Cabinet Office, had passed the memo to Leo O'Connor, a researcher working for Tony Clarke, a Labour MP who was opposed to the war. Keogh and O'Connor were both arrested after O'Connor slipped the memo into a batch of papers that were to be read by Clarke, who – no doubt fearing prosecution – had promptly called the police.

The sensitive nature of the document became clear when its contents were disclosed to reporters at the *Daily Mirror*. 'Bush Plot to Bomb His Arab Ally,' read the newspaper's subsequent headline. 'Top Secret Madness of War Memo.' The *Mirror* reported that Bush told had Blair that he wanted to attack the headquarters of Al Jazeera television in Qatar, a friendly Arab nation. 'But he was talked out of the attack . . . by Tony Blair, who said it would spark a backlash.'[38] The White House suggested that Bush had been joking, while Blair suggested, falsely, that the *Mirror*'s report was founded on a 'conspiracy theory'. The truth, however, was so disturbing that the judge who presided over the subsequent trial ordered that the contents of the memo could be raised only while the court was sitting in camera, with the press and the public excluded. Keogh admitted that he had passed on the memo, but said its contents, which he described as 'abhorrent' and 'illegal', would cause embarrassment rather than damage to the national security. O'Connor's defence was that he passed the document to Clarke in order for it to be handed to the police. Both men were found guilty after a four-week trial.

On jailing Keogh for six months and O'Connor for three, the judge issued a sweeping injunction that prohibited the media from mentioning the contents of the memo – despite the fact that the report had already appeared on the front page of the *Mirror*. It also barred publication of three words that Keogh had uttered when asked in open court about what preyed on his mind when he first saw the document.[39]

On appeal by lawyers representing the media, the Court of

Appeal ruled that the contents of the memo, as reported by the *Mirror*, could be reported, as long as it was not suggested that this accurately represented what was said during the in camera court sessions. If this were not tortuous enough, the court also ruled that the media could report that Keogh had described the contents of the memo as 'abhorrent' and 'illegal', but could not repeat the three specific words he had used when asked in court about its contents.[40] Even today, disclosing what Keogh had said would constitute a criminal offence.

The D-Notice system continues to operate. In 1993, the notices were renamed DA – or defence advisory – Notices, to reflect their voluntary nature, and the committee of government officials and journalists that oversees the system became known as the Defence, Press and Broadcasting Advisory Committee.

In 2015, in the wake of Edward Snowden's revelations, which were read largely online, there was another change of name to the Defence and Security Media Advisory Notice System, or DSMA.

By this time the notices had been whittled down to five standing categories, covering military operations, plans and capabilities; nuclear and non-nuclear weapons; ciphers and secure communications; sensitive installations and home addresses; and the intelligence services and Special Forces. If the committee's secretary believed one of them was about to breached, he simply sent out a letter – nowadays an email – drawing editors' attention to the relevant Notice.

As in Sammy Lohan's day, the relationship between the DSMA Committee secretary and individual proprietors, editors and journalists has remained crucial, because the system has no legal status. The Official Secrets Act continues to stand behind the DA-Notice system, however. Journalists know that they may face prosecution if they decline the committee secretary's friendly request that they do not publish or broadcast a particular piece of information.

The force of the system is perhaps best illustrated by how rarely it is breached, and how infrequently advisory letters are dispatched. On most occasions, British journalists continue to collaborate with a system of self-censorship that works to suppress material that is subject to the standing notices. In 2013, the committee estimated that around 80 to 90 per cent of the news reports that journalists believed might contain material subject to one of the standing notices had been submitted for scrutiny in advance of publication.[41]

The most recent and most high-profile illustration of the efficacy of this system came in June 2013, when the *Guardian* began to publish reports based upon the GCHQ and NSA documents leaked by the whistle-blower Edward Snowden. The DA-Notice committee immediately sent an advisory email to every major news organisation in the UK as well as to dozens of individual journalists, most of them editors, political correspondents or defence specialists.

'There have been a number of articles recently in connection with some of the ways in which the UK Intelligence Services obtain information from foreign sources,' the email said. 'Although none of these recent articles has contravened any of the guidelines contained within the Defence Advisory Notice System, the intelligence services are concerned that further developments of this same theme may begin to jeopardise both national security and possibly UK personnel.

'May I take this opportunity to remind editors that DA-Notice 05 advises, inter alia, that the following should not be published: "(a) specific covert operations, sources and methods of the security services, SIS [Secret Intelligence Service, or MI6] and GCHQ, Defence Intelligence Units, Special Forces and those involved with them, the application of those methods, including the interception of communications and their targets; the same applies to those engaged on counter-terrorist operations."'

This may partly explain the way in which most sections of the

British media subsequently ignored the almost daily revelations about the way in which the two intelligence agencies aimed to capture the digital communications of everyone on the planet. Elsewhere around the world the media did not turn a blind eye, however, thus exposing the system's greatest weakness: the fact that the modern media is a global affair, and digital publishers outside the UK are highly unlikely to heed an essentially British arrangement.

The system is also still capable of getting itself tied up in knots of its own making when trying to censor information about its own operations. Nowhere was this better illustrated than when a former secretary, Rear Admiral Nicholas Wilkinson, wrote the official history of the committee.

Wilkinson had completed *Secrecy and the Media* in 2008 and submitted it to the committee. It was cleared for publication after checks by MI5, MI6 and GCHQ; the Foreign, Cabinet, and Home Offices; the Treasury solicitor; and the Attorney General. But the Ministry of Defence sent the manuscript to Wilkinson's successor, who apparently complained that the book should have been written by a 'trained historian'.[42] A compromise was eventually agreed, and the book was published in 2009 without five chapters that covered the committee's activities following the election of the Labour government that was still then in power.

The censored chapters contained numerous examples of the media suppressing stories at the committee's request. The *Sunday Times*, for example, when preparing a report on the way in which MI5 had bugged the High Commission of an allied country, agreed to not identify the country concerned.*

Some of the material within the censored chapters was mildly amusing. The Ministry of Defence was jittery about the BBC television series *Spooks*, a fictitious drama about MI5, because

---

* It was Pakistan.

it referred to the agency working alongside Special Forces troops. It seemed that the ministry was concerned that the public might conclude that this cooperation existed in real life, apparently not realising that most people would have assumed this kind of collaboration went on anyway. At another point in the book, Wilkinson wrote that the MoD had made an attempt to impound all copies of a magazine that it had published itself.

The censored chapters also contain a number of more sobering disclosures. They describe the way in which one author who refused to cooperate with the committee before publication of his book about the conflict in Northern Ireland was subsequently arrested and questioned, because he was suspected of having seen a classified document.

Wilkinson had also detailed the way in which the government was once again resorting to injunctions to prevent publication. Realising that the 1989 Official Secrets Act was something of a blunderbuss that could sometimes backfire, government departments began obtaining injunctions from the civil courts, instead of resorting to the criminal law. During the 1990s, they were seeking three or four of these injunctions a year, including one in 1997 to prevent publication of some of the disclosures that the former MI5 officer David Shayler wished to make about an IRA bomb attack in the City of London. When *Punch* magazine breached the injunction and published an article headlined 'MI5 Could Have Stopped the Bomb Going Off', its editor was fined £5,000 for contempt of court. His conviction was overturned on appeal.[43]

The censored chapters also made clear that in 1999, the MoD had gone a step further and started asking the courts to issue so-called super-injunctions – court orders that not only prevent publication of a news report, but actually prohibit anyone from revealing the existence of the injunction. Wilkinson was appalled as he realised that such measures would undermine the goodwill upon which his committee's work depended.

After the 9/11 terrorist attacks, Wilkinson found himself having to persuade the MoD not to push for formal censorship measures that would prevent all publication of reports on Special Forces operations. He also argued against proposals to 'punish' journalists who published unwelcome material.

After Labour failed to be returned to office in the 2010 election, much of the material censored from Wilkinson's book was placed in the National Archives and made available to the public. However, twenty-eight separate redactions have been made to that material.[44]

It seems that the official history of this quintessentially British form of guided self-censorship will itself remain permanently censored.

3

Don't Mention the Wars

The Secret Battles of a Peaceful People

In the months after the surrender of Japan on 14 August 1945, the British people were ready to believe that war was behind them. The newspapers were full of stories about possible home rule for India, and dockers going on strike in London, Liverpool and Hull. It is questionable how many readers of the *Manchester Guardian* on 6 December 1945 saw, let alone read, a short item that was tucked away at the foot of page six, nestling between a reader's letter about the Nuremberg war crimes trials and a leading article about the foundation of the United Nations.

Under a headline 'British in Indo-China' appeared a copy of a letter that had also been sent to Ernest Bevin, the Foreign Secretary. 'It appears that we are collaborating with Japanese and French forces against the Nationalist forces of Việt Minh,' the letter read. 'For what purpose is this collaboration? Why are we not disarming the Japanese? We desire the definition of Government policy regarding the presence of British troops in Indo-China.' The letter was signed by the 'British other ranks' of the signal section of an infantry brigade based in Saigon.[1]

It was highly unusual – notwithstanding the egalitarian spirit of those post-war days – to see a group of low-ranking British troops so publicly demand that the Foreign Secretary explain his government's policies. But what was truly extraordinary was the disclosure that British troops were fighting in the former French colony against the local population, and that they were doing so alongside their former enemies: the Japanese army and the Vichy French.

Few members of the public were aware that the British government had been so anxious to see the French recover control of their pre-war colonial possession that the entire 20th Infantry Division of the British Indian Army had been airlifted into the country the previous August, with orders to suppress the Vietnamese people's attempts to form their own government. There were almost 26,000 men with 2,500 vehicles, including armoured cars. Three British artillery regiments had also been dispatched, the RAF had flown in with fourteen Spitfires and thirty-four Mosquito fighter-bombers, and there was a 140-strong contingent from the Royal Navy.[2]

On landing, the British had rearmed the Vichy troops with new .303 British rifles. Shortly afterwards, surrendered Japanese troops had also been rearmed and compelled to fight the Vietnamese – some under the command of British officers.[3]

The British were operating in accordance with an order that they should show a ruthless disregard for civilians, who, consequently, were killed and maimed in large numbers. 'There is no front in these operations,' the order said. 'We may find it difficult to distinguish friend from foe. Always use the maximum force available to ensure wiping out any hostilities we may meet. If one uses too much force, no harm is done. If one uses too small a force, and it has to be extricated, we will suffer casualties and encourage the enemy.'[4]

Many of the troops who were expected to act on such orders were appalled. One of the signatories to the letter to Bevin was Dick Hartmann, a thirty-one-year-old soldier from Manchester. Hartmann later recalled: 'We saw homes being burned and hundreds of the local population being kept in compounds. We saw many ambulances, open at the back, carrying mainly – actually, *totally* – women and children, who were in bandages.

I remember it very vividly. All the women and children who lived there would stand outside their homes, all dressed in black, and just grimly stare at us, really with . . . hatred.'[5]

Back in the UK, Parliament and the public knew next to nothing about this war, the manner in which it was being waged, or Britain's role in it. And it appears that the Cabinet and the War Office wished their state of ignorance be preserved.

At the Allies' Southeast Asia headquarters in Ceylon, however, and at the War Office in London, British commanders and senior defence officials were enraged by the letter. Hartmann and his comrades were warned that a brigadier was coming to see them. 'He just came in one morning and gave us a haranguing about the evils of our ways. He said a few years before we would have been shot, but unfortunately he couldn't do that now.' Hartmann was worried. But some of his comrades had many years of jungle combat behind them and were unimpressed by the brigadier and his bluster. They told him, bluntly, that they believed Britain's cause in the country to be unjust, and that he should make himself scarce. The brigadier turned on his heel, and did just that.

But there were no more letters from Saigon, there was little press attention, and almost no comments were made in the Commons.

Despite the size of its military commitment to Indo-China, this was to be a British military operation that would be kept out of sight, and largely out of mind. And it would not be the last such campaign.

Almost seventy years later, in September 2014, the British Prime Minister David Cameron gave a statement in which he prepared the country for the resumption of military action in Iraq, this time against Islamic State forces. 'We are a peaceful people,' Cameron said, standing in front of two Union Jack flags. 'We do not seek out confrontation, but we need to understand we cannot ignore this threat to our security . . . we cannot just walk on by if we are to keep this country safe. We have to confront this menace.'[6]

Nobody doubted that the Prime Minister was under pressure to act after the Islamic State had filmed the brutal murder of a British aid worker and threatened the slaughter of a second. Moreover, nobody disputed his assertion that the British are 'a peaceful people' who do not seek confrontation.

In fact, since the outbreak of the First World War in 1914, not a single year has passed when Britain's armed forces have not been engaged in military operations somewhere in the world, very often fighting in several different theatres at once. The British are unique in this respect: the same could not be said of the Americans, the Russians, the French or any other nation. Only the British are perpetually at war.

One possible reason for this could be that in the years following the Second World War, and before the period of national self-doubt that was provoked in 1956 by the Suez Crisis, Britain engaged in so many end-of-Empire scraps that military activity came to be regarded by the British public as the norm, and therefore unremarkable.

Another is that since 1945, British forces have engaged in a series of small wars that were under-reported and now all but forgotten, or which were obscured, even as they were being fought, by more dramatic events elsewhere. On one occasion, they fought a war that was successfully concealed from the public for the better part of a decade through the careful application of secrecy.

Very often, the official silence surrounding these wars has relied as much upon an incurious media as it has upon the Official Secrets Acts, D-Notices and the paraphernalia of official secrecy. The consequence is that a great deal is known about some conflicts, such the 1982 Falklands War and the 2003 invasion of Iraq, and Britain's role in the two world wars has become in many ways central to the national narrative. But other conflicts are remembered only dimly or have always remained largely hidden.

The Second World War was not yet over when Britain began to wage the first of the wars that would later be forgotten, entering into the civil war in Greece at the end of 1944. By mid-December, British troops were fighting house to house in Athens against men and women who had been allies a few weeks before, while the RAF dropped 500-pound bombs and strafed targets across the city.

More damage was done to the buildings and infrastructure of Athens during the first three months of British liberation than had been inflicted in more than three years of Nazi occupation. One BBC correspondent described many years later how 'British troops set about the task of clearing Athens and Piraeus street by street and block by block, ferreting out the enemy through tunnels of mouse-holed houses. The scale of the fighting in the last phase of the battle can be judged from the fact that the British dead numbered about two hundred and fifty. Rebel losses were much greater; they were never exactly counted.'

Not that this correspondent was able to inform the BBC's listeners about this. 'This period, murky in itself, was made murkier in its passage, or rather non-passage, through British military censorship.' For war correspondents who were attempting to negotiate censorship and official secrecy at that time, 'dissension among allies was one of the taboo subjects'.[7]

Just a few months later, Dick Hartmann and his colleagues found themselves in Saigon on that brutal mission to prop up the French in an effort to ensure that Britain should not be the last remaining imperial power in Southeast Asia.

Within hours of the Japanese capitulation in August 1945, the nationalists of the Communist-dominated Việt Minh – which had been battling against the Japanese occupation, with allied support, for more than three years – had declared independence and formed administrations in both Saigon in the south and Hanoi in the north. There was little doubt that the new administration enjoyed popular support. Germaine Krull, a French photographer in the city, described in her diary how 'all the streets were hung with large banners and all the walls and official buildings bore inscriptions: "Down with French Imperialism" and "Long live Liberty and Independence"'.[8]

France had too few troops of its own to crush this spirit of independence and to reimpose the pre-war status quo on its former subjects. Nor did it have any ships to transport those troops that were available, Britain's Royal Navy having sunk a large number of them in 1940. Instead, the British went to war on behalf of France and against the Vietnamese people.

By the end of January, the British commander, Major-General Douglas Gracey, was estimating that forty Indian and British troops had been killed, along with 106 French and 110 Japanese. On the Vietnamese side, there were 3,026 dead.

By early April 1946 British soldiers had handed over to French troops, but the campaign that they fought had already kick-started the thirty-year conflict now known as the Vietnam War.

British troops performed exactly the same service in the Netherlands East Indies. With the Dutch unable to muster enough troops to displace a genuinely popular Indonesian administration that had stepped into the power vacuum created by Japanese capitulation, the British agreed to do the fighting for them. In just one three-week battle in October and November 1945 in the city of Surabaya, the British deployed one-and-a-half divisions, supported by dozens of tanks and aircraft, against thousands of Indonesians, some of whom fought with rifles, knives and even their bare hands.[9]

It remains one of the largest single engagements fought by British troops since the end of the Second World War. The British lost 600 men, including their commanding officer, a brigadier, and estimated that they had killed around 10,000 Indonesians.[10]

The Indonesians put their death toll at 15,000. So unpopular among its own troops was the British government's intervention, and so vicious the fighting, that a number mutinied, refusing to fight on against the Indonesians and threatening to turn their weapons against returning Dutch troops, whom they accused of carrying out atrocities against civilians.[11]

But just as all recollection of the 22nd Division's campaign in Vietnam has vanished from the collective British memory, so too the Battle of Surabaya has disappeared from view, although in Indonesia it is regarded as the key event in the country's struggle for independence.

Less than twenty years later, in 1963, UK forces were again fighting Indonesians, this time alongside Malaysian and Commonwealth forces on the island of Borneo. The four-year struggle for the control of the north of the island was euphemistically described as a 'confrontation' rather than a war, yet by its conclusion 295 British and allied soldiers had been killed or wounded, many of them Gurkhas; an estimated 812 Indonesian troops and 89 civilians had been killed or injured.[12]

There were occasional media reports on the war, but they were few and far between. Correspondents were not encouraged to visit, and editors were discouraged from publishing: in May 1964, for example, the secretary to the D-Notice Committee wrote to all editors, asking them not to publish or broadcast any reports 'referring to operations in Borneo against Indonesia'.[13] The absence of the media from the war zone meant that the world was unaware that the British were operating deep inside Indonesian territory.[14]

On entering Downing Street in 1964, Harold Wilson inherited the UK's war against Indonesia. When he came to publish his account of the Labour administration that governed until 1970, the other Southeast Asian war, that which the United States was waging in Vietnam, was mentioned almost 250 times. Wilson mentioned his own war with Indonesia just six times, *en passant.*

He described it as a war between Malaysia and Indonesia, and omitted to mention the UK's leading role, although he did at one point admit to committing 30,000 men, the largest deployment of Britain's armed forces since 1945 and one that was made at enormous strain to both the military and the Exchequer.[15]

There were many other small and little-noticed British wars. In the immediate wake of the Second World War, British servicemen also fought in Eritrea, Palestine, Malaya, China, Egypt and Oman. During the twenty-two years between 1949 and 1970, the UK initiated thirty-four foreign military interventions.[16] Later came the Falklands, Iraq – four times – Bosnia, Kosovo, Sierra Leone, Afghanistan, Libya and, of course Operation Banner, the British Army's thirty-eight-year deployment to Northern Ireland.[17]

The quietest year was probably 1961. A British task force was dispatched to newly independent Kuwait that year to deter an Iraqi invasion, but no shots were fired and it appeared that an entire calendar year might pass without any members of the British military killing or being killed. Then, in the run-up to a referendum in October that year which resulted in British Cameroons being divided between Nigeria and the Republic of Cameroon, British troops engaged with Chinese-backed rebels, twice crossing the border to attack their camps.

Normal service had resumed.

Making sense of war is a notoriously challenging exercise. War correspondents, trying to write what might be described as the first draft of history, face physical danger, suspicion and deception. The belligerents can be expected to attempt to limit journalists' movements and control their output. Witnesses to events are frequently too involved in the conflict to give accounts that are reliable, or too psychologically damaged to give any account at all.

The greatest difficulties for such correspondents – often unseen by consumers of their work – are logistical. How does one enter the war zone? How best to assess whether it is safe to travel from A to B? Where can one find a reliable local guide, and how can one avoid putting them at risk? Where does one obtain clean drinking water in a region where the infrastructure has been shattered? How does one transmit words or pictures from a land where there is no longer any electricity?

The military historian may not face such practical and pressing problems but must, like the war correspondent, attempt to make sense out of chaos. And, like the war reporter, the historian may be susceptible to myth-making: to the temptation to embrace a selective and heroic view of events. Military history, as one of its more eminent practitioners has put it, is on occasion 'liable to be regarded as a handmaid of militarism' rather than a genuine endeavour to establish what actually happened.[18]

During the second half of the twentieth century, as British governments waged one war after another, year after year, the making of myths was encouraged both among the media and among those members of the military who were often the first to attempt to write a history of the conflict in which they fought.

During the twelve-year war in Malaya between 1948 and 1960 – or the Malayan Emergency, as it was euphemistically termed – the expression 'winning hearts and minds' entered the British military lexicon. Often, during the years that followed, the hearts and minds at stake were to be found not in the territories where the fighting was taking place, but back home, among the British electorate. As a consequence, persuading the British media to report favourably upon the wars that successive governments were waging became a preoccupation of the military and the Ministry of Defence.

However, one strategically vital war, fought by Britain for more than a decade, was thought to be so politically repugnant that even those reporters and commentators most supportive of the country's military adventures were unlikely to be impressed. As a consequence, a decision was taken that this war should be fought in complete secrecy.

And that is what happened: from the mid-1960s to the early 1970s, the British public knew nothing about this conflict. Even today, some British soldiers refer to 1968 – the year sandwiched between withdrawal from Aden and deployment to Northern Ireland – as the Year of Peace, believing it to be the one year during which British troops were not on active service somewhere in the world. They could not be more mistaken.

In June that year the explorer-to-be Ranulph Fiennes was a twenty-four-year-old junior officer in the Royal Scots Greys who had volunteered to serve in this most clandestine conflict. While waiting for the aircraft that would take him on the final leg of his journey, he watched an ambulance pick up a casualty who had been landed at the airfield: 'A stretcher case with a blood drip attachment; an officer . . . whose upper chest and shoulder had been ripped apart by a bullet.'[19]

In the 'Year of Peace', Fiennes was part of a secret contingent of troops deployed to Southern Oman, where the British had been fighting for the past three years. It would be a further four years before the British press got wind of the war.

The first hint of the story came in early January 1972, when a report about Omani political developments appeared on page four of the *Daily Telegraph*. This mentioned in passing that two soldiers from the Special Air Service regiment had died while fighting in the country.[20] One of these men, Christopher Loid, had died two months earlier, while the other, John Moores, had been shot dead several weeks before that.

In January 1972, readers of the *Observer* opened their newspaper to see a report headlined 'UK fighting secret Gulf war?' On the same day, the *Sunday Times* ran a very similar article, asking: 'Is Dhofar Britain's hush-hush war?' British troops, the newspapers revealed, were engaged in the war that the Sultan of Oman was fighting against guerrillas in the mountains of Dhofar in the south of the country.[21]

This was something of a surprise for readers of both news-papers, as four years earlier the devaluation crisis had forced the Wilson government to pledge that British forces would be with-drawn from all points east of Suez by December 1971, the only exemption being a small force that was to remain in Hong Kong.

Now the *Observer* article was demanding to know: 'Has Britain really withdrawn all her forces from the Persian Gulf and the Arabian Peninsula? Or is the British government, like the Americans in Laos, waging a secret war without the full knowledge of Parliament and public?' The *Observer* located one of the insurgency's leaders, who told its reporter that the war had begun with an 'explosion' in the country on 9 June 1965, triggered by what he described as poor local governance and 'the oppression of the British'. But the newspaper failed to grasp the significance of this statement: Britain had been at war in Oman for the previous six-and-a-half years.

Situated on the south-east corner of the Arabian Peninsula, the Sultanate of Oman is bordered by the United Arab Emirates to the north, and by Saudi Arabia and Yemen to the west and south-west. The country also sits alongside the Strait of Hormuz, the thirty-three-mile wide waterway through which oil from the Persian Gulf makes its way to market. In the 1960s, more than sixty per cent of the western world's crude oil came from the Gulf, a giant tanker passing through the Hormuz bottleneck every ten minutes. As the oil flowed, local economies flourished and became important markets for exported British goods: London became even more anxious to protect its interests in the region and the local rulers who supported them. In 1967, oil was extracted from Oman itself for the first time, and within six years the country was annually producing more than 100 million barrels.

Most of the population of Oman are Arabs living in the north of the country, on the coastal plain upon which the capital,

Muscat, is situated. To the south-west, beyond 500 miles of desert, is the province of Dhofar, linked to the capital at that time by a single unpaved road. The only towns in Dhofar, including the provincial capital Salalah, lie on a coastal strip that is just thirty-seven miles long and nine miles deep, and thick with tropical vegetation, due to the monsoon that visits each year between June and September. Inland is a 150-mile-long plateau known as the Dhofari Jebel − *jebel* being Arabic for highlands − that rises steeply to 4,500 feet in places.

In the late '60s, around a million people lived in Oman. An estimated 150,000 of them were in Dhofar. Around 10,000 were nomadic herdsmen, the *jebelis* of the plateau, ethnically distinct from their countrymen, and speaking a language closer to Aramaic than Arabic.[22]

There are some who believe Dhofar to have been Sheba, the land of the queen who visited Solomon; others claim that it is Ophir, the biblical source of frankincense, the aromatic resin that once was as valuable as gold. Even today, frankincense trees grow in profusion across the mountains. What is not in dispute is that the poor roads of Dhofar made movement difficult for anyone attempting to put down an insurgency; the monsoon rendered air support impossible for almost four months of each year; and the heavy, rolling surf made it all but impossible to land boats along the coast.

When the *jebelis* began to rebel, they discovered that Dhofar is probably the best guerrilla warfare country in the whole of the Middle East. And the Sultan of Oman would need some outside help to fight it.

Britain's relationship with Oman dates back to 1798, when it secured the Sultan's support against France following Napoleon's invasion of Egypt. Throughout the nineteenth and twentieth centuries, Britain maintained control of successive sultans to prevent any other colonial power gaining a foothold in the region. It achieved this through a simple means: money. In the mid '60s, Sultan Said bin Taimur, who had ruled the country since 1932, received more than half his income directly from London. Only from 1967, when Omani oil was pumped from the ground for the first time, did Oman begin to generate most of its own income.[23]

Even then, Britain exercised enormous control over the Sultan. His defence secretary and chief of intelligence were British army officers, his chief advisor was a former British diplomat, and all but one of his government ministers were British. The British commander of the Sultan of Oman's Armed Forces met daily with the British defence attaché, and weekly with the British ambassador.[24] He had no formal relationship with any government other than the UK.

The official British position was that the Sultanate of Muscat and Oman was a fully sovereign and independent state.[25] In truth, it was a de facto British colony. As such, successive British governments were responsible for the woeful political, social and economic conditions that the Sultan's subjects endured, and which both created and fuelled the popular revolt.

In the mid-1960s, Britain's south Arabian colony might charitably have been described as medieval. It had one hospital, which struggled to deal with endemic malaria, trachoma and glaucoma. Its infant mortality rate was seventy-five per cent and life expectancy around fifty-five. A broken bone could prove fatal. One visitor to the hinterland in the 1950s commented that 'there is often not a single healthy inhabitant in sight'.

There were just three primary schools – which the Sultan frequently threatened to close – and no secondary schools, with the result that just five per cent of the population could read and write.[26]

There were no telephones or any other infrastructure worthy of the name, other than a series of ancient water channels. The Sultan banned any object that he considered decadent, which meant that Omanis were prevented from possessing radios, from riding bicycles, from playing football, from wearing sunglasses, shoes or trousers, and from using electric pumps in their wells.[27]

The gates of Muscat – a walled city, where the only impressive buildings were the Sultan's palace and the British embassy – were locked each night and a curfew enforced. And Omanis were forbidden to leave the country. If they did succeed in crossing the border, they were not permitted to re-enter.

Those who offended against the Sultan's laws could expect savage punishment. There were public executions. Conditions in his prisons – where Pakistani guards received their orders from British warders – were said to be horrendous, with large numbers of inmates shackled together in darkened cells, without proper food or medical attention.[28]

The people of Oman despised and feared both their Sultan and the British who kept him in place and colluded with his policy of non-development. Ranulph Fiennes had been in the country for just a few hours when he began to sense how deep this enmity ran. He walked to a town near his base, 'and everywhere saw poverty and dirt; disease and squalor'. His fellow officers, he noticed, carried revolvers at their waists as they strolled around the market. 'The people jostled past and spat and stared from dark, proud eyes, with hate I thought.'[29]

Unsurprisingly, the Sultan often had to call upon the British to provide the military force required to protect him from his own people.

In 1955, a rising by the *jebelis* of the mountains in the north of the country, led by the Imam of Oman, was suppressed with the help of British forces. Two years later the rebellion flared up again, culminating in a two-year struggle for control of the 10,000-foot Jebel Akhdar, or Green Mountain, which stands at the heart of the range. The Sultan's own forces were supported by a squadron of SAS troops, two companies of British infantrymen and a squadron of armoured cars, but several hundred of the rebels held out. The mountain was eventually captured by the SAS, an achievement that is said to have saved the regiment from disbandment.

Just as critical to the eventual success of the counter-insurgency operation was the RAF, however. Between July and December 1958, the RAF flew 1,635 sorties, deploying Shackleton bombers with 500-pound bombs and Venom fighter jets equipped with 60-pound rockets and cannons. They dropped 1,094 tons of bombs and fired 900 rockets at the insurgents and their mountain-top villages and irrigation works.[30] This was more than twice the weight of bombs that the Luftwaffe dropped on Coventry in November 1940.[31]

In 1966, after surviving an assassination attempt, the Sultan and his Dhofari wife retired to his palace on the coast at Salalah. He was so rarely sighted that many of his subjects became convinced that he must have died, and that the British were concealing this from them.

For the new Labour government, the close relationship with the client sultanate presented an ideological problem. The Labour Party had been elected in 1964 on a manifesto that included a pledge to wage a new 'war on want' in the developing world, and to fight for 'freedom and racial equality' at the United Nations General Assembly, and it would cause the most excruciating humiliation were it to become known more widely, at home and abroad, that Oman was the last country on earth where slavery remained legal.

Slavery had been abolished in Bahrain in 1937, in Kuwait in 1949 and in Saudi Arabia in 1962.[32] In Oman, it flourished. The Sultan himself owned around 500 slaves. An estimated 150 of them were women, whom he kept at his palace at Salalah; a number of his male slaves were said to have been physically deformed by the cruelties they had suffered.[33]

Wilson's Foreign Secretary Michael Stewart was a leading member of the Fabian Society, which was dedicated to advancing the equality of power and wealth within the UK. Stewart was fully aware that slavery still existed in Oman, yet he made no effort whatsoever to intervene to end it. Some of his senior civil servants appear to have considered it acceptable: one drafted a minute in which he claimed that 'slavery can be regarded in some respects as the local equivalent of the welfare state'.[34]

At the conclusion of the Jebel Akhdar War of 1959, the Sultan of Oman's Armed Forces were reorganised, with British advice, training, equipment and funds. More Omanis were recruited into the ranks, along with a number of Baluchis from Pakistan, but all of the officers were British. Some were 'seconded officers' – volunteers, like Fiennes, from the British Army or Royal Marines – while others were so-called contract officers, or mercenaries. These were mostly men who had previously served in Oman with the British Army and who had chosen to return to earn handsome rewards. The Sultan of Oman's Air Force was created, with British, Australian and Rhodesian pilots. This branch of the Sultan's service was, according to one seconded officer, 'really the RAF in disguise'.[35]

Young men in search of adventure and good money and who were in possession of military experience found that entry was simple. When Ray Kane, a young Irishman serving as a junior officer in a British infantry regiment, applied to join the Sultan's Armed Forces as a contract officer in 1968, his interview was held at the Old War Office in Whitehall, and consisted of just five questions. 'Not queer are you?' was the first, followed by: 'Not running away from your wife, someone else's wife, a pregnant mistress or a pack of creditors are you?' After Kane answered 'no' to each question, his interviewer – a man in a suit who declined to identify himself – said: 'You're in, nice to have met you, goodbye.'[36]

Initially, the rebels they faced were Arab nationalists, members of an organisation called the *Jabhat Tahrir Dhofar*: the Dhofar

Liberation Front. It was organised around a nucleus of men who had been trained in Iraq, and was supported by *jebelis* who were desperate to rid themselves of Omani rule from distant Muscat and see their homeland developed.

To the west of Dhofar lay Aden, from which the British were forced to withdraw at the end of 1967 in the face of increasingly violent rebellions by two separate groups of insurgents. In their absence a Marxist state, the People's Democratic Republic of Yemen (PDRY), was established. The rebellion in Dhofar moved into a new phase – a perilous one for the Sultan and his British backers – as increasing numbers of men and weapons were slipped across the border. The PDRY was receiving aid from both China and Russia, and before long a number of Dhofaris were receiving military training in China. The Dhofar Liberation Front changed its name to the Popular Front for the Liberation of the Occupied Arabian Gulf. A nationalist insurgency with local aims was developing into a revolutionary movement with pan-Arabian ambitions. To the British officers, however, the foe was always simply the *adoo* – Arabic for enemy.

The fighting intensified during 1968 – the Year of Peace – and again in '69, particularly during the monsoon seasons. Armed with Soviet and Chinese small arms and artillery, the insurgents drove the Sultan's Armed Forces out of one position after another. They are said to have slaughtered any prisoners they took, although some of the atrocities attributed to them are now acknowledged to have been merely British propaganda.[37] By the end of 1969, the *adoo* had captured the coastal town of Raysut, and by early the following year they controlled most of the *jebel* and were within mortaring distance of the RAF base at Salalah. The new oil fields on the desert between Dhofar and Muscat were beginning to look vulnerable; some in London were developing a fearful Middle Eastern domino theory, in which they envisaged the Strait of Hormuz falling under Communist control.

The British response was merciless. 'We burnt down rebel villages and shot their goats and cows,' one officer wrote. 'Any enemy corpses we recovered were propped up in the Salalah *souk* as a salutary lesson to any would-be freedom fighters.'[38] Another officer explained that unlike in Northern Ireland, where soldiers were anxious to avoid killing or wounding non-combatants, he believed that in Dhofar there were no innocents, only *adoo*: 'The only people in this area – there are no civilians – are all enemy. Therefore you can get on with doing the job, mortaring the area and returning small arms fire without worrying about hurting innocent people.'[39]

In their determination to put down a popular rebellion against the cruelty and neglect of a despot who was propped up and financed by Britain, British-led forces poisoned wells, torched villages, destroyed crops and shot livestock.[40] During the interrogation of rebels they developed their torture techniques, experimenting with noise, the infliction of which became the fifth of the so-called Five Techniques that would later be used in Northern Ireland and condemned by the European courts.[41] And areas populated by civilians were turned into free-fire zones.

Little wonder that Britain wanted to fight this war in total secrecy.

There was no need to resort to the Official Secrets Acts or the D-Notice system in order to conceal the Dhofar War, and the ruthless manner in which it was being fought, from the outside world. Two simple expedients were employed: nobody in government mentioned the war,* and journalists were not permitted into the country.

The last journalist allowed to roam around Oman had visited

---

* While Harold Wilson's published account of the Labour government of 1964–70 may be rather coy on the subject of the UK's war against Indonesia in Borneo, he appears almost in denial about the Dhofar War: he does not mention it once.

in 1962. When the Irish journalist and academic Fred Halliday decided to attempt a visit in February 1970, he tried to prepare for the trip by reading British press reports of the war, only to discover that there weren't any.[42]

John Akehurst, who commanded the Sultan's Armed Forces from 1972, believed such secrecy to be entirely understandable at a time when Oman was, as he euphemistically put it, 'in the throes of dragging itself from the seventeenth to the twentieth century in a decade, and . . . not ready to show itself off'.[43] Not that the Sultan's cruelties were particularly reprehensible, to Akehurst's way of thinking: the lopping off of hands and stoning people to death were mere 'extravagances', he later wrote, matters which were misunderstood by westerners.[44] Akehurst later explained how this policy of secrecy was exercised: 'The Sultan of Oman had total control over entry into his country. He simply didn't allow the world's press in. They could speculate as much as they liked outside but they had very little hard fact to go on.'[45]

Tony Jeapes, who commanded the first SAS squadron to be sent to Dhofar, believes it would have been more difficult to fight the war if the Labour government, which was attempting to disengage from Britain's colonial commitments, had been obliged to admit 'that some of its troops were engaged in the biggest campaign in which British troops had been involved since Korea'. Because it wasn't, he says, 'the campaign was conducted in a security blackout. Press, radio and television commentators were just not allowed into the country'.[46]

Two journalists working for the German magazine *Stern* did manage to slip into the country and report on the war in 1969. After being informed by a contract officer whom they had met that 'Britain has clamped a strict news embargo on the area', they travelled to South Yemen, made their way by foot across the border and linked up with Popular Front fighters in the mountains. 'Every day we met refugees who reported that the

British mercenaries burned down their villages and filled their wells with cement,' they wrote.

'The men were either killed or put in prison in the capital. The women did not complain. They simply told us about the enemy's cruelty.' The journalists also reported that their Popular Front escort had told them: 'The English have sworn that you will not leave Dhofar alive; they want to kill you, we've found out. They do not want the world to know what they are doing here.'[47]

When Halliday eventually reached the region, he heard similar accounts of the way in which the war was being fought. One woman demanded to know why a Labour government which called itself socialist was killing the peasants of Dhofar.[48]

There were additional reasons for the all-embracing secrecy. This was an era in which the developing world and the United Nations had rejected colonialism; Arab nationalism had been growing in strength for decades. It was vital, therefore, for the credibility of the UK in the Middle East, that its hand in Oman should remain largely hidden.

Akehurst, the commander of the Sultan's Armed Forces, suggests a further reason for the British government not wishing to draw attention to its war in Dhofar: 'They were perhaps nervous that we were going to lose it.'[49]

By the summer of 1970, Britain's secret war was going so badly that desperate measures were called for.

On 26 July, the Foreign Office in London announced that Sultan Said bin Taimur had been deposed by his twenty-nine-year-old son, Qaboos bin Said, in a palace coup. A spokesman explained that the palace had been surrounded by hostile tribesman, and the old man slightly wounded. By the time British forces arrived at the scene, the Sultan had agreed to abdicate in favour of Qaboos, and was asking to be settled in London.[50]

There was no suggestion of any British involvement in the

coup, the British press reported; however, the possibility that the British officers of the Sultan's Armed Forces 'had an under-standing with Qaboos, under which they would not intervene', could not be ruled out.[51]

In fact, the coup was a British affair, and a key role was played by Ray Kane, the young infantry officer who had joined the Sultan's Armed Forces after a cursory interview two years earlier. Kane had been chosen to lead the troops who fought their way through the Sultan's palace. 'We charged upstairs into a labyrinth,' he recalled years later. 'We rounded blind corners to right and left. We blundered into a cavernous, dark walk-in cupboard opening and walked out again. Ahead, heavy double doors led into a windowless, carpeted *majlis* room lit by chandeliers. On its floor – as though ready for a Monopoly session – piles of stacked banknotes, and some, tipped in the same direction, suggested a hurried departure. A burst of gunfire whipped past our heads. We had not found the Sultan. The Sultan had found us.

'I jumped down onto a patio next to a glass door. I tried the door handle – locked . . . armoured.' A fellow officer rested his light machine gun on a soldier's back and, maintaining the same aim point, fired two-round bursts at the glass panel from about fifteen metres. A hole appeared in the glass and began to expand. 'Using his given name, Said, as though we had been schoolmates, I ordered the Sultan to surrender, adding that otherwise all inside would be burnt to death by the phosphorous grenade I threatened to throw into his room. In perfect English, calm and unflustered, the Sultan offered his surrender.'

The old man had been hit by several ricochets, his torso 'sliced horizontally as though sabre-slashed'. He was ordered to sign a prepared abdication agreement, and Kane watched as he was then laid on a stretcher and taken to hospital. 'As I hobbled down the ornate stairway I had previously sprinted up, I passed the new Sultan, Qaboos, armed with a small-calibre pistol and ascending alone.'[52]

The coup had been planned in London by MI6 and by civil servants at the Ministry of Defence and the Foreign Office, with little reference to elected ministers.[53] The Foreign Office had prepared the ground earlier in the year by spreading rumours among British journalists that the old Sultan was preparing to stand down. Harold Wilson had sanctioned the coup, but appears to have been reluctant to give the go-ahead before the general election he was about to fight.[54] The planning took on a greater sense of urgency in mid-June, after a group of northern allies of the Dhofari rebels renewed their attacks on the Sultan's troops in the Green Mountain region. Eight days later, the Conservative Party led by Edward Heath won the general election and within days the new Foreign Secretary, Sir Alec Douglas-Home, had given his enthusiastic permission for the coup to go ahead and for Qaboos to be installed.[55]

The son of the Sultan by his third wife, Qaboos had been raised in his father's palace and looked after by slaves. At the age of eighteen he had been sent to a small public school in the east of England, to be 'crammed' in preparation for entry to the British military academy at Sandhurst.

He served briefly as a junior officer with one of the British regiments that had suppressed the revolt against his father's rule on Green Mountain, before being taken on a tour of Western Europe, the Far East and North America, escorted by Foreign Office officials. His preparation for eventual rule, under British tutelage, was rounded off by a two-week placement with a town council in Ipswich, Suffolk.[56]

On Qaboos' return to Oman, his father had placed him under virtual house arrest. However, he was permitted to receive visits from one of his old Sandhurst classmates, who was serving as an intelligence officer in Dhofar, and who talked him into cooperating with the coup.

After the forced abdication, Whitehall officials – who had conspired with the old Sultan for years to keep the media away from their secret war – wasted no time in arranging flights to usher Fleet Street's finest and the BBC into Oman, to bear witness to the son and heir's entry into Muscat.

The *Guardian*'s Michael Lake recalls the Foreign Office calling him the morning after the coup and asking him if he would like to fly to Muscat. 'I can't remember such a call before.' Oman's Military Secretary, Colonel Hugh Oldman, who escorted the visiting press, told them that he had no idea that the coup was going to be mounted. Lake and the other journalists were sceptical about this claim, but had no way of proving it to be a lie. 'You couldn't grab Oldman warmly by the throat and say: "Now come on, Hugh old boy, tell us the truth." I mean, that just wasn't on.'[57] The reception was carefully stage-managed. There were red carpets, a guard of honour and a speech in which Qaboos pledged to 'pull us out of our backwardness'. Some of the visiting journalists were duly impressed. 'It was,' gushed the man from the *Express*, 'like Wembley Cup-tie Day, Epsom Downs on Derby Day, and a fairground fantasy all in one.'[58]

The slaves were set free, and a few were put on display for the visiting press. The journalists were also briefed about the Sultan's many crimes. However, few appear to have asked themselves who had sustained the regime for so many years; nor do any of them seem to have realised that 500 miles to the south-west, in Dhofar, their own country was entering its sixth year of war.

The deposed Sultan, meanwhile, was patched up at an RAF medical post before being flown to Bahrain for further treatment. Then he was flown to London, where he spent the rest of his days in secluded luxury in a suite at the Dorchester Hotel, dying of natural causes in October 1972, at the age of sixty-two.

After abolishing slavery,* the new Sultan and his British mentors

---

* A number of the Sultan's slaves, although technically emancipated, continued to serve Qaboos at the palace, where they were known as *Abeed al-Sultan*: the slaves of the Sultan.

began to consider how best to spend the oil revenues his father had been banking, in order to develop the country. Qaboos began immediately to improve the irrigation infrastructure in order to increase his people's agricultural yields. He decided also – on British advice – to expand still further the Sultan's Armed Forces. Over the next two years it grew in strength from 3,000 to more than 10,000 men and acquired more aircraft, including, critically, its first helicopters.[59] By 1974, the Sultan's air force comprised four squadrons, including one of Strikemaster jets.[60] That year, the war began to move into its final stage.

Troops from the SAS arrived, first as bodyguards for the new Sultan, then as trainers who had been given the task of helping the Omani troops overcome what was termed *jebelitis*: the belief that the *jebel* could never be conquered. Finally, they arrived in squadron strength.

One of the first SAS troops to be dispatched recalls being briefed at the cookhouse at the regiment's base at Hereford. 'The brigadier told us that we needed to find small wars, in order to keep the regiment going, and that he had found the ideal war for us in a place called Dhofar. We didn't discuss with other people in the regiment where we were going. That's the way it was: if you went on a team job you didn't discuss it with people who weren't part of the team. It would be considered unethical. But the brigadier talked at that time about the need for even greater secrecy.'[61]

Employing a tactic they had used in Malaya and Borneo, the SAS began to recruit the *adoo* as allies: Dhofari tribesmen were offered an amnesty if they agreed to serve the Sultan, and were paid rewards if they surrendered with their rifles or a mine or two. The rebels called these men *mutasakiteen* – the fallen ones – while the British organised them into units that they called *firqats*. They were well fed, clothed and armed; by 1976, there were 3,000 of these irregular troops.[62]

The people of Dhofar would continue to be governed by an

absolute monarch who would be reliant upon British patronage, and they would continue to be killed by British bullets and bombs. But a new era had begun for Oman, one in which those people who accepted the Sultan as their ruler would enjoy some of the benefits of the burgeoning oil revenues, something which had been impossible before the coup.

As more of the *jebelis* surrendered, the Sultan's Armed Forces changed their tactics from stick to carrot. Instead of pouring concrete into wells to cut off the water supply to a community, they would now drive the rebels out of a location chosen by the *firqat*, who would then occupy the area. A track to the area would be cleared, and then a drill brought along the track to bore a new well. SAS medics provided some medical and dental aid; and finally a shop, clinic and mosque would be built.[63] A model farm was established on the plain near Salalah, and army vets imported Hereford bulls to improve the local livestock.[64] One SAS officer even took a local soil sample back to Britain for analysis by agronomists, who advised on ways to improve fertility.[65]

At the same time, it was made clear to the local civilian population that the supply of both aid and water would be cut off if the rebels became active in the area once more.[66] Water and improved livestock became the currency of persuasion.

A new Ministry of Information was established, a printing press was purchased and an official newspaper launched from offices in Muscat. A radio station was also set up, staffed by British officers, and, because the old Sultan had banned radios, an SAS corporal was dispatched to buy several hundred cheap Japanese transistor sets, which were distributed around the *jebel*, free of charge.[67]

Pauline Searle, the British wife of an oil industry executive, who had produced anti-communist propaganda during the Malayan Emergency, was also recruited to the radio station. A few months later she was permitted to open a bureau for Reuters, the news agency, but was prevented from reporting on the war, and confined to regurgitating official communiqués. Her work was censored, sometimes by Ministry of Information officials, sometimes directly by senior officers of the Sultan's Armed Forces, and she could not travel outside the capital without permission.

In October 1971, Searle wrote to Colonel Hugh Oldman, the Sultan's Defence Secretary, to complain about the restrictions that were being placed upon her. 'I cannot be committed to publishing nothing but Defence Dept. handouts,' she complained. 'So far, as I can prove to you, all my material has been based on military communiqués and I have toned down as much as possible the British involvement side. But there is a difference between toning down and complete silence.'

Searle added that she had met a number of British soldiers who had been 'sworn to secrecy by their officers'. Most of them, she said, 'seemed very unhappy about the whole state of affairs'. Finally, she demanded to know: 'What sort of a war is this?'[68] The only response appears to have been that the Ministry of Information produced a greater number of official communiqués.

Meanwhile, some pockets of resistance remained and there was still some hard fighting, particularly along the Yemeni border, as the Sultan's Armed Forces, the SAS and the *firqat* began to cut off the insurgents' supply lines. The conflict began to be a little more widely reported, although visiting journalists remained unwelcome. In 1972, when the Shah of Iran agreed to send troops to fight alongside the British and recently committed Jordanian forces, the British military attaché in Muscat advised that although the first reports on the war had already appeared in the western media, the utmost secrecy was still required: the British and their Omani clients did not wish to see the Iranian contribution widely advertised around the Arab world.[69] After Labour won the February 1974 general election, Harold Wilson decided that British involvement in the conflict should remain as obscure as possible.[70]

Eventually, in December 1975, Sultan Qaboos was informed by the British that order had been restored in Dhofar, and the following month most of the *adoo* withdrew across the border to Yemen. At this point, the media ban was lifted and the world's press were finally welcome in Muscat. A handful of rebels remained in Dhofar, mounting sporadic artillery operations until late April 1976, and by June of that year, the British troops had ceased operations. There was one final, isolated skirmish in May 1979, in which a young New Zealander became the last of the Sultan's officers to be killed.[71] And then it was over.

During the course of the eleven-year war, twenty-five British soldiers were killed, along with an uncertain number of British contract officers.[72] Around 190 Omani troops died, and seventy-two Iranians. It remains unclear how many of the *adoo* perished, although the figure is certain to be many hundreds and possibly thousands. Civilian casualties were never counted, although one estimate puts the number as high as 8,000.

Pauline Searle eventually concluded that the secrecy surrounding the war had impeded the Sultan's Armed Forces – that a degree of publicity would have resulted in greater military support from other countries in the region. 'But there was always a clampdown on news from the war-zone by misguided men who should perhaps have been swept away with the old guard in 1970.'[73]

Strategically, the Dhofar War was one of the most important conflicts of the twentieth century, as the victors could expect to control the Strait of Hormuz and the flow of oil. Thousands died, the British won and the West's lights stayed on. Today, the war is still studied at the British Army Staff College. But because of the way in which information about the long campaign was so successfully suppressed at the time that it was being waged, it has been all but blanked out of the nation's memory. Like the British wars in Greece, Eritrea, Indo-China, the Dutch East Indies and Borneo, it is remembered in Britain only by those men who fought it, and their families.

Some aspects of Britain's role in the coup and the war remain among the deep secrets of the British state: Harold Wilson's correspondence on Oman, for example, and that of his successor Edward Heath, are to remain closed to historians and the public until 2021.[74] In 2005, a Foreign Office memo was briefly made public which describes the way in which the old Sultan's own Defence Secretary, Colonel Hugh Oldman, had taken the lead role in planning the coup that deposed him – in order to safeguard British access to Omani oil and military bases. It was then hurriedly withdrawn: its release, the Foreign Office said, had been an unfortunate error.[75]

The war in Dhofar coincided with the final stages of the Vietnam War, a conflict that was fought in full view, as far as the world's media were concerned. Ian Gardiner, a Royal Marines officer who served as a seconded officer in Dhofar, says: 'Journalists were drawn to Vietnam like moths to a light and this tended to obscure Oman which was arguably of greater strategic signif- icance. Unsurprisingly, virtually no Americans have ever heard of the Dhofar War. But they surely would have heard about it if we had lost it.'[76]

The US military had welcomed correspondents to Vietnam. They fed them, briefed them, defended them against the enemy and drank with them. Most of the journalists responded by attempting to give their readers, listeners and viewers an honest account of what they witnessed. It was the first time that the truth had not become the first casualty of a war, and the military did not enjoy the experience. Nor did the American public, who could read about the horror of the conflict each morning at their breakfast tables, and see images of it each evening in the corner of their living rooms. The public's support for the campaign soon dwindled, and during the post-mortem examination of their defeat, some in the US military blamed the media; a handful of journalists agreed.[77]

The British drew lessons from their victory in Dhofar, and from their ally's humiliating defeat in Vietnam: lessons that would shape their future military adventures. One of the most important was that the media was best excluded from the battlefield. If that could not be achieved, journalists needed to be very strictly controlled. Tony Jeapes, who commanded the SAS in Dhofar, says the news blackout was 'for both the SAS and the British government . . . an ideal state of affairs'.[78]

In fact, this was not a new lesson: by 1914, it was apparent to governments across Europe that the management of public opinion was an inescapable element of large-scale wars. On the Western Front, six correspondents had been 'embedded' within the British Army; they produced what some believe to be the worst reporting of any war, before or since, and all were knighted for their services.[79] Their editors knew that these correspondents were concealing the horrors of trench warfare: the Prime Minister, David Lloyd George, told C. P. Scott, editor of the *Manchester Guardian*: 'If people really knew, the war would be stopped tomorrow. But of course they don't know and can't know. The correspondents don't write and the censorship would not pass the truth.'[80]

The UK's next major war after Dhofar was in 1982, against Argentina, for control of the Falkland Islands, or Malvinas. The Ministry of Defence mounted a media management operation that was a classic of its kind: one that the Pentagon could only stand back and admire.

Because the campaign was to be fought by a seaborne task force, sailing to a group of islands 8,000 miles from the UK and 400 miles from the nearest land mass, in the midst of a bitter south Atlantic winter, no journalist could reach the war zone unless the Ministry of Defence took them. The only other sources of information would be official communiqués from London and Buenos Aires.

The MoD agreed to take a couple of dozen reporters and

photographers. All were to be British – there was no room on board for 'neutrals' – and no journalists considered to have had an unhelpful track record were admitted, with the result that the veteran war photographer Don McCullin was excluded. All were obliged to agree to censorship of all their material. There was no way around this, because the military controlled the means of transmitting their words and pictures back to London. No pictures of the war were transmitted for fifty-four of the seventy-four days of war. Two correspondents attempted to preface their bulletins with the rider that they were being censored. This fact was itself censored. Finally, they were each issued with an MoD booklet informing them that they would be expected to 'help in leading and steadying public opinion in times of national stress or crisis'.[81]

None of this was done to deceive the Argentinians. Indeed, the enemy had learned the numbers of aircraft, warships and supply ships being mobilised against them – and even the names of many of the vessels – when government ministers informed MPs of their plans during two Commons debates.[82]

Once the war was over, the correspondents rushed into print and onto the airwaves with their 'untold stories' of the war: the material that the military censors had refused to pass. Once read and viewed, it was clear that this material would have been of little value to the Argentinians, consisting as it did of descriptions and pictures of the exhausted, the wounded and the traumatised fighting men, and of Royal Navy warships burning and sinking. It would, however, have been deeply distressing for the British people. The celebrations that marked the return of the task force may have been a little more muted had the public already seen the close-up images of burned flesh peeling from young Welsh Guardsmen as they were rescued from the blazing troop-landing ship, *Sir Galahad*.

In 1991, the United States and the United Kingdom both expanded the embedding system for journalists as they prepared to drive invading Iraqi forces out of Kuwait. They were less successful than the British had been in 1982, because the war in Iraq was to be fought across the desert. Embedded journalists later complained that they could see or hear little of the conflict, while those journalists who remained free of military restraint and censorship – so-called unilaterals – enjoyed considerable freedom to do their jobs.*

Ten years later, in 2001, the West's war in Afghanistan that followed the al-Qaida attacks of 9/11 began as an even greater free-for-all for visiting correspondents. There was more time to plan for the 2003 invasion of Iraq, however, and this time round there were determined attempts to restrict access to the war zone to those journalists who were embedded, and new levels of danger for unilaterals.

Subsequent studies of embedded reporting of the Iraq war found that 'embeds' generated a number of reports based on information supplied by the military escorts which was simply untrue. Some broadcasts reported that Saddam Hussein's forces had fired Scud missiles into Kuwait City, for example, while others announced a popular uprising against the dictator in the southern city of Basra. There were no Scud attacks and there was no such rebellion.[83] They also, unsurprisingly, produced reporting that was more positive in tone regarding the military.[84]

There was no censorship of the work of embedded reporters. But seventeen journalists were killed during the invasion, and most of them were killed by the US military.[85] While some of

---

* The author, reporting on the 1991 Gulf War as a 'unilateral', found that the military checkpoints intended to prevent the press from travelling along the straight desert roads could be easily overcome by turning around and driving five miles; performing a ninety-degree right turn and driving five miles into the desert; turning ninety degrees to the right once more and driving ten miles; then performing a final ninety-degree right turn, to rejoin the road five miles beyond the checkpoint. At the front-line positions that were reached in this way, most officers and men were found to be remarkably welcoming.

these were victims of friendly-fire incidents, the British government subsequently went to great lengths to suppress the minutes of a conversation between Tony Blair and George Bush, which betrayed the US President's eagerness to bomb the headquarters of Al Jazeera television in Qatar in 2004; US forces had already bombed the network's office in Kabul. The Pentagon subsequently said that the office was a legitimate target because it had 'repeatedly been the location of significant al-Qaida activity'.[86] This activity, it transpired, consisted of interviews conducted with Taliban officials, something that Al Jazeera had regarded as journalism, rather than terrorism. A suspicion arose among some experienced journalists that the senior US commanders did not wish there to be any 'unilateral' reporting of the invasion, and hoped that a few deaths would discourage the practice.[87]

There is no evidence of the British military having deliberately targeted journalists, but there is evidence that the Ministry of Defence has come to regard accurate reporting as a subversive activity, one to be guarded against by the same security measures that are deployed against terrorists and foreign intelligence agencies. The department's *Defence Manual of Security*, redrafted in the weeks after the al-Qaida attacks of September 2001, and subsequently leaked, warns military personnel that the greatest security threats are those posed by 'foreign intelligence services, subversive and terrorist organisations, investigative journalists and criminals'.[88]

This comment still stands as an explanation for much of the secrecy that surrounds modern warfare. Journalists are excluded, deceived and controlled, words and pictures are censored, facts suppressed, and an information vacuum is carefully cultivated as a space within which lies and propaganda can thrive; and all this is done not to confuse the enemy, but to prevent the public from learning the truth about the violence that is being carried out in their name. The morale of the Home Front remains as crucial in 2016 as it did in 1916.

*

Judging from the last decade and a half, there is little sign that the British state is about to lose its appetite for war. The first conflict of the new century in which the UK became involved was the post-9/11 assault against the Taliban regime in Afghanistan. This war enjoyed early success, but stuttered and soured after the UK's mission expanded to Helmand in the south of the country. The war dragged on, costing an estimated 95,000 lives over thirteen years, including those of 453 British servicemen and women, and brought little discernible benefit to the people of the country. The twenty-first century's second war – the 2003 invasion of Iraq – was possibly the UK's greatest foreign policy disaster since Suez. Casualty estimates vary widely, from 150,000 dead to more than a million. What cannot be disputed is that 179 of the dead were British. More than a decade later, Iraq remains in chaos.

The post-9/11 conflicts in Afghanistan and Iraq were fought in the full glare of the media and came to haunt the politicians who had initiated them. Despite this, Britain continued to invest in war – politically, technically and financially – as a means of projecting power and securing influence among key allies, and also, it seemed at times, in an attempt to impose order and a degree of familiarity upon a chaotic and unpredictable world.

But could this be done in secret? Surely, in the age of global media, twenty-four-hour rolling news, social media, and the troops' own ability to record and instantly share images of conflict, it would be impossible for a British government to go to war and conceal its actions, in the way that Britain's war in Dhofar was hidden from the public for six-and-a-half years? Tony Jeapes, who commanded the SAS squadron that was covertly deployed to Oman, considered this question, and concluded that while such secrecy was desirable, it would probably be impossible to achieve.[89]

However, in the years since the Dhofar war, the UK's Special

Forces have been gradually expanded, and from 1996, all its members have been obliged to sign a confidentiality agreement. This has reinforced the discretion with which members of this elite unit within the military traditionally perform their duties, and it has rarely been broken.

Meanwhile, the evolution of successive generations of un-manned aerial vehicles, or drones, along with advances in the development of the weapons they carry and their communications and targeting systems, has presented military planners with greater opportunities to mount operations that could remain unknown, other than to those who are ordering, planning and executing them, and to those on the receiving end.

The enormous reliance of modern societies on the Internet and the increasing frequency with which states probe and attack each other's cyber defences have led to some analysts talking of hybrid warfare, combining regular and irregular operations with information and cyber attacks, many of which are shrouded in deniability, with the result that the line between war and peace is increasingly blurred.

In the years after 9/11, hints began to emerge, in the footnotes of the budget statements of the Ministry of Defence, and from scraps of evidence salvaged from the coastal villages of Somalia, the mountains of Yemen and the cities of Libya, that the British were once again waging war in secret. It appeared that a lethal trinity of Special Forces, drones and local proxies (i.e. fighters like the *firqat* of Dhofar) was being brought to bear in a way that would spare the British public the disagreeable details of the nature of modern war, and relieve Parliament of the need to debate the wisdom of waging it.

In July 2007, less than a week after succeeding Tony Blair as Prime Minister, Gordon Brown had announced a series of sweeping constitutional changes that he said would make the British government 'a better servant of the people'. One measure

– clearly a response to the deeply unpopular war in Iraq and the calamitous and costly expedition into Helmand – was to give Members of Parliament the final say on declarations of war.

Six years later, in August 2013, Parliament exercised its new right when MPs rejected a government motion that would have authorised military intervention in Syria's bloody civil war. Ministers of the coalition government were appalled by the vote – it was said to be the first against a British Prime Minister's foreign policy since 1782 – and argued that it not only blocked the deployment of British troops, it also prevented the UK from providing any military assistance whatsoever.[90]

Prime Minister David Cameron acknowledged that the vote ruled out any involvement in military intervention in Syria. 'It is clear to me,' he told the Commons, 'that the British Parliament, reflecting the views of the British people, does not want to see British military action. I get that and the government will act accordingly.'[91]

But those words – 'act accordingly' – were not quite what they seemed.

In July 2015, the Defence Secretary, Michael Fallon, gave MPs an update on the renewed military operations in Iraq – the campaign that David Cameron had announced while standing before two Union Jack flags and declaring the British to be 'a peaceful people'. The RAF, he said, had carried out 300 air strikes, there were 900 UK personnel engaged, and the operation had cost £45 million in the previous twelve months. He reassured his audience that 'our position remains that we would return to the House for approval before conducting air strikes in Syria'.[92]

Before making this statement, Fallon was said to have been unsettled by talk in Washington political circles that the UK's refusal to act in Syria could be seen only as a sign of British decrepitude.[93] His statement was deeply misleading: for at least eighteen months, RAF pilots who were said to have been 'embedded' with the US and Canadian military had been carrying out air strikes against targets in Syria. Others had been flying combat missions with the French military over Mali. They were said to be under the command of these foreign forces, but they were clearly a British contribution to a war that MPs had decided the country should avoid.

Two weeks later the truth was out, and Fallon was back on his feet in the Commons, explaining himself to angry MPs. 'Embedded' service personnel were nothing new, he declared; they comply with UK law, but 'have to comply with the rules of engagement of the host nation'. He had not publicised what had been happening because these pilots had been assisting with other countries' operations. Moreover, he made clear that the failure to publicise what was happening should be regarded as 'standard practice'.[94]

In December 2015, MPs voted that overt military action against Islamic State forces should finally proceed. The government was given parliamentary approval for military operations that had already been covertly under way for two years.

In the Gulf, meanwhile, it was disclosed that British military personnel were sitting in the control rooms from which the Saudi Arabian air force was guiding its bombers onto targets across Yemen. The British were helping their Saudi counterparts key in the codes that would help them select and attack their targets.[95] The Saudis were not only flying British-built aircraft and dropping British-made bombs, they were dropping vast numbers of them. Over a three-month period in 2015, the value of exports of British-made bombs and missiles had increased by 11,000 per cent, from £9 million to £1 billion.[96]

This bombing campaign has been heavily criticised by rights groups for causing thousands of civilian deaths. In Parliament, the British government has had little to say about this, other than to insist that it 'obeys the norms of humanitarian law'.

Once again, the government appeared to be quietly pulling the country into a Middle Eastern war without any parliamentary oversight or approval. And covert, undeclared and unreported warfare could be seen to be not merely a possibility, but the reality of many of the UK's military operations.

4

Sinning Quietly

Operation Legacy and the Theft of Colonial History

An hour's drive north of London, little more than a stone's throw from the M1 motorway and surrounded by farmland, lies Hanslope, a quiet village of thatched cottages and modest nineteenth-century terraces that can trace its origins back to the Norman invasion and beyond.

Hanslope is a sort of company village: many of its 2,000 or so inhabitants travel a short distance each day to the same place of work, or are related to people who are employed there. Should you ask, however, about the work carried out within the large fenced-off government compound on the edge of Hanslope, people tend to fall silent. At Tompkins the butcher's, the big men behind the counter politely change the subject; at the Globe Inn the tattooed barman says: 'I never ask my customers about what they do, and they never tell me.'

The people of Hanslope are in the business of protecting official secrets by any means technically possible. And that is the way it has been for generations.

The compound to the south of the village is known informally as Hanslope Park, after the old manor house that stands at its heart. During the Second World War the manor house was the headquarters of the Radio Security Service, a division of MI6 tasked with the interception of wireless signals from the German intelligence agency, the Abwehr. It was one of a string of intelligence facilities established north and west of London on the outbreak of war: close enough to the capital for ease of access but far enough from the south-coast beaches where a German invasion was feared to be imminent. Ten miles to the south of Hanslope Park is Bletchley Park, the wartime home of the fabled code-breakers of the Government Code and Cypher School, the forerunner of today's GCHQ. Whaddon Hall, the home of the MI6 signals centre that was known as Station X, is four miles west of Bletchley Park. Towards the end of the war, Alan Turing, the pioneering mathematician and computer scientist, was based at Hanslope Park, working on speech-scrambling technology.

After the war, the Radio Security Service was absorbed into GCHQ, but staff at Hanslope Park continued to develop technical aids for MI6 and MI5. They were the real-life counterparts of the quartermaster in the James Bond films who is known as Q. The site was largely redeveloped in the 1990s and is today the home of Her Majesty's Government Communications Centre, a joint MI6, MI5 and Foreign Office research and development facility. HMGCC is dedicated to providing the UK government with effective electronic, acoustic and cyber security. At the same time its staff work to discover novel ways of breaching the security measures deployed by other governments. It is also concerned with physical security: within one group of buildings, a team from the Foreign Office's technical security department develops locks, doors, windows and walls that are intended to be impregnable, while outside, an MI6 team endeavours, equally diligently, to find ways of breaking in.

The compound is surrounded by trees, and most people driving along the narrow lane that skirts its north-western perimeter could pass by without noticing anything out of the ordinary. Behind the trees, however, stands a seven-foot-high chain-link fence. Beyond that is a ten-foot-high fence topped with coils of razor wire. Along the no man's land that runs between the two fences is a series of signs warning of the presence of intruder alarms. There are closed-circuit television cameras and floodlights every few yards. Anyone approaching the outer perimeter can expect to be watched and overheard. In 2011, a press photographer paused outside for a few minutes to take a picture of the main gate, and was promptly detained by police.[1]

Only from the air can the enormous scale of the compound be comprehended: it measures almost half a mile across and contains half a dozen large office blocks, living accommodation, warehousing, libraries, a manufacturing zone, waste-disposal facilities, a crèche, tennis courts, running and bike tracks, a helipad and more than a thousand car-parking spaces.

Hanslope Park is the size of a small town, and its obsession with security does not end at its gate. There are small stickers on the safes that are to be found in almost every office, bearing the warning: 'Have you put away all papers? Locked up? Made a final check? Be quite sure before you leave. Keep our secrets secret.' Members of staff are discouraged from discussing work outside the small teams within which they operate. To reinforce the point, there are posters on the walls of the corridors that are based upon the British Second World War propaganda posters that cautioned civilians against the careless talk that could cost lives. 'Careless Talk Costs Jobs', the posters warn. It is not a joke. At Hanslope Park, staff are under no illusion that careless talk could cost more than their jobs: it could cost them their liberty.

Hanslope Park is one of the most secure facilities operated by any government, anywhere in the world. It is largely unobtrusive. Its staff are governed by the Official Secrets Act, and their relatives, friends and neighbours have learned to say nothing.

It is a perfect place to bury difficult secrets.

In 2001, a small team of British personal injury lawyers flew to Kenya to prepare a damages claim on behalf of the families of scores of Masai people who had been killed after stumbling upon unexploded shells on the British Army's practice ranges in the country.

At the same time, a number of historians, from the United States and Europe as well as Kenya, were beginning to re-examine the British response to the Mau Mau insurgency that had resulted in the end of colonial rule over the country in 1963.

It had always been acknowledged that the decolonisation conflict that preceded British withdrawal from Kenya had been among the most bloody of the many small wars that Britain fought at the end of Empire. Terrible atrocities had been committed by the Mau Mau, and the manner in which the insurgency was fought continues to be a divisive issue within Kenyan society today.

Throughout the conflict, those atrocities were always assidu-ously recorded by the authorities in Kenya and reported to the British public by a media that tended, very often, to take its lead from the Colonial Office. Any misconduct on the part of the British, in the prison camps and out in the forests, was hidden from view. As a consequence, British government ministers and officials had been able to maintain that any acts of brutality inflicted by the colonial authorities had been isolated and unauthorised, rather than systemic. It was a claim that took root and flourished, in the British national memory, and across much of the West.

Repeatedly, however, the lawyers and historians who were in Kenya in 2001 heard stories from elderly people that suggested that this was not true: that the British authorities had been responsible for atrocities that had been well organised and committed on a previously unimagined scale. If the old people were telling the truth, hundreds of thousands of Kikuyu, the country's largest ethnic group, had been incarcerated by the colonial government, abused, tortured and not infrequently raped. The network of prisons that would have been needed to contain so many people would have been so extensive that it would have resembled the Soviet Union's Gulag.

There were allegations that some prisoners had been horrifically mutilated, and that some jailers, in their determination to force their prisoners to disavow the oaths that were thought to bond them psychologically to the Mau Mau cause and the war against the British, had beaten inmates to death, and even burned men alive.

Bewilderingly, the available official documents from the period did not support these lurid tales of British colonial bloodlust. The Kenyan archives in Nairobi held few files of any sort that detailed the treatment of prisoners. It was known by those who worked at the archives, however, that on 3 December 1963, nine days before Kenya formally achieved independence, four large wooden packing crates had been loaded onto a British United Airways flight bound for Gatwick Airport south of London; there were persistent rumours in Nairobi that those crates contained hundreds of sensitive files. Some Kenyans spoke of other crates being flown over the Indian Ocean to be dumped at sea.[2]

At the British government's Public Record Office at Kew, south-west of London, meanwhile, there was a wealth of material that appeared to show that the colonial authorities had approached their responsibilities to their prisoners in a largely humane and civilising manner. Any acts of brutality that the documents described appeared, on the basis of the evidence within the records, to be one-off incidents.

But there was also some evidence suggesting that there were gaps in the official archives: that a great many records were absent. The British were known to be meticulous record-keepers in Kenya – no less than three different departments within the colonial administration kept individual records on more than 100,000 prisoners – yet only a few hundred appeared to have survived.

And while a handful of memoirs, letters and contemporary

newspaper reports did contain fragments of evidence that suggested the official account may have been false, many government files remained classified, more than half a century after the events that they described.

In 2005 an American historian, Caroline Elkins, published a history of the Mau Mau insurgency that relied heavily upon the accounts of the elderly people who were imprisoned by the British during the insurgency. Elkins depicted a prison regime of almost unspeakable barbarity, and a conflict in which the British colonial administrators, police and soldiers – the agents of what was supposed to be a civilising force for good – had sunk to a moral depth that would be difficult for many members of the British public to comprehend. Her work was condemned by many of her peers for relying so heavily upon oral history techniques rather than documents – which had largely vanished – and her book, *Imperial Reckoning*, came under attack. One reviewer, for example, condemned it as 'rigidly one dimensional', while another wrote: 'I shudder for those of her students who expect academic rigour.'[3]

In the absence of a large body of indisputable documentary evidence to support Elkins' view, it remained possible for many historians to take a largely benign view of the dying days of Empire in East Africa and the civilising mission of the British. Niall Ferguson, for example, barely mentions Kenya in his 2003 book about the Empire, other than to describe his time in the country as a small boy. 'Thanks to the British empire, my earliest childhood memories are of colonial Africa,' he wrote. The country had gained independence three years earlier, but thankfully, 'scarcely anything had changed . . . we had our bungalow, our maid, our smattering of Swahili – and our sense of unshakable security. It was a magical time, which indelibly impressed on my consciousness the sight of the hunting cheetah, the sound of Kikuyu women singing, the smell of the first rains and the taste of ripe mango. I suspect my mother was never happier.'[4]

Two years after that book was published, Gordon Brown, then the Chancellor of the Exchequer, declared during a visit to East Africa: 'The days of Britain having to apologise for its colonial history are over. We should move forward; we should celebrate much of our past rather than apologise for it. We should talk . . . about British values that are enduring, because they stand for some of the greatest ideas in history: tolerance, liberty, civic duty, that grew in Britain and influenced the rest of the world.'[5]

The truth about the recent past – about what actually happened in 1950s Kenya – remained largely obscured, and a subject of bitter dispute. It would be a number of years before it was revealed, before the veil would be drawn back to expose one of the most extraordinary secrets that lay behind the ten-foot fences and razor wire at Hanslope Park.

By late 2002, the British personal injury lawyers at work in Kenya had interviewed scores of elderly people who had been imprisoned by the British authorities during the 1950s, and were convinced that there was a case for the government in London to answer. The number of potential claimants ran into several thousand. Many of them were Mau Mau veterans. Some had played no part in the conflict but had been imprisoned nonetheless, and alleged that they had suffered appalling abuse.

The lawyers selected five Kenyan pensioners as test claimants. One of them, Jane Muthoni Mara, aged sixty-five, had been fifteen when she was arrested and taken from her home in the Embu district. While being interrogated, she said, two men held her down while a third raped her with a heated glass bottle. She then faced daily beatings for around three months.

Another, Paul Nzili, said he had been forced to join the Mau Mau in 1957, and was arrested after leaving the movement six months later. During his year in captivity he was castrated. 'I was taken to an open area in the camp where Luvai [the nickname of a colonial official] stripped me of my clothes in front of all the other detainees.' Nzili's arms and legs were tied together. 'Luvai then approached me with a large pair of pliers which were more than a foot long and castrated me.'

Wambugu Wa Nyingi, seventy-five, was arrested on Christmas Eve 1952. He had never joined the Mau Mau. Nevertheless, he was imprisoned for nine years. During that time he was beaten unconscious in a particularly notorious episode at a prison camp at Hola in the south-east of the country, in which eleven men were clubbed to death. He still bore the marks from leg manacles, whipping and caning. 'When I was released I would have nightmares about three times a week,' he said. 'I would dream about the murder of people at Hola. These nightmares continued for about four years.'

It was another six years before the case reached the High Court in London, by which time one of the claimants, Susan Ngondi, had died. The Foreign Secretary of the day, David Miliband, argued that the government should settle and offer a statement of regret. He was overruled by officials within his own department.[6]

Instead, the government's lawyers attempted to have the claim against it struck out on the grounds that the elderly Kenyans should have been suing the Kenyan government, and not the British authorities. Under the law of state succession, they argued, the British government was not responsible for the actions of the British colonial authorities: all legal liabilities had been inherited by the post-independence Kenyan government.

This argument did not succeed, with the judge ruling that it might be considered 'dishonourable' for the courts to refuse to hear such a claim. After all, if the British were not responsible for what happened in Kenya prior to independence, he asked, who was? So the British government's lawyers tried a different tack: the claim was time-barred, they argued, and should have been brought many years earlier.

When the claim was first lodged, a judge had ordered the

Foreign Office to disclose all relevant material. Foreign Office officials signed a number of witness statements asserting that this had been done. All Kenyan files had been sent to the National Archives, they said, and they specifically denied holding any files relating to the Mau Mau insurgency. It is unclear whether the officials who signed those statements were aware that this was not correct.

However, three historians, including Elkins, who were acting as expert witnesses for the elderly Kenyans' lawyers, realised that the historical documents handed over in court could not possibly represent full disclosure: some of the papers made references to other files which had not been delivered up. Some events, committees and policies received no mention whatsoever in the papers that had been handed over. The minutes and decisions of the colonial administration's war council, for example, were missing. In reply, the Foreign Office gave a sworn undertaking to the court that it was not holding back any Kenyan files.

At this point, one of the historians, Professor David Anderson, then of Oxford University, drew upon a forty-year-old Foreign Office minute to submit a witness statement to the court in which he concluded that the Foreign Office was deliberately withholding some 1,500 files, in 300 boxes, which would take up around 100 feet of shelf space.[7] At this point, in May 2011, two years after the claim had been lodged, the Foreign Office finally admitted the truth: it was indeed holding a further 1,500 historical Kenyan files.

The files had been concealed for years, held where no historian or lawyer or interested member of the public could find them. So voluminous was the cache that it occupied even more than the estimated 100 feet of shelving. The files took up almost 200 feet at Hanslope Park.

The rumours in Nairobi had been correct. The packing crates loaded aboard a British United Airways flight to Gatwick on the eve of independence had contained the 1,500 files. The consignment had been met by a civil servant from the Colonial Office who had supervised the loading of the four crates onto a van that was then driven to a storage facility in the west London suburb of Hayes. The papers would be held there for more than thirty years before being transferred to Hanslope Park, where a purpose-built three-storey repository was opened in November 1992. Inside the crates were some – but not all – of the British colonial authority's most sensitive documentary archives.

Once these papers were finally disclosed to the lawyers representing the elderly Kenyans and to the expert witnesses, the reason that they had remained hidden for so long was immediately clear. They detailed the way in which suspected insurgents had been beaten to death, burned alive, raped, castrated – like two of the high court claimants – and kept in manacles for years. Even children had been killed.

Among the most damning papers were a number of letters and memoranda written by the colony's Attorney General, Eric Griffith-Jones. At one point, Griffith-Jones describes the mistreatment of detained Mau Mau suspects as 'distressingly reminiscent of conditions in Nazi Germany or Communist Russia'. Despite this, in June 1957 he agreed to draft legislation that sanctioned a new regime of abuse known as the 'dilution technique', as long as the beatings were carried out with care. 'Vulnerable parts of the body should not be struck, particularly the spleen, liver or kidneys,' Griffith-Jones wrote. Anyone who protested would have 'a foot placed on his throat and mud stuffed in his mouth . . . in the last resort [would be] knocked unconscious'. While Griffith-Jones may not have been too concerned with the victims of this abuse, the papers showed him to care deeply about the future well-being of those who were to inflict it. 'The psychological effects on those who administer violence are potentially dangerous; it is essential that they should remain collected, balanced and dispassionate.'[8]

These proposed instructions were contained in a memo that Griffith-Jones sent to the colony's governor, Sir Evelyn Baring. It went almost without saying, of course, that the redrafting of the law and the introduction of the dilution technique would be enshrouded in complete secrecy. 'If we are going to sin,' Griffith-Jones advised Baring, 'we must sin quietly.'

Baring forwarded the memo to Alan Lennox-Boyd, Secretary of State for the Colonies, in London, with a covering letter which asserted that inflicting 'violent shock' was the only way of dealing with Mau Mau insurgents.

The documents also contained accounts of torture that colonial officials were writing and passing on to their superiors throughout the eight years of the insurgency. One described how an African employee of Special Branch 'pushed pins into their [i.e. detainees'] sides, buttocks, fingers and, on at least one occasion, the head, and . . . pinched the sides of their bodies, penis and scrotum with pliers. He crushed the fingers of one detainee.'

Also buried away within the 1,500 files at Hanslope Park was a letter to Baring from Colonel Arthur Young, a veteran police officer and Christian socialist who had lasted less than a year as commissioner of the Kenyan police before handing in his resignation. Young had told Baring in December 1954 that the prison camps in which the Mau Mau suspects were detained 'present a state of affairs so deplorable that they should be investigated without delay so that the ever-increasing allegations of inhumanity and disregard for the rights of the African citizen are dealt with'.

Many of the documents addressed the requirement that British officers and their African subalterns should escape prosecution for their acts. In January 1955, for example, Baring informed Lennox-Boyd that eight European officers were facing accusations of a series of murders, beatings and shootings. They included: 'One District Officer, murder by beating up and roasting alive of one African.' All eight received an amnesty.

Despite having received such clear briefings, Lennox-Boyd and the officials around him had repeatedly denied that the abuses were happening, and publicly denounced those colonial officials who came forward to complain.

With the disclosure of the Hanslope Park archive, the fiction that the abuses in Kenya had been isolated and unauthorised could no longer be maintained. The torture and murder had been systemic – choreographed, in fact, by colonial administrators and the colony's law officers – and ministers and officials in London had been fully aware of the details of the abuses for which they were responsible: abuses that the British public had repeatedly been assured, throughout the 1950s, were not happening.

This was not all. In an announcement in the House of Lords in April 2011, the government admitted that Hanslope Park was holding a total of 8,800 files, containing hundreds of thousands of pages of official documents, from thirty-seven former colonies. Some, such as Palestine, Cyprus and Aden, had been territories from which the British had withdrawn amid bloody conflict.

Most of the documents had been removed secretly from the colonies in line with a telegram of 3 May 1961 from Colonial Secretary Iain Macleod that set down four main criteria for selection. The documents that were to be sent back to Britain would be those that might embarrass Her Majesty's Government; that might embarrass members of the police, military forces, public servants or others, such as informers; that might compromise sources of intelligence information; or that 'might be used un-ethically by ministers in a successor Government'. They were to be loaded aboard RAF aircraft or a British-owned airliner and flown to London. If they must be transported by sea, they could be entrusted only to the 'care of a British ship's master on a British ship'.[9]

The Foreign Office had given its enormous hidden cache of colonial-era papers a name. It called it 'the migrated archive', as it was said to contain files that had 'migrated', in some ill-defined way, to London from the former colonies. Some of the files were still arriving in London as recently as the late 1970s.

Being forced to admit the existence of the archive was a deeply humiliating episode. The Foreign Office maintained that the vast hoard of documents had been misplaced and overlooked. William Hague, the Foreign Secretary, announced that there would be an inquiry headed by the former High Commissioner to Canada, Anthony Cary. 'It is my intention,' Hague told MPs, 'to release every part of every paper of interest subject only to legal exemptions.'[10]

Then in June 2013, following months of negotiations with the Mau Mau claimants' lawyers, Hague told the House of Commons that the British government was finally settling the case. It would pay £19.9 million in compensation and costs to 5,228 claimants. The British government would also fund the construction of a memorial in Nairobi to victims of torture during the colonial era. 'The British Government sincerely regrets that these abuses took place and that they marred Kenya's progress towards independence,' Hague said. 'Torture and ill treatment are abhorrent violations of human dignity, which we unreservedly condemn.'[11]

A Foreign Office spokesperson added: 'We believe there should be a debate about the past. It is an enduring feature of our democracy that we are willing to learn from our history.'

Caroline Elkins and her work on the Mau Mau conflict were exonerated: much of the documentation corroborated the oral evidence she had gathered. David Anderson, the historian whose High Court witness statement had forced the Foreign Office to acknowledge its hidden archive, wrote that he believed the contents of the files would lead to a significant revision of the history of British decolonisation. 'It is somewhat ironic that what began as a quest to find documentary evidence of systematic British torture in Kenya should end up revealing a potential treasure trove of documents on the decolonisation of Britain's vast empire in the years following the Second World War,' he wrote.[12]

Later that year in Cyprus, veterans of the armed rebellion against British rule that was waged by Ethniki Organosis Kyprion Agoniston, or EOKA, for three-and-a-half years in the '50s announced that they too were bringing proceedings against the British government. The old men had been watching the Mau Mau proceedings closely. They alleged that at least fourteen Cypriots, including two seventeen-year-old boys, died under interrogation, and that hundreds more were beaten and water-boarded – allegations that appeared to be supported by some of the Hanslope Park papers, as well as by International Committee of the Red Cross reports of the time.

The inquiry got under way and eventually Anthony Cary's findings about the 'migrated archive' were made public, albeit in a document that was itself redacted, with a number of passages blacked out. Cary had established that the Kenyan government had repeatedly asked for the return of its 1,500 files, but this had been refused on the grounds that they were said to be the property of the British government. Privately, the Foreign Office had been concerned that returning the Kenyan papers would advertise the existence of the thousands of files taken from other colonies. The minute from November 1967 which had been the basis for Professor Anderson's High Court witness statement, for example, warned that sending the documents back to Kenya could 'set a precedent and encourage other governments to follow suit . . . [and demand] the documents of other former Dependent Territories which are now held here'.

A Commonwealth Office memo on the same subjected warned: 'The fact that it has always been British policy to withdraw or destroy certain sensitive records prior to Independence has never been advertised or generally admitted. The reply we give to Kenya could affect the treatment of records and files withdrawn from other former Colonial Territories.'

It was now clear that over the course of three decades, the British government had stuck to the line that the 'migrated archive' was the property of Her Majesty's Government and that it did not intend to part with any of it. At Hanslope Park, a convenient lie was put about – 'a canard widely shared and passed down during handovers', in Cary's words – that the files were being held on behalf of a company or agency called Hayes, where there had been a fire.

On a number of occasions, the National Archives was asked whether it wanted to take possession of the documents. But staff at the National Archives persistently refused, on the grounds that they did not believe colonial administration documents to be covered by the Public Records Acts. In this way, the documents were tossed into a legal limbo, with the National Archives claiming that they were not official British government papers, and the British government determined not to relinquish ownership.

In 2007, senior staff at the National Archives, officially described as 'the guardians of some of our most iconic national documents', were still attempting to wash their hands of the papers. While accepting that the files had been removed from former colonies because 'they were deemed too sensitive for whatever reason', they proposed a simple solution: 'We are content for the FCO [Foreign and Commonwealth Office] to dispose of these records by destruction without further reference to TNA [The National Archives].'

A number of Foreign Office archivists objected, on the grounds that they knew the files to contain material of unique historical interest. Moreover, the archive was a useful working resource for a department such as this that had a continuing historical interest in most corners of the globe. The files were consulted, for example, by the Foreign Office during its legal battle with Chagos Islanders who had been forcibly removed from their homes on Diego Garcia, the largest of the islands comprising the Chagos Archipelago in the Indian Ocean, in order to make way for a US military base.

According to Cary, Foreign Office archivists were 'conscious of the files as a sort of guilty secret'. One junior documents retrievals officer told him: 'People tried to ignore the fact that we had them. We weren't really supposed to have them so it was thought best to ignore them for the purpose of [Freedom of Information–related] requests.'

Cary was reluctant to conclude that there had been a conspiracy to conceal the documents. Instead, he said, there had been 'a failure by successive senior managers to grip what should have been seen to be an unresolved and potentially explosive problem'.[13] But even if Cary was correct to conclude that muddle and carelessness accounted for the 'loss' of such an enormous archive – an explanation that Professor Anderson dismisses as 'incredible' – his report made clear that the system for storage and declassification of government papers was woefully inadequate and excessively secretive.

After the existence of the colonial–era files was exposed during the Mau Mau case, the Foreign Office asked an independent historian, Tony Badger of Cambridge University, to oversee their declassification and transfer to the National Archives. Badger described it as an 'embarrassing, scandalous' episode. After he began his task, he wrote: 'It is difficult to overestimate the legacy of suspicion among historians, lawyers and journalists. For years, the FCO . . . denied its existence. Only belatedly did the FCO acknowledge its existence and hand over relevant documents for the court case. The decision by the foreign secretary to order the release of all the documents of interest has not allayed the suspicions of historians that the Foreign Office is "up to its old tricks".'

Badger established that the 'migrated archive' did not contain 8,800 files, as Parliament had been told: the true figure was higher than 20,000. He found that their contents gave an illuminating insight into the mindset of British colonial administrators. 'The files confirm the casual disregard of the rights or the fate of the indigenous islanders of Diego Garcia,' he wrote. They also 'convey a sense of how the business of government carried on on a day-to-day basis as administrators continued with the mundane tasks of running a country while momentous events went on round about them.'[14]

As well as the Kenyan files that had led to the government throwing in the towel in the High Court Mau Mau case, the 'migrated archive' yielded official papers from Cyprus which contained 'very full descriptions of the allegations of police brutality'; revelations about the ruthlessness with which Chagos Islanders were forcibly removed from Diego Garcia to make way for a US military base; and new details about the politics of decolonisation around the globe.

However, Badger and other historians quickly realised that the hidden archive was as remarkable for what it did not contain as for what it did. There were just five boxes of files from Aden, for example, a colony from which the British extracted themselves after a particularly bloody four-year rebellion, and where there was a policy of removing as many documents as possible for fear they would be discovered by a successor government. When the boxes from Aden were opened, it was found that half the files inside were personnel records of low-ranking officials, while most of the remaining papers concerned agriculture.

Similarly, there were substantial numbers of files from Malaya, but very little material about the British war against the Malayan Communist Party, which was waged for twelve years from 1948 at a cost of more than 11,000 lives.

And there were no files whatsoever from British Guiana, a colony where the democratically elected government had been overthrown by British troops in 1953, where there had been a covert Anglo-American campaign of bombings, and where politicians had been detained in the early 1960s.

It was, one historian commented, 'almost as if the material now made public had also been screened according to the same criteria applied *circa* 1960 – preventing potential prosecutions, protecting collaborators, and protecting the reputation of Britain'.[15]

The truth was that the missing material had not merely been screened, it had been subjected to one of the most extraordinary clandestine processes of the end of Empire: Operation Legacy.

When the final retreat first began, the British had made no great attempt to conceal the manner in which they were weeding the annals of Empire for destruction.

On the partition of India in August 1947, for example, one Colonial Office official noted that 'the press greatly enjoyed themselves with the pall of smoke which hung over Delhi during the mass destruction of documents'.[16] Four months later, after the British announced plans to withdraw from Palestine, a correspondent in Jerusalem reported that 'government officials have . . . been instructed to prepare their effects for dispatch to England. The burning of files is progressing satisfactorily; slow withdrawal of troops has already begun . . .'[17]

The following year, as first Burma and then Ceylon broke free, colonial officials began to give greater thought to the future of the archives under their control. In Ceylon, officials who were considering how they might take 'proper steps to safeguard secret material' decided to find out what had happened on Irish independence twenty-six years earlier. They noted, however, that all they could find in the Colonial Office records was 'the version of what happened to the Eire papers as given to the public',[18] suggesting that they had little confidence that that version had been the truth.

One legal advisor thought the Ceylon material should be handed to the post-independence government, but Colonial Office officials said they feared the contents of some of the documents would cause embarrassment of 'monsoon proportions'. The best option, they concluded, would be remove any sensitive material to London, and let the Colonial Office

– rather than the newly appointed British High Commissioner – take any subsequent blame.[19]

By the 1950s, it was clear that the British would soon be withdrawing from one territory after another: the imperial adventure was entering its endgame, but its legacy was yet to be shaped. It would be difficult to maintain the boast that the British Empire had been a uniquely gracious and charitable enterprise – compared with, say, that of the French or the Portuguese – if its final days were seen to be accompanied by a frenzied destruction of the papers that documented the day-to-day running of that empire. A greater degree of secrecy was called for.

On the morning of 19 August 1957, a civilian truck driven by a British soldier set off from Kuala Lumpur, the capital of British Malaya, for the 220-mile drive to Singapore. It was the first of five journeys that would be made that week. Military police provided escorts, but at a discreet distance, as they were under orders not to draw attention to the trucks: the loads they carried were of inestimable value.

Over the previous eight months, British officials across Malaya had been working steadily through all of the files in their possession in preparation for the country's independence. They were under instructions to weed out every document that it might be considered undesirable to hand over to the newly independent government of the Federation of Malaya, either because 'the information they contain reflects the policy or point of view of the UK Government which it is not desired to make known to the Federation Government', or because 'they might give offence on account of their discussion of Malayan problems and personalities'. Some of these papers were destroyed immediately by burning, while others were removed to the Governor's office for further inspection.

That morning in August, independence was just twelve days away. The Army provided crates, civil servants packed them with official papers and soldiers loaded the crates aboard the trucks. One colonial official later wrote, in an account of the operation, that 'the files . . . were driven down to the naval base at Singapore, and destroyed in the Navy's splendid incinerator there'. He added that 'considerable pains were nevertheless taken to carry out the operation discreetly, partly to avoid exacerbating relationships between the British government and those Malayans who might not have been so understanding . . . and partly to avoid comment by the press. These efforts were successful.'[20]

So successful were these efforts that the account of the Malayan document destruction remained concealed for more than half a century before it turned up among the papers that had been hidden away for decades at Hanslope Park, and which the Foreign Office was compelled to hand over to the National Archives during the Mau Mau case.

From the moment that the 'migrated archive' became available for public scrutiny at Kew in 2012, it was clear that it contained numerous other papers that testified to a worldwide purge of sensitive or damning documentation: there was correspondence that described the laborious burning of papers; there were telegrams from London giving precise instructions for methods of destruction; there were even 'destruction certificates', signed and witnessed by colonial officials to confirm that certain classes of documents had been incinerated.

Acting under directions from London, colonial officials had also created an extraordinarily elaborate system of document classification and a series of code words in order to conceal evidence of the purge from post-independence governments. Eventually, as that system was developed, government clerks working in colonies that were on the brink of independence were creating entire parallel registries: one containing files that were to be handed over at independence, and a second that would be destroyed or returned to London.

An overview of the system was included in a Foreign Office

background report that was prepared for ministers in 1982, before it too was hidden away in Hanslope Park. During the transition to independence, the report explained, successor governments would establish unofficial cabinets of local ministers, and very often ask the British colonial authorities for help in understanding the archives of official papers that they were to inherit. At this point, the defence, intelligence and security departments of the Colonial Office, along with the relevant geographical department, would send a dispatch to the Governor, setting out the principles to be kept in mind when either destroying records, shipping them to London, or handing them over to the post-independence government.[21]

On 15 May 1953, British Guiana became one of the first colonies to adopt the practice of parallel filing.[22] This was less than three weeks after the leftist People's Progressive Party won a landslide victory in a general election – a result that disturbed London and terrified Washington. The poll result had prompted Winston Churchill to write to his colonial secretary, Oliver Lyttelton, suggesting it was time to ask for US assistance to topple the democratically elected government. 'We ought to get American support in doing all that we can to break the Communist teeth in British Guiana,' he wrote.[23] Five months later, Operation Windsor was launched, with British troops landing in British Guiana to overthrow the government.

Another early adopter of the double filing system was Uganda, where a handful of local ministers had been in office for seven years by the time the country achieved independence in 1962. It was in Uganda that the term Operation Legacy was first coined. The covert parallel files were given the simple codename 'Personal', so that any Ugandan inquiring about their contents could be told that they contained only personal and confidential correspondence.[24]

In truth, the Foreign Office background report made clear that these 'Personal' papers were to be seen only by the British

Governor and his senior aides: they were for UK eyes only. 'The Personal series was in fact a covert system of correspondence,' the author of the 1982 background report explained. 'All Personal correspondence, whether by mail or by telegram, was numbered in a separate series so that there was no indication in the normal overt series of its existence, and its existence was scrupulously protected. Introducing the Personal system meant that there were two sets of files for classified material, the overt (including material up to secret) to which [local] ministers had access, and the covert, which no-one but the [British] Governor and his expatriate staff in the dependent territory knew about.'

This system was expanded over time, with new security classifications known as 'DG' (short for Deputy Governor) and 'Watch' being introduced, to allow documents to be seen by lower-ranking white officials, or by officials of the governments of Australia, New Zealand or Canada.

In March 1961, Bill Marquand, senior assistant secretary of the colonial government in Uganda, wrote to his old friend and colleague Fernley Webber at the Colonial Office in London. Marked 'Secret and Personal', the letter explained the latest arrangements. 'Dear Webber,' he wrote, 'You should know that at the moment we are carrying out an exercise throughout Uganda of "purging" all files and papers which may prejudice the defence of the Commonwealth in times of war; embarrass HMG or any other government or the present government of Uganda; lead to the identification of a "source" and thereby to the possible victimisation of that source; provide information that may lead to the victimisation of any person.

'This operation is known as "Operation Legacy" and steps are being taken to ensure that such papers are only seen and handled by Civil Service Officers who are British subjects of European descent employed by the Protectorate Government. Such officers are known for these purposes as "Authorised Officers" and for as long as practicable the papers will be retained by such officers in their offices. In the future, as these officers are replaced by unauthorised officers or at any time that the Government thinks appropriate, these papers will be gradually destroyed or withdrawn to higher offices which remain under the direct control of authorised officers until the papers are all held in the Deputy Governor's office, eventually to be destroyed there or removed to the United Kingdom.

'All papers in the "Personal" series with the Colonial Office etc. are of course regarded as falling within this category. The main purpose of this letter is to warn you that you may receive some papers in the future with the magic letters "D.G." (standing for "Deputy Governor") in the top right-hand corner. This mark has no significance insofar as the Colonial Office is concerned, but in Uganda the mark means that the letter is only to be seen and handled by an authorised officer.'

Webber wrote back congratulating Marquand on the steps being taken and suggesting that a small committee of two senior administrators and a Special Branch detective might examine each document to advise on concealment or destruction.[25]

The teams responsible for the purges worked in line with the broad instructions that had been issued by Colonial Secretary Iain Macleod in May 1961: that nothing should be handed over that might embarrass HMG; that might embarrass members of the police, military forces or public servants; that might compromise sources of intelligence information; or that might be used 'unethically' by a post-independence government.

Further detailed instructions issued by the colonial government made it clear that 'DG' papers should include those that contained information about political parties and trade unions; those containing details of individuals' involvement in politics or unions; 'all intelligence summaries, appreciations and reports from other Governments, except those that have been deliberately issued in the knowledge that they may be seen by unauthorised persons'; all papers relating to Special Branch training and organisation; 'any papers which might be interpreted as showing religious intolerance on the part of HMG', and 'all papers which might be interpreted as showing racial discrimination against Africans (or Negros in the USA)'.

Those files that were to be handed over to the post-independence government of Uganda were to be known as Legacy files. To be sure they fully understood their responsibilities, the weeders were reminded: 'Legacy files must not contain any reference whatsoever to the subject of DG files or papers. A DG file may contain some Legacy papers but a Legacy file must never contain any DG papers. Similarly, Legacy papers may be kept on a DG file to complete the story.'[26]

Early in 1961, the system was extended to Kenya, and the following year to Northern Rhodesia. In a memo headed Operation Legacy, colonial officials in Nairobi were informed that some DG files could be destroyed immediately, while those that were to be kept must be 'filed in clearly marked "DG" files which can be picked up and removed to a safe office at very short notice'. DG papers could be transported only in envelopes marked Personal.[27] What was described as a 'thorough purge' was soon under way in Kenya. Instructions were issued that only an individual who was 'a servant of the Kenya government who is a British subject of European descent' could participate in the operation. This was enforced by Special Branch police officers, who were under orders to prevent any African from stumbling upon the process.

In February 1962, the Kenyan colonial government's Director of Intelligence and Security wrote a slightly impatient note to the administration's Permanent Secretary for Defence, reminding him: 'My view for some time is that we need a protective code word to indicate that documents so marked are for sight by expatriate European officers only . . . and I think we ought to introduce it very soon if we are not to run into trouble. You were going to take this up with the Colonial Office. Perhaps you could hurry them up?'[28]

The documents that survived the purge and ended up at Hanslope Park depict a period of mounting anxiety as independence for Kenya approached, amid fears that some of the incriminating files might be leaked. Officials were warned that they would be prosecuted if they took any paperwork home, and some were. A new security classification, the 'W', or 'Watch', series, was introduced, and sensitive papers were stamped with a red letter W. As independence grew closer, large caches of files were removed from colonial ministries to governors' offices, where new safes were installed.

Again, painstaking measures were taken to prevent post-independence governments from learning that the Watch files had ever existed. One instruction stated: 'The legacy files must leave no reference to Watch material. Indeed, the very existence of the Watch series, though it may be guessed at, should never be revealed.' When a single Watch file was to be removed from a group of Legacy files, a 'twin file' – or dummy – was to be created to insert in its place. If this was not practicable, the documents were to be removed en masse and destroyed or flown to London.

A handful of 'destruction certificates' that are to be found scattered among the 'migrated archive' give a hint of the sort of documents that were routinely set ablaze during the purge. One completed at the residency at Zanzibar in 1963, for example, certifies the destruction of dozens of files, including those entitled 'Codewords and Nicknames', 'The Immediate Outlook in Iraq', 'Egyptian Activities in East Africa' and 'Subversive Activity in Zanzibar'.

Across the Empire, the weeders were urged not to follow the example set by their colleagues in Malaya a few years earlier, it by then being the view that the Singapore incineration operation, while no doubt 'splendid' in its own way, had been far too zealous. 'It is better for too much, rather than too little, to be sent home – the wholesale destruction, as in Malaya, should not be repeated.'

Nonetheless, the emphasis was on secrecy. Officials engaged in the purge in Kenya were even warned that they must keep their W stamps in a safe place.

Following destruction, no trace of the act of destruction was to remain. When documents were burned, 'the waste should be reduced to ash and the ashes broken up'. In some circumstances, officials in Kenya were informed, 'it is permissible, as an alternative to destruction by fire, for documents to be packed in weighted crates and dumped in very deep and current-free waters at maximum practicable distance from the coast'.[29]

In June 1960, the Colonial Office authorised the introduction of an additional code word, 'Guard', which was to be stamped on papers that could be seen by senior officials of the so-called Old Commonwealth – Australia, New Zealand, Canada and South Africa – but not, intriguingly, by the Americans.

The following year, Macleod's successor at the Colonial Office, Reginald Maudling, sent a circular to senior colonial officials across the Empire marked 'Confidential, Personal and Guard', which reminded them that papers stamped 'Guard' must be kept out of the hands of the Americans. 'The British governments and the governments of the old Commonwealth countries collaborate so closely with the Government of the United States in certain fields,' Maudling said, 'that a special warning is required to indicate that certain documents should not be made available to the Americans.'

The document notes that such advice need not be extended to the colonial authorities in the so-called New Commonwealth – in Africa and the Caribbean – as they did not receive 'Guard' material. However, officials serving in 'more advanced Colonial territories' may be shown 'Guard' material on a strict 'need to know' basis and always in paraphrased form. 'If considered necessary the information should be accompanied by an oral warning that it must not be communicated to the Americans.'

Maudling made it clear that South Africa was to be kept out of the picture altogether, giving notice that 'an amendment covering the exclusion of South Africa from the "Guard" procedure will . . . shortly be issued.'[30]

In 1961, British territories in the Caribbean prepared for independence. Colonial officials in Jamaica, Trinidad and the Leeward and Windward Islands were given the instructions for the destruction and removal of documents that were by now routine. They were also introduced to the parallel-files system of the Personal system.

By this time, Operation Legacy had become a source of amusement for some in the upper reaches of Whitehall. In December that year, for example, the Colonial Office wrote to Sir Solomon Hochoy, the British Governor of Trinidad and Tobago, suggesting he make an early start on the weeding of official papers. 'It is a long job that needs doing thoroughly and it would perhaps be a little unfortunate to celebrate Independence Day with smoke.' Helpfully, the civil servant at Whitehall added: 'You may like to know that, as an alternative to fire, it is permissible to pack documents in well weighted crates and sink them in current free water at the maximum practicable distance from the shore.'[31]

The following year, in Belize, as with other colonies in the region, there was a shortage of trustworthy officials 'of European descent' who were considered qualified to perform the task of weeding and destroying documents. The task was left to a visiting MI5 officer, who decided that every sensitive file should be destroyed: 'In this he was assisted by the Royal Navy and several gallons of petrol.'[32]

In British Guiana – which had been placed on the Personal network in 1953 in advance of the landing of British troops during Operation Windsor – the burning of documents did not get under way for another twelve years. In late 1965, six months before independence, a British official at Government House in Georgetown wrote to London to complain about the requirement to complete destruction certificates, when so few staff were available to perform the task. 'It has not yet been possible to record for you the correspondence which has been or is about to be destroyed,' he wrote. Two women employees were working alone, burning papers in a single forty-four-gallon drum in the grounds of Government House, and it was a far from easy task. 'The daily burden of work resting on Miss Dalgleish and Mrs Sutherland leaves insufficient time in which they can identify, record and type as necessary, the identities of the Colonial Office correspondence which you need to know about, as well as enduring the hot and wearing work of actually burning the files.'

The official added that he was 'hoping that a period of relative quiet will descend on Government House for a week or so from 1st November and that an orgy of destruction will then become a practical proposition'. In the event, the military came to the rescue, as in Malaya and Belize, 'to provide more adequate facilities for disposal by burning'.[33]

Meanwhile, colonial officials scattered around what remained of the Empire were looking for clear guidance on what should and should not be destroyed, and they turned for advice to the Colonial Office and Foreign Office records keepers.

The Public Records Act, which had come into force just a short time before, made clear that these government archivists were responsible for ensuring that their departments met their legal obligation to preserve and eventually declassify important official papers. Yet far from creating and preserving an official archive of record, they were the very people who had been given the responsibility for the destruction and concealment of papers, under Operation Legacy.

In August 1963, Robert Turner, the Chief Secretary of the British protectorate of North Borneo, wrote to senior officials and records officers at the Colonial Office a few weeks before his colony gained independence and merged with Malaya. Turner explained that his subordinates' monthly reports – 'which would be unsuitable for the eyes of local ministers' – were being saved and sent to London, rather than destroyed. 'I . . . have been prevailed upon to do so on the grounds that some at least of their contents may come in handy when some future Gibbon is doing research work for his "Decline and Fall of the British Empire".'[34] Turner clearly had no idea that the documents he was preserving would be concealed from historians for decades, until their disclosure was forced upon the Foreign Office by the Mau Mau case.

Later that year an official in Malta asked London for advice about which files should be 'spirited away out of the country', noting that while some documents could be handed over to the post-independence government, 'there may . . . be others which could be given to them if they were doctored first; and there may be files which cannot be given to them under any circumstances'.[35]

In June 1966, Fernley Webber, by now the High Commissioner in Brunei, consulted Bernard Cheeseman, chief librarian at the Commonwealth Relations Office, about the disposal of sixty boxes of files. 'My Dear Cheese,' he wrote, 'I should be very grateful if you could give me some advice about my Records. I have inherited rather over sixty boxes of files from my predecessors. Can you tell me what the procedure is? Can I, off my own bat, destroy some of these papers, or should the whole lot be sent home for weeding or retention in your records?'[36]

Finally, before the British withdrawal from Aden the following year, civil servants engaged in what one described as 'an orgy of burning'. Those files that were returned to London were 'severely weeded' beforehand, 'to destroy the more embarrassing papers'. As a consequence, one of the weeders later wrote, 'details of tribal affrays, secret counter-insurgency operations funded out of the coded-worded money bags . . . and many examples of less sensitive "keeni meeni" * are all gone and are not duplicated elsewhere'.[37]

Operation Legacy continued for more than two decades, until the early 1970s. Hundreds if not thousands of British colonial officials were involved, as were Special Branch officers and local MI5 liaison officers, all three branches of the armed services, and countless servicemen and women.

And it achieved its aim. For more than half a century, the bonfires that accompanied the end of Empire went largely unreported and without comment. The former colonies had been robbed of the documents that would have mattered most to them at the moment of their independence: they contained evidence of the methods of subjugation that had helped to shape their new national identity. And the duplicity and deception of the Personal double-filing system led to post-colonial governments attempting to conduct their business on the basis of incomplete or bogus records, or no records at all.

In the late 1970s, British diplomats around the world were asked to discreetly inquire as to which nations that were formerly part of the Empire were aware that their colonial-era records had been destroyed or removed to London. Only the governments of Kenya and Malta knew: the other thirty-five governments remained in the dark. The Foreign Office was determined that they should stay that way.[38]

It is difficult to sift through the surviving papers without being overawed by the scale of the operation and the all-encompassing secrecy surrounding the destruction of such a large amount of the annals of Empire, and the removal of what remained to London.

---

* From the Swahili term that describes the slithering of a snake.

Why was it done? The desire to protect British officials from 'embarrassment' – or prosecution – is an explanation that can readily be understood. Equally explicable would be an inclination to place at a disadvantage those post-colonial governments whose allegiance may not have been completely assured, particularly at a time when Britain, the United States and other western governments were seeking to manage the process of decolonisation in a way that advanced their Cold War objectives.

That might help to explain the destruction and concealment of official archives in British Guiana in 1965 and '66, say, and certainly it would explain the bonfires that were set alight the following year in Aden. But it is more difficult to see how Cold War anxieties could explain the deployment of Operation Legacy in Malaya or Brunei, where the loyalty of the post-independence governments was not in doubt.

Nor could a determination to protect the reputations of the dead explain a clandestine operation that was global in scope, that ran for decades, and which must have been exorbitantly expensive.

The answer, of course, is in the name: Operation Legacy. By the time the greatest of empires was finally being dissolved, the most important considerations for those in government, in Whitehall and in the colonies, were that the British way of doing things should come to be recalled with fondness and respect, and that the retreat should be recorded as a dignified affair.

Alan Lennox-Boyd, the Secretary of State for the Colonies who was ultimately responsible for the appalling abuses inflicted on Mau Mau suspects, and who presided over the cover-up, was once said by his arch-enemy Barbara Castle, the Labour politician, to be 'imbued with the conviction that the British ruling class, both at home and overseas, could do no wrong'.[39] In fact, Lennox-Boyd, and many others around the Empire, were perfectly aware that they were capable not only of doing wrong, but also of great folly and cruelty. A flattering official narrative needed to be established and protected.

Operation Legacy allowed the British to nurture a memory of Empire that was deeply deceptive – a collective confabulation of an imperial mission that had brought nothing but progress and good order to a previously savage world, unlike the French, Italians, Belgians, Germans and Portuguese – those inferior colonial powers whose adventures had been essentially brutal, cynical and exploitative.

As a consequence, some historians would in future be able to enjoy the smell of the first rains in Kenya and the ripe mangoes, and the singing of the Kikuyu women, rather than concern themselves with the castrations, and the water-boarding, and the roasting alive.

With forced disclosure of the 20,000 files of the 'migrated archive' that had been hidden at Hanslope Park, this carefully constructed narrative of Empire had begun to unravel, and new questions were being asked about each and every one of Britain's former colonies, questions that historians will be attempting to answer for many years.

But there was another question. Of all the locations at which the Foreign Office could have stored its Special Collections, why did it choose Hanslope Park?

The answer, it appeared, lay in a scientific discovery that was made on the other side of the Atlantic at the height of the Second World War, and which itself became a closely guarded official secret.

One morning in the summer of 1943, at the laboratories of the Bell Telephone Company in downtown New York, a technician saw something that made him put his coffee cup to one side and take a deep breath. A few feet from where he was working was an oscilloscope. And every few minutes, for no apparent reason, the oscilloscope would spike. He observed the machine for some time, and after roaming around the lab to see what else was going on, the technician realised that the spikes coincided with the moments at which a teleprinter machine, several yards away on the opposite side of the lab, would start operating.

This was a phenomenon that was not merely fascinating, it was deeply alarming: Bell had sold large numbers of identical teleprinters to both the US Army and the US Navy, asserting that they were entirely secure. Far from being secure, it was now clear that the machines were sending out signals that could be captured and read.

Bell alerted the US Army's signals corps, whose technicians were so incredulous about what Bell was claiming that the phone company offered to stage an experiment. The army's signallers sent messages for several hours from an office in Varick Street in lower Manhattan, while the Bell technicians, sitting in their lab across the street, not only picked up the signals, but deciphered around three quarters of them.

The potential that this discovery offered to those working in the realms of signals intelligence was obvious — as were the dangers that it flagged up to their colleagues operating on the other side of the coin in communications security. And others had also made the same discovery: not long after the Second World War ended, the US Army Security Agency, forerunner of the National Security Agency (NSA), and its close friends across the Atlantic serving with the British government's newly formed Government Communications Headquarters both noticed that the Soviets appeared to be insulating their teleprinter machines.

The exact nature of the phenomenon and the scale of both the problem and the opportunity that it created were set out succinctly several years later in an article in the NSA's internal bulletin, *Cryptological Spectrum*: 'At any time a machine is used to process classified information electronically, the various switches, contacts, relays and other components in that machine may emit radio frequency or acoustic energy. These emissions, like radio broadcasts, may radiate through free space for considerable distances – a half mile or more in some cases. Or they may be induced on nearby conductors like signals lines, power lines, telephone lines or water pipes and be conducted along those paths for some distance – and here we may be talking of a mile or more.

'When these emissions can be intercepted and recorded, it is frequently possible to analyse them and recover the intelligence that was being processed by the source equipment. The phenomenon affects not only cipher machines but *any* information processing equipment – teletypewriters, duplicating equipment, intercoms, facsimile, computers – you name it.'

The article went on to explain that the interception of emissions from encryption machines was a serious danger as it could lead to the reconstruction of the daily changes to the NSA's keying patterns – and that, it claimed, from the point of view of communications security, 'is absolutely the worst thing that can happen to us'.

The author added: 'The problem of compromising radiation we have given the cover-name TEMPEST.'[40]

As GCHQ began to grow in the post-war years, first at an RAF station in west London and then at its own site in Cheltenham, Hanslope Park continued to operate as an out-station where technicians grappled with the Tempest problem. They and their colleagues in the United States experimented by erecting control zones around electronic equipment, and developed ways of shielding machines – and sometimes entire rooms and buildings – with copper or other conductive materials. It is work that continues today – hence the use of a degausser to eliminate magnetic emissions from the *Guardian*'s computer hard drives during the heavy-handed visit that followed publication of the first news reports based on the GCHQ and NSA files that had been leaked by Edward Snowden in 2013.

The opportunities that Tempest offered were quickly exploited, meanwhile: in his autobiography *Spycatcher*, the MI5 officer Peter Wright described the way in which a body called the Radiation Operations Committee coordinated Tempest surveillance operations against the Egyptian embassy in London during the Suez crisis, and against the French embassy during Britain's negotiations to join the European Economic Community. Soon, Wright recorded, he was 'reading the Frog's traffic' with such ease that he was thanked in person by the Permanent Secretary at the Foreign Office.[41]

The technicians at Hanslope Park realised that the safest way to make sure that no foreign intelligence agency captured compromising British radiation was to use machines that do not create any. As a consequence, in the twenty-first century, some of the offices inside the compound contain manual typewriters. The ribbons are produced by a government agency. And in the corner of each office is a small incinerator, into which the ribbons are placed after use.

Hanslope Park is a facility that is at the vanguard of technological development and experimentation, and, at the same time, curiously low-tech. It is also a place that is accustomed to generating, transporting, storing – and destroying – prodigious amounts of paper.

As such, it was the ideal location for the Foreign Office to hide the evidence of Operation Legacy. And it would turn out that the 'migrated archive' at Hanslope accounted for only a small proportion of the vast repositories of 'public' documents that are being unlawfully withheld from the public.

Locks, Keys and Responsible Custodians

The Misnomer of Public Records

The British government's official position on public documents is that it is 'committed to openness and transparency in public affairs' as it believes this to enhance good governance. 'When the public can access as much public information as possible,' it says, 'society benefits from a wider range of contributions to public debate; public authorities are held to account by those they serve; and the way Government has handled recent events can be analysed better.'[1] But the reality has never been quite so clear cut, and those with direct experience of government's approach to public documents – the historians, lawyers, journalists and other members of the public – find at times that it appears rooted in a culture of concealment and retention, rather than one of openness.

Following the disclosure of the existence of the 'migrated archive', Foreign Office ministers made a number of statements to Parliament, announcing a thorough investigation and promising to declassify 'every part of every paper'. At no point, however, was there any hint that the department might be unlawfully hoarding other records.

In fact, in addition to the 20,000 colonial-era files, the Foreign Office was holding on to no less than 170,000 other historical files at its offices in the UK and in missions overseas.[2] These were said to have been discovered during an exhaustive search of filing cabinets.

And then there was Hanslope Park. Occasionally, the department's records keepers in London would let slip that a particular file was held at an unnamed location nicknamed 'Up North', although the facility is only sixty miles north of London. But there was never any suggestion, while the Foreign Office was finally coming clean about its 'migrated archive', that it was holding any further historical files there.

When Foreign Office archivists held a clear-the-air conference for historians in London two years after the 'migrated archive' was disclosed, the department's senior records officer went so far as to give a presentation entitled 'Myth and Reality' in which she denounced 'inaccurate' media reporting of the scandal, and suggested that only a few other papers were held at Hanslope Park, trivial items that she dismissed as 'odd collections of material'.[3]

In fact, the Foreign Office staff at the 'clear-the air' conference were aware that it was not some small and barely significant collection of papers that the department had been concealing; it had been struggling with a shameful and unlawful secret of colossal proportions.

There were not thousands of files of public documents being held there, but anything up to 1.2 million, containing millions and millions of individual pages. Far from taking up a few hundred feet, or even a few hundred yards, of shelving, the Foreign Office's invisible cache of historical records took up fifteen miles of floor-to-ceiling shelving.

The Foreign Office had given its enormous secret a name: the 'Special Collections'. The archive did not just detail the final days of the Empire: its contents related to events stretching back to 1662, and spanned the slave trade, the Boer War, two world wars, the Cold War, the relationship with the United States, and Britain's entry into the European Common Market.

The 'Special Collections' archive was so vast that a basic inventory compiled by Foreign Office archivists catalogued the files by the metre. There were six metres and two centimetres dedicated to files about Rhodesia, for example, and four metres and fifty-seven centimetres taken up by files about Guy Burgess and Donald Maclean, the KGB spies who operated inside the Foreign Office and MI6. There were fifty metres of Hong Kong papers, 100.81 metres about the United States and 97.84 metres of 'private office papers'.

There were files from the Colonial Office in London that had not been declassified and sent to the National Archives. No length of shelving was given for these, nor for the stored records from the Permanent Under-Secretary's department, the point of liaison between the Foreign Office and MI6.

There was said to be 'one bag' of records from the Information Research Department, the Foreign Office's Cold War propaganda unit, including several files about its activities in Northern Ireland during the early years of the conflict in the province. There were German-language files about the Holocaust, which may have been recovered from post-war Germany. Tucked away in one corner of the archive, wedged between files from the British military government in post-war Germany and lists of consular officials, were papers about the treaty of Paris, which had brought the Crimean war to an end in 1856.[4]

The list went on and on.

After the humiliating disclosures during the Mau Mau court case, the Foreign Office realised it was not going to be able to conceal its Special Collections for ever. Quietly, officials approached the Ministry of Justice and asked it to declare that the entire archive had been placed on a legal footing. This was done: in November 2012, an authorisation was signed off.

As a result of the furtive manner in which this was arranged, it was to be a further twelve months before any knowledge of the Special Collections was made public. When this happened, following a tip-off to the author, historians realised the scale of the material that had been concealed from them and many were both angry and bewildered.

One of them questioned whether the existence of these collections had the potential to force historians to revise their explanations of such major diplomatic questions as the partition of Africa and the origins of the first and second world wars.[5] Another warned that it would be a mistake to assume that the sense of resentment felt in those countries affected by British imperial policy would diminish as the years pass, and said that it was vital for the UK's international reputation that it can prove it is not seeking to whitewash the historical record.[6]

With its Special Collections no longer a secret, the Foreign Office announced that it would release the ten per cent of the documents that it considered to be of the greatest interest over a six-year period. But when it presented its declassification plan at the National Archives, it did so at a meeting that was held entirely behind closed doors.

Subsequently, the Foreign Office claimed there were not 1.2 million files in the archive, but 600,000. The remaining 600,000 files, it said, were not yet due for release, although some of them dated back to 1852. The Foreign Office has refused to answer questions about the 600,000 files that it maintains are not due for declassification, and has also refused to say publicly how long it might be before those papers that it did not consider to be of the highest public interest would finally see the light of day.

The Public Records Acts, and their constitutional role as a means of democratic accountability, were being subverted on an industrial scale. But it appeared that the handling of 'public documents' remained, as far as the Foreign Office was concerned, a private affair.

Until the late 1950s, historians and members of the general public had no right of access to British government papers, such as those created by the Kenyan colonial authorities. Before then, the assumption in Whitehall was that almost every request for access would be turned down. The general rule was that no documents created after 1793 would be made available unless the individual requesting to see it was considered by government officials to be an 'impartial' historian.[7]

During one debate on the matter in Parliament in 1899, MPs heard that an Irish member had been refused permission to see papers about the Irish rebellion of 1798, on the grounds that his 'political credentials' were considered unsatisfactory, while a distinguished American scholar had been denied access to a document about the American War of Independence, on the grounds that it remained secret.

Herbert Asquith, the future Prime Minister, urged his fellow MPs to be cautious: official documents 'ought to be kept under lock and key and under a responsible custodian', he said, rather than becoming 'accessible to what I may call, for want of a better phrase, the man in the street'. Asquith was equally suspicious of historians: 'I do not believe there has ever been an historian who has not exhibited some amount of partisanship; it is a common infirmity of the tribe.'[8]

Until the mid-1940s, sensitive government papers were indeed stamped with the words 'To Be Kept Under Lock and Key',[9] and it would be almost sixty years before the man in the street and historians, partisan or otherwise, would be granted the right to access official papers. In 1958, the first Public Records Act introduced what the Solicitor-General of the day described as 'modern and apt' provision for public access to such documents. Modern and apt meant that even with the passing of the Act, official papers would remain closed for half a century after being created, and even then would not be open to scrutiny if the department that held them believed that the documents should be retained for a longer period.

The committee that recommended the introduction of this legislation believed that it was necessary to delay declassification for fifty years in order to allow civil servants a degree of what it described as 'unselfconsciousness' at the point at which they were helping to formulate public policy. Ministers of the Conservative government of the day appeared more concerned with their own reputations, however, and were particularly concerned that there should be no disclosure of Cabinet minutes during their lifetimes. Eventually, they were told that the minutes would be recorded in an 'impersonal style',[10] which helps to explain why records of Cabinet meetings shed so little light on the views expressed by individual ministers.

Rather than satisfying the curiosity of the public and the requirements of historians, the Fifty-Year Rule aroused a great deal of indignation – it was, one historian said, 'inimical to the existence of a properly informed public opinion in this country' – and it compared unfavourably with the more liberal policies of the United States and Germany. As a consequence, in 1967 the law was amended by a second Act that introduced the Thirty-Year Rule. In the absence of a written Constitution, the Public Records Acts joined those other pieces of statute that contribute to the British constitution: in theory, they were tools of democratic accountability.

At the time of writing, in 2016, the Thirty-Year Rule is being reduced still further, to twenty years, under the terms of the Constitutional Reform and Governance Act 2010, a piece of legislation that was introduced after a committee that reviewed the Thirty-Year Rule reported that 'the UK now operates one of the less liberal access regimes to its official records'.[11]

Under the Public Records Acts, any document that is created or received by a government department or public body, and which is considered to be worthy of permanent preservation, must be selected for transfer to the National Archives or another suitable location, such as the British Museum.

The selection of material is the responsibility of the chief executive of the National Archives, but in practice the staff of individual government departments decide what to select for transfer, working to criteria laid down by the National Archives. Material that is not considered to be of historical significance is destroyed. Most departments destroy more than ninety per cent of the paperwork they possess once it is thirty years old; in 2013, for example, Ministry of Defence archivists said they were destroying ninety-seven per cent of the department's old papers.[12]

Section 3(4) of the 1958 act allows government departments to hold back documents that are more than thirty years old, and of historical interest, 'provided . . . they are required for administrative purposes or ought to be retained for any other special reason', which the National Archives interprets as meaning for reasons of national security.

Within each department there are officials known as Sensitivity Reviewers who consider whether historical documents should remain classified under Section 3(4). A review is carried out when records are twenty-five years old to consider whether they are no longer of value and should be destroyed; whether they are of historical significance, and should be handed to the National Archives after a further five-year delay; or whether they are too sensitive to be made public, and should, in the opinion of the reviewer, be withheld.

The Sensitivity Reviewers are staff from the department or, occasionally, retired members of staff, who can be expected to have the departments' interests at heart. At the Foreign Office, for example, the reviews are conducted by retired diplomats, who see no conflict of interest in their making decisions about the non-disclosure of documents created by old colleagues. 'We've had a situation where one Reviewer was reviewing something he had written to another person – who was by then a Sensitivity Reviewer – about the work of a third person, who was also by then a Sensitivity Reviewer,' one says. 'I've even reviewed myself.'[13]

Papers may be retained under Section 3(4) only once the Lord Chancellor has issued an authorisation known as a Lord

Chancellor's Instrument, or LCI.* The Lord Chancellor, in turn, can sign an LCI only once the application from the department has been considered and approved by a body at the National Archives called the Advisory Council on National Records and Archives. The council is chaired by the Master of Rolls, the most senior civil judge in England and Wales, and also includes a number of historians, archivists, and retired diplomats and intelligence and defence officials.

As part of the application, an individual identified in a schedule to the Act as 'a listed person' is required to declare that public access would 'create a real risk of prejudice to national security'. The sensitivity of documents classified in this way is said to be indefinite, as is the period they may remain hidden from the public. 'Listed persons' include not only the Prime Minister, the Chancellor of the Exchequer and the Attorney General, but the company secretary of the telecommunications company BT Group plc; the company secretary of the postage company Royal Mail plc; the head of the National Audit Office, the body that scrutinises central government expenditure; and the Secretary of State for Education.[14]

In addition to individual Instruments that deny public access to individual documents or files, the Lord Chancellor (now the Culture Secretary) is empowered to sign 'blanket Instruments', denying public access to entire classes of documents – even entire departmental archives. In 2013, blanket Instruments covered the records of MI5, MI6 and GCHQ; the records of Scotland Yard's Special Branch; all documents about the defence application of atomic energy; the personal files of civil servants and members of the armed forces created before 1990; and the pension files and misconduct records of teachers created between 1914 and 1978.[15] A blanket Instrument was

---

* Responsibility for the National Archives – and for issuing LCIs – was transferred from the Justice Secretary to the Secretary of State for Culture, Media and Sport in December 2015.

issued in order to put the Foreign Office's enormous Special
Collections archive at Hanslope Park on a legal footing.

Such is the volume of applications that in practice members
of the Advisory Council on National Records and Archives
see very few of the files concerned, and instead read lists of file
names attached to requests. In 2013–14, for example, the council
requested further information about just sixty-nine files that it
was advised should remain hidden from public view: two per
cent of the total.[16] It rarely rejects applications by government
departments. In 2013, it accepted ninety-six per cent of government arguments for closure.[17] And there are any number of
imaginative means by which government departments can
ensure that 'public' documents remain anything but.

Section 10(2) of the 1958 act allows government departments
to retain files that have been gathered in 'assemblies' until thirty
years after the date at which the most recent file within the
assembly was created. In this way, new documents can simply
be added to an assembly to enable the papers within it to be
withheld indefinitely.

In 1984, for example, the British Museum refused to release
papers about the way in which museum staff had badly damaged
the Elgin Marbles in the 1930s by scraping away their surfaces
at the request of a wealthy benefactor who believed they were
not quite white enough. The museum initially refused to release
its records about this scandal on what it described as 'security
grounds', and then said it was withholding them because one
of the documents in an 'assembly of files' had been created in
1967. When the papers were eventually released in the late '90s,
historians could see that they had been deliberately brought
together in one 'assembly' that was so large that it could not be
picked up. Lawyers who examined what the museum had been
doing concluded that it had unlawfully contrived to evade the
provisions of the Act.[18]

When papers are deemed no longer to be sensitive, it is not unknown for them to be slipped quietly back within the file at the National Archives from which they had been withheld. No note appears on the file to explain that this has been done. The result is that the concealment of state secrets within government departments is followed by their being hidden in plain sight within the National Archives.

Furthermore, as the gradual introduction of the Twenty-Year Rule brought more recent documentation under review, some government departments began to consider that increasing amounts of its historical documentation were too sensitive to release. In December 2015, for example, the Cabinet Office, which usually transfers around 500 files to Kew at the end of each year, produced just fifty-eight. The omissions included papers about the Lockerbie bombing which claimed 270 lives; the Special Air Service shootings in Gibraltar of members of the IRA who may have been attempting to surrender when they died; and the decision to press ahead with a controversial poll tax.[19] In effect, a measure that was intended to bring greater transparency and accountability to government was being used to justify continuing secrecy.

Similarly, it was not long before the Foreign Office appeared to turn the scandal of the Special Collections to its own advantage. When the gradual transition from the thirty-year to the twenty-year regime began in 2013, the Foreign Office was the one department that failed to take steps to start the process. Apparently it was too busy clearing up the mess of its 'migrated archives' to be able to meet new legal obligations intended to provide greater transparency and accountability.

Occasionally, papers that senior officials wish to withhold from the public have been known to slip through the Sensitivity Reviewers' net. In January 2014, for example, a series of thirty-year-old Downing Street papers released to the National Archives showed that an officer of Britain's SAS had played a role in planning the Indian military's 1984 attack on the Golden Temple in Amritsar, which was under the control of Sikh militants. Hundreds – and possibly thousands – of people died during the assault. When the papers were discovered in the National Archives, Prime Minister David Cameron announced that an inquiry, headed by the Cabinet Secretary Jeremy Heywood, would be held. Heywood's conclusion, 'based on the available written records in UK government files', was that the advice offered by the SAS played no part in the slaughter. *En passant*, however, he also noted that the key Ministry of Defence documents on the episode had been destroyed in 2009. 'I understand,' Heywood reported, that 'this was part of a routine process.'[20]

Heywood had made clear that the twenty-five-year review was being used not as a means of identifying records of historical value – which the Amritsar papers clearly were – but as an opportunity to weed out documents that contained embarrassing material about the government, the MoD or the armed forces. And as the Cabinet Secretary noted, the complete destruction of these records was a 'routine' affair.

Even those government papers that are transferred to Kew and become part of the public record may on occasion become official secrets again, disappearing from the National Archives after new concerns about their contents have emerged. This happened, as we have seen, with a Foreign Office memo that described the way in which the old Sultan of Oman's Defence Secretary, Colonel Hugh Oldman, a Briton, had planned the coup that deposed the Sultan in 1970. It also happened in 1982, shortly before the Falklands War, to a number of papers that discussed the basis for Britain's claims to the Falklands Islands.[21] Ten years later, following the 1991 Gulf War, papers that detailed British plans to drop bombs containing mustard gas on Kurdish villages in 1919 similarly vanished.

In 2013, a historian researching a biography of Klaus Fuchs, the German-born scientist who betrayed America's atomic bomb secrets to Moscow, found at Kew a twelve-page document that indicated that Fuchs had also been spying for Britain. The historian wrote about his find for a nuclear history website. On his return to Kew the file had vanished: it had been taken away by Ministry of Defence officials shortly after the website post had appeared.[22] At the time of writing, three years on, the file was still being hidden from public view at the MoD.

All requests by government departments for the withdrawal of previously released documents are considered by a committee of archivists at Kew known as the Reclosure Panel. This panel removes any file that has been requested by a government department, and then considers whether or not it should remain at the National Archives. It usually complies with the government department's request. In 2014, for example, the panel considered forty requests, covering more than forty files. In eighteen cases, the files were fully reclosed, and in a further fourteen, they were partly reclosed. Only eight remained open to the public.[23]

The loan system operated by the National Archives provides another means by which files that have been placed in the public domain can be recovered and effectively hidden by government departments. The department simply asks for the return of the file, and while, according to the National Archives, the department is 'strongly encouraged' to return it promptly, it is not under any obligation to do so. This happened to 9,308 files in 2011, to 7,122 the following year and to 7,468 in 2013. As of early 2014, almost 3,000 had not been returned to the National Archives.[24]

While all Whitehall departments appear at times to approach their legal obligations over historical records from a position that is rooted in a culture of concealment, it is often the Foreign Office that shows the greatest sensitivity around disclosure.

After the Foreign Office had been forced to confess the

existence of its hoard of colonial documents at Hanslope Park, and the Foreign Secretary promised 'to release every part of every paper of interest', the declassification of the 'migrated archive' and its transfer to Kew took place gradually over a period of eighteen months. Only when it was completed did it become clear that the Foreign Office would not be releasing every part of every paper that was of interest.

The department is withholding around one per cent of the archive. While this may appear to be a modest amount, it adds up to hundreds of files and thousands of pages. It includes a file that contains the minutes of every cabinet meeting of the British colonial government in Kenya throughout the twelve months prior to independence in 1963; a file concerning the 1946 bombing of the British military HQ at the King David Hotel in Jerusalem; and a file containing telegrams that British diplomats sent to London from Mauritius in 1968, the year in which that colony proclaimed independence. The Mauritius papers could be particularly sensitive as they could shed further light on the expulsion of the Chagos Islanders a few years earlier.[25]

Furthermore, the most sensitive files within the 'migrated archive' have vanished altogether. Among those files flown to Britain during Operation Legacy there had been 170 boxes marked 'Top Secret Independence Records 1953 to 1963'. These had always been kept separate from the rest of the archive, and stored in Whitehall rather than at Hanslope Park. Their contents were thought to be the most threatening of all the colonial papers that had been removed to Britain rather than destroyed *in situ*.

Tony Badger, the independent historian overseeing the declassification of the 'migrated archive', established that these 'Top Secret' files had been in Foreign Office storage as recently as March 1991, when an inventory listed them as taking up seventy-nine feet of shelf space in Room 52A at the Old Admiralty Building in Whitehall. Thirteen of the 170 boxes contained files from Kenya. The boxes of files from Singapore took up forty-eight feet of shelving, and those from Malaya took nine feet, while there were smaller amounts from Palestine, Uganda, Malta and fifteen other colonies. In September 1992, a removals firm was contracted to transport Foreign Office papers from that building to Hanslope Park, using two vehicles each day. A detailed schedule kept by the firm showed that none of the 170 'Top Secret' boxes was among that consignment, and since then no trace has ever been found of them.

Badger is certain that these 'Top Secret' colonial files no longer exist. 'The implication is that the remaining files had been destroyed,' he says, adding: 'If, as I believe, almost all the top secret files were destroyed at some point between March 1991 and September 1992, it is profoundly disturbing that there are no destruction certificates for such a large body of records.'[26]

It is entirely possible that the contents of the 170 'Top Secret' boxes were destroyed on the eve of the 1992 general election, at a time when the opinion polls were predicting – incorrectly, as it transpired – that there was about to be a change of government for the first time in thirteen years.

And it may not have been the only cull of secret colonial-era files. Historians of British Guiana such as Richard Drayton believe it is inconceivable that the British authorities would have destroyed all of its files from that colony at independence, yet none survive in the 'migrated archive'. 'The decolonisation of British Guiana was part of the Cold War,' Drayton says. 'The security files kept at Government House would have been recognised to have potential future operational value and would have been repatriated. The British government would not have destroyed resources for its foreign and security policy, in particular the kind of thick data on local people which the Government House files would have held.'[27]

What did survive is an inventory of the thirteen of the 170 'Top Secret' boxes that contained files from Kenya. It is sketchy, but the information that it contains shows that those files included documents about the abuse of prisoners and about psychological warfare. The inventory also contains a curious warning about one batch of papers from 1953: 'This file to be processed and received only by a male clerical officer.' Its title was: 'Situation in Kenya – Employment of Witch Doctors by CO [Colonial Office].'[28]

So while it may be profoundly disturbing, as Badger says, that no destruction certificate was completed at the point at which the 'Top Secret' colonial files were destroyed, it is perhaps not surprising. The 170 boxes no doubt contained some of the most invaluable records of the final days of Empire, as well as some of the most unsettling.

By law, the contents of all of the boxes should have been considered for declassification and transfer to Kew, or at least made the subject of a Lord Chancellor's Instrument after scrutiny by the National Archives' advisory council, and a date given for their eventual release.

Instead, the contents were covertly expunged from the record, destroyed at the heart of Whitehall, thirty or forty years after the events that they described.

The Foreign Office was not the only British government department with a secret archive of historical documents it was keen to keep secret. During the summer of 2013, the author discovered that the Ministry of Defence also had a large, hidden repository. Eventually, inquiries led to the small town of Swadlincote in Derbyshire, where the MoD was leasing two large warehouses from a private company.

Like other government departments, the MoD possessed several archives that contained files that were held perfectly lawfully, either because the papers were less than thirty years old, because they were required for administrative purposes, or because a Lord Chancellor's Instrument had been issued to authorise their retention.

At Swadlincote in 2013, however, there were more than 66,000 files that were being held unlawfully. It later became clear that this was just a small part of the entire archive. The MoD was holding around 8.5 million files at Swadlincote, and had been able to place their retention on a legal footing because the National Archives' advisory council had granted Lord Chancellor's Instruments without carefully examining their contents. Some of the Instruments that were issued did not refer to individual files. 'They may refer to records by subject matter or length of shelf,' one MoD official said. Staff at the MoD had realised that legal cover could be obtained for its enormous accumulation of files without anyone outside the department knowing what it was hoarding. Even the MoD's own archivists were unaware of what lay inside some of the files.[29]

The MoD made it clear that it would never admit the author into its secret archive. Asked to describe the interior of the warehouses at Swadlincote, one archivist cited the final scene in the Hollywood film *Raiders of the Lost Ark*, which features a giant US government warehouse within which countless artefacts are stored, buried away, never to be seen again. 'Do you remember that warehouse scene?' the archivist asked. 'Well, I've got two of those.'[30]

Swadlincote is not the only location outside London at which the MoD has an archive. Around 100,000 of its most sensitive files are held on a Royal Navy base at Portsmouth.[31]

At Portsmouth, Navy officers have – at least until recently – been employed not only as Sensitivity Reviewers, examining files and recommending which should be retained at the MoD and which handed over to Kew, some have also worked as 'weeders', removing individual pages from within files in a manner similar to the work that was carried out during Operation Legacy. One former Navy officer who worked as a weeder at Portsmouth during the 1980s explained how the process worked at that time. 'Weeding was conducted once the file had been inactive for one year, and again when it was five years old,' he said. 'The work would be carried out by a relatively junior officer – a Sub-lieutenant in the Royal Navy – who would consult upwards if in doubt. Anything that was not needed for the future, but which was potentially embarrassing, would be destroyed.' Two more senior officers would sign an authorisation for the documents to be destroyed; the MoD's civilian staff would not be permitted to be involved in the process.

'Anything that was needed in future, but which was sensitive, would be placed in a confidential file, and marked for destruction in 25, or 50 or 100 years. And then "weeding certificates" would be placed within the registry to show what was happening.'

In addition to the MoD's archives, the individual branches of the armed services kept their own records. The Royal Navy, for example, maintained an archive in a series of tunnels deep beneath Mount Wise in Plymouth, Devon. 'Services would keep records from each other, and there was secrecy within the services,' he said.

'There would be no regard for the Public Records Acts. If you needed to see a particular file, you had to know who to talk to about it – you needed to know that you should go to see Charles or Julian or whoever. You relied on informal networks of knowledge, rather than a catalogue. Particularly sensitive documents were known as "burn *before* reading" papers. These were documents that would not even be kept within an individual unit's registry; they could be disavowed even at unit level. These would be kept in a safe that would be opened with a combination lock, behind which would be a 14-lever lock known as a Mersey lock.'

The former Royal Navy weeder added that some of the documents that were destroyed had detailed operations 'that were exceptionally dark', including incidents in which British servicemen's lives had been sacrificed in order to conceal intelligence-gathering capabilities. Documents of such sensitivity would be shredded – 'sometimes double shredded' – and then burned.[32]

A handful of highly sensitive files whose existence had already been acknowledged to the National Archives were dealt with by other means. First, the MoD said that their transfer had been delayed, as they had been found to have been stored in a building in London where asbestos was said to have been discovered. The department was unable to withhold the names of its 'asbestos files' however, and a Freedom of Information (FoI) request disclosed that they included such titles as 'Sale of Arms to Saudi Arabia', 'An Improved Kiloton Bomb', 'Medical Aspects of Interrogation', 'Special Operations and How They Effect Deception', 'Project R1' and 'SAS Regiment: Borneo Operations'.[33]

Five years later, the MoD informed the National Archives that thirty-one of the files would never be declassified, as they were said to have suffered severe water damage during the 'decontamination' process. The thirty-one lost files had dealt with subjects that included some of the most secretive Cold War military operations; military operations within British territory; the introduction of judge-only courts in Northern Ireland; the mysterious R1 weapon; the involvement of British troops in far-right groups; and the treatment of German prisoners at the British Army's Second World War and post-war interrogation centre, the London Cage.

Some of the most intriguing and perhaps controversial MoD documentation of the past fifty years had been destroyed. There was never any evidence that the papers had actually been contaminated with asbestos: the MoD maintained that drastic measures were required simply because they had been stored in a building where asbestos had been found.

Throughout the 1970s and '80s, the clamour for reform of Section 2 of the Official Secrets Act had often been accompanied by a demand for greater transparency in government, and by calls for greater access to the bulk of the information held by government. Most other mature democracies had passed freedom of information legislation many decades earlier: the United States had passed its own Act in 1966, while New Zealand, Australia and Canada had adopted freedom of information laws in 1982 and '83. In Sweden, the legal regime granting access to official documents had been in place since 1766. Writing in 1990, after his own Section 2 trial, Clive Ponting noted that while many governments had passed legislation granting access to all but a small number of carefully defined official papers, 'in Britain the concept of public records still appears to be something of a misnomer'.[34]

The Conservative governments of 1979 to 1997 steadfastly refused to countenance freedom of information legislation. In 1992, as the pressure of public opinion mounted, the government embarked upon an open government initiative that saw historians being invited to identify the official papers that they believed had been withheld beyond thirty years without justification. Significant material was released for the first time, but the government resisted the call for freedom of information legislation, believing that the status quo – with a presumption against disclosure of information, rather than a presumption in favour of its release – should be maintained.

By the mid '90s, however, the campaign for a Freedom of Information Act was fast gathering pace, and it had found an enthusiastic champion: a political leader who appeared to see that such legislation could help to transform government in Britain from an essentially private affair into a public enterprise, and who was about to find himself in a position to bring about this change.

In March 1996, Tony Blair was the highly popular leader of a Labour Party which knew that it was almost certain to win the next general election. That month he gave a speech in which he set out his view that the manner in which governments control information defines their relationships with the people they govern.

'Information is power,' he said, 'and any government's attitude about sharing information with the people actually says a great deal about how it views power itself, and how it views the relationship between itself and the people who elected it. Does the government regard people's involvement in politics as being restricted to periodic elections? Or does it regard itself as in some sense in a genuine partnership with people? The government's attitude to what it is prepared to tell people and the knowledge it will share with them says a great deal about where it stands on that matter.'

As matters stood in the UK, Blair said, 'the culture of secrecy permeates almost every single aspect of government activity'. A Freedom of Information Act was years, perhaps decades overdue. It would do more than simply sweep away 'the obsessive and unnecessary secrecy which surrounds government activity': it would empower the people, helping them to become partners in government, he declared. 'I don't believe it is possible for government to govern effectively now, unless it governs in some sense in a relationship of partnership with the people whom it is governing.'[35]

Under the next Labour government, a Freedom of Information Act would be introduced, and as a consequence, Blair said, the presumption would be that information should be, rather than should not be, released. It was a measure that he believed would deliver not just more open government but more effective and efficient government.

Fifteen years later, after leaving office, Blair gazed back on his Downing Street years, and his volte-face over the free flow of information from government could not have been more complete. 'Freedom of Information,' he wrote in his memoirs. 'Three harmless words. I look at those words as I write them, and feel like shaking my head till it drops off my shoulders. You idiot. You naive, foolish, irresponsible nincompoop. There is really no description of stupidity, no matter how vivid, that is adequate. I quake at the imbecility of it.

'Once I appreciated the full enormity of the blunder, I used to say – more than a little unfairly – to any civil servant who would listen: Where was Sir Humphrey when I needed him? We had legislated in the first throes of power. How could you, knowing what you know, have allowed us to do such a thing so utterly undermining of sensible government?'[36]

Blair went on to claim that his antipathy to freedom of information came about because it was used largely not by members of the general public, but by journalists who wanted to deploy it as a political weapon. 'For political leaders, it's like saying to someone who is hitting you over the head with a stick, "Hey, try this instead", and handing them a mallet.'

The problem with this claim is that no journalist was able to use the Act until it came into force in 2005, almost eight years after Labour came to power, and more than four years after the law was passed. There was a gap of more than four years between the Act being passed and it being implemented because Blair had intervened personally to prevent it coming into effect.[37] The fact that he impeded its implementation for so many years shows that he had become hostile to freedom of information long before there was any such freedom, and before any journalist, or anyone else, had been able to make use of the Act.

Blair also claimed in his memoirs that the Act impeded the ability of civil servants to offer frank advice in confidence. But the Information Commissioner and the Information Tribunals that enforce the Act take this requirement into account before deciding whether information should or should not be released. Blair himself admits that he did not see this as a problem until long after the Act came into force. And just eighteen months after that happened, he proposed a series of amendments that would make it far easier for public bodies to refuse access to information.

So why did Blair become so hostile to freedom of information, a principle that he had once regarded as empowering for the people and essential for good government? One explanation is that New Labour had a culture of secrecy that was further ingrained by office. During the war in Kosovo, for example, Blair is said to have been horrified when Bill Clinton told him that he could not write down the advice he was receiving from military advisors for fear of public exposure.[38] This may partly explain the penchant for what became known as sofa government: ministers and officials conducting government business during informal meetings, with no records kept.

But a more complete explanation can also be found within Blair's memoirs. In opposition, he wrote, 'we made a very big mistake in allowing the impression to be gained that we were going to be better than the Tories; not just better at governing, but more moral, more upright'. The consequences of exploiting the Tories' involvement in so-called sleaze were disastrous, he said. 'What I failed to realise is that we would also have our skeletons rattling around the cupboard, and while they might be different, they would be just as repulsive. Moreover, I did not at that time see the full implications of the massive increase in transparency we were planning as part of our reforms to "clean up politics". For the first time, details of donors and the amounts given to political parties were going to be published. I completely missed the fact that though in opposition millionaire donors were to be welcomed as a sign of respectability, in government they would very quickly be seen as buying influence.

'The Freedom of Information Act was then being debated in Cabinet Committee. It represented a quite extraordinary offer by a government to open itself and Parliament to scrutiny. Its consequences would be revolutionary; the power it handed to the tender mercy of the media was gigantic. We did it with care, but without foresight. Politicians are people and scandals will happen. There never was going to be a happy ending to that story, and sure enough there wasn't. The irony was that far from improving our reputation, we sullied it.'[39]

Blair goes on to explain his position by writing about two 'scandals' that arose during the first months of the new Labour administration. One was a personal matter which resulted in Blair telling his Foreign Secretary Robin Cook to decide between his wife and his assistant, after a newspaper reported that he had been having an affair; the second was a major funding scandal, engulfing Blair's government not long after he had accused his predecessor John Major of bowing to 'the squalid monetary interests of the Conservative Party'.

In January 1997, Bernie Ecclestone, the chief executive of Formula One motor racing, had secretly donated £1 million to the Labour Party. It was money that had been used during the election campaign that brought the party to power in May that year. The donation did not become public until the following November, however, after the government had announced that Formula One would be exempt from the ban on tobacco advertising in sport that the party had promised in its election manifesto. Ecclestone had lobbied for the exemption during a meeting with Blair at Number 10, five months after the election.

Amid the growing controversy over the donation, Blair told Parliament that no decision had been taken as a result of the meeting with Ecclestone. Years later, after a two-and-a-half-year battle with government, journalists acquired secret papers that showed that very shortly after Blair's meeting with Ecclestone, the Prime Minister informed his health ministers that he wanted Formula One to be exempt from the ban. The same papers also showed that when the facts began to emerge, senior civil servants warned Blair that a form of words proposed in answer to a parliamentary question risked misleading Parliament.[40]

The papers were obtained under the Freedom of Information

Act: had Blair not impeded the Act's implementation for more than four years, they may well have emerged while he was Prime Minister, rather than after he had left office, and he would have faced calls for his resignation.

In the event, the Ecclestone donation affair died down only after Blair gave a television interview in which he apologised for his government's handling of the matter. Sweating heavily under the studio lights, Blair insisted he was 'a pretty straight sort of guy', a phrase that came to haunt him. Ecclestone admitted being asked to make a donation in January 1997 and doing so, adding, 'I never sought any favour from New Labour or any member of the government, nor has any been given.' The donation was eventually repaid.

It was Blair's first scandal, a humbling episode that inflicted considerable damage on the reputation and public image of the previously spotless young Prime Minister. It erupted just as the Cabinet Office was putting the finishing touches to the Freedom of Information White Paper, entitled 'Your Right to Know'. The first clause of the White Paper declared: 'Unnecessary secrecy in government leads to arrogance in governance and defective decision-making.' Its preface had already been written – by Tony Blair – and stated: 'The traditional culture of secrecy in Britain will only be broken down by giving people in the United Kingdom the legal right to know.' The document proposed that information should be released on request unless it could be demonstrated that this would cause harm to any of seven clearly defined interests.

Transparency campaigners were delighted. One described the White Paper as stunning. Their delight was to be short-lived. Blair and a number of close Cabinet colleagues had already decided that the Act itself would differ in a number of significant ways from the White Paper. Following the Ecclestone funding scandal, a number of ministers had become deeply resistant to the principle of freedom of information. One former government minister recalls that the body drafting the new Bill – the Constitutional Reform Policy Freedom of Information Committee, or CRP FoI – was derided by a number of his ministerial colleagues as 'crap fooey'.[41]

Some of the committee's meetings were ill-tempered affairs, with the Home Secretary, Jack Straw, being particularly hostile to a Bill that he regarded as extravagant and implausible.[42] Responsibility for steering the Bill through Parliament was taken from the Cabinet Office and handed instead to Straw's Home Office, which produced a draft Bill that was widely condemned for the number of exemptions it contained. One extraordinary clause was intended to prevent individuals who received information under the Act from sharing that information with anyone else, effectively meaning that it couldn't be discussed, published or in any way made public.

In the event, the Act that was passed was far better than the draft Bill, and over the years it has been used by many individuals and groups to bring into the public domain useful information that would otherwise have remained buried. Nevertheless, it contains no less than twenty-four separate exemptions that can, and often do, prevent information from being made public. Some of these are qualified exemptions, which require public bodies to weigh the competing interests between disclosure and retention of the information being requested. Some, however, are blanket exemptions: information that falls within these categories will not be released regardless of whether to do so would be harmful. One exemption – allowing the retention of information deemed to be 'prejudicial to effective conduct of public affairs' – is far narrower even than the voluntary code of conduct that preceded the Act. Furthermore, the Act does not extend to police forces, or to private contractors running public services, including some prisons and National Health Service care.

Yet even in this shape, the Act was unpalatable for Blair, who delayed its implementation for more than four years. Blair's aversion to the free flow of government information appeared to be rooted not only in the Ecclestone funding scandal, but in his realisation that his persona might not always stand up to the sort of scrutiny that freedom of information legislation was intended to facilitate – that the public might discover that their new Prime Minister was not always a straight sort of guy.

Shortly before the Act came into force, the Cabinet Office warned its staff that they should delete old emails and destroy electronic versions of letters.[43] Downing Street went one step further, surreptitiously installing a new email system which guaranteed that all emails would self-destruct after three months. This system – recommended by the National Archives – was said to be tremendously disruptive to government, as it meant that officials had different recollections of what had been agreed at meetings.[44]

Once it finally came into force, the UK's Freedom of Information Act was seen to compare unfavourably with the FoI legislation of many other major democratic states, at least from the point of view of those who wanted to see greater openness in government. While it does impose significant duties and responsibilities on British public authorities to grant access to information, and offers strong oversight by the Information Commissioner, the range of exemptions that allow public bodies to refuse to declassify information is far wider than in many other countries.

While the date for transfer to Kew remained at thirty years, the Act created a new class of inaccessible papers known as Closed Records – documents that are passed to the National Archives, but opened to the public only following a successful FoI request. Two of the exemptions allowed some papers to be withheld for far longer: papers concerning the award of honours can be held back for sixty years, and those concerning law enforcement for 100 years. As a result, the Freedom of Information Act can be deployed to suppress, rather than liberate, some historical information.

Furthermore, no sanction is imposed on those authorities that choose to ignore the time limits contained within the Act, which call for a response to a request for information to be provided within twenty working days. In 2012, for example, the Treasury took more than 120 working days to answer each of seventy-eight requests, including sixty-nine requests that had been lodged the previous year but not answered until 2012. That same year, hundreds of requests to other departments remained unanswered for more than 120 working days.[45] *

It is not unknown for some government officials to avoid providing information for two years or more, during which time they will claim to be weighing up the competing interests between disclosure and retention, or will cite exemptions that they will eventually acknowledge do not apply.[46]

The FoI system allows people requesting information to ask for an internal review if the information is refused, and then permits a complaint to be lodged with the Information Commissioner. There can then be an appeal to a court known as the Information Tribunal, followed by an appeal to an upper tribunal. Some requests can eventually end up with the Court of Appeal. Government departments are permitted to refuse to disclose information if the cost of meeting a request would cost more than a set sum – in 2013 the figure was £600 for central government, Parliament and the armed forces, and £450 for all other public authorities.

Even parliamentary questions about the government's compliance with the Act have gone unanswered on the grounds of cost. In November 2013, for example, the Labour peer Lord Kennedy tabled a question asking how many FoI requests which had been turned down since the coalition government was

---

* At the Foreign Office, the unit responsible for delayed responses to FoI requests is called the Knowledge Management Department.

formed in 2010 had subsequently been upheld on appeal. Lord McNally, the Minister of State for Justice, replied that 'to obtain this information we would have to ask each central government body to investigate the outcome of each appeal individually. Therefore it would only be possible to provide this information at disproportionate cost.'[47]

Meanwhile, some government departments have spent hundreds of thousands of pounds on legal fees, as requests drag on through Information Tribunals and the courts, in an attempt to avoid the declassification and release of information. The flaws within the UK's freedom of information legislation were such that some legal academics denounced it as a sham within months of its receiving royal assent in November 2000. Despite these weaknesses, from the moment it came into force in January 2005, some government officials appeared to be desperate to find ways to undermine it still further.

An early dodge was for departments to disclose the information requested, but then maintain that it remained subject to Crown Copyright, and so could not be disseminated further; this appeared to be an attempt to dissuade journalists from making use of the Act.

Public bodies can also change their minds over the reason for refusing to declassify documents, substituting one claimed exemption for another, time after time. In 2005, for example, a historian who was researching the nineteenth-century inter-national anarchist movement asked Scotland Yard if he could see Special Branch files from 1884 to 1905. He had already been welcomed into the police archives of France, Belgium and Russia.

The Yard did not want people looking at its historical Special Branch records, however, and provided the historian with a series of ever-changing reasons why it was not possible. These included health and safety concerns; national security; the need to protect personal data; and Scotland Yard's need to meet its obligations under the European Convention on Human Rights to protect both family life and the right to life itself.

The matter dragged on, with the Yard failing to respond to some of the historian's requests for an internal review, while at the same time asking the National Archives' advisory council for permission to keep the documents hidden from public scrutiny – a request which was granted. Eventually an Information Tribunal ordered that the Yard must allow access to some of the material. The entire process had taken more than three-and-a-half years.[48]

At times, some ministers and officials have seemed desperate to conceal their actions from scrutiny under FoI. One ploy has been to use their personal rather than official email accounts. They appear to have been inspired by the Alaskan Governor and Republican vice-presidential candidate Sarah Palin, who attempted to use an account named gov.palin@yahoo.com in a bid to circumnavigate the freedom of information legislation of the United States. Palin was ultimately unsuccessful. Later, Hillary Clinton would also be found to have used her family's private email server while conducting business as US Secretary of State.

In December 2010, for example, the Education Secretary, Michael Gove, sent an email about government business through an email account in the name of his wife – an account known to his close advisors as the 'Mrs Blurt account'. A few weeks later, a journalist – who had already been shown the email – decided to submit an FoI request to Gove's department, asking to see the contents of the email. The department replied that it did not possess the information.

It is not against the law for ministers or officials to use private email accounts for government business; but it is illegal to intentionally conceal the information within the emails once they are subject to an FoI request. Personal emails sent by ministers and officials are subject to the Act, but it remains to be seen whether those British civil servants who are responsible for responding to FoI requests would be able, or willing, to demand access to the

Hotmail or Yahoo accounts of ministers or senior colleagues.

Two months later, one of Gove's most senior political advisors sent an email to another of the Education Secretary's advisors, copying in Conservative Party officials. In it, he advised: 'i will not answer any further emails to my official DfE account or from conservatives.com – i will only answer things that come from Gmail accounts from people who I know who they are [sic].' He went on: 'i suggest that you do the same in general but thats obv up to you guys – i can explain in person the reason for this . . .'[49]

After these practices were exposed in the media, some officials from the Department for Education apparently decided that they would resume use of their departmental email accounts, rather than risk their personal email accounts being scrutinised under FoI, but would then destroy their email correspondence. In so doing, they appeared to have overlooked rules laid down by the Lord Chancellor which stipulated that government officials destroying documents must keep deletion logs with which 'to defend themselves against a charge . . . that records were destroyed in order to prevent their disclosure'.[50]

Under the law, anyone who 'alters, defaces, blocks, erases, destroys or conceals any record' in an attempt to avoid disclosure in response to an FoI request is committing an offence. Section 77 of the Act says that anyone convicted can be fined up to £5,000. Nobody has ever been prosecuted, however, and it is highly unlikely that anyone ever will be: the law also states that prosecutions must be brought within six months of the offence being committed, but such are the delays to official responses to FoI requests that it could be years before such an offence came to light.

Another method of circumventing that Act saw ministers and civil servants cease the practice of writing observations in the margins of documents, writing them instead on Post-it notes that could be attached to documents, read and then discarded.[51]

Finally, the UK's freedom of information regime has allowed

government ministers who are dissatisfied with any direction made by the Commissioner – or any court – to simply overturn it. There is no requirement for such ministers to lodge an appeal against an order that their department should declassify information: they can simply tear that order up.

This ministerial veto was deployed five times in the eight years after the Act came into force. It was used to prevent publication of the minutes of Cabinet discussions about the 2003 invasion of Iraq; to suppress Cabinet minutes about devolution of the governments of Wales and Scotland; to halt the publication of the Department of Health's analysis of the damage that might be caused by its own reconstruction of the National Health Service; and to halt the publication of a sample of the letters that Prince Charles, the heir to the throne, writes regularly to government departments in an attempt to influence public policy – a practice that some consider to be highly unconstitutional.

The royal family's own archives, held at Windsor Castle, are completely exempt from the Public Records Acts. A number of historians believe that these papers were severely weeded in 1945 – although not so thoroughly as to prevent the leak of film showing the future Queen, aged around six, being encouraged by her mother and uncle to give a Nazi salute[52] – and some have condemned what they see as attempts by the royal family to censor and suppress the history of their role in British public life.[53]

Nor does the Freedom of Information Act apply directly to the royal family, which is not included in the law's definition of a public body, although correspondence to and from members of the royal family was initially subject to FoI – but also to a qualified exemption test.*

---

* This theoretical access to royal correspondence ended in 2011 when the Constitutional Reform and Governance Act – the law that reduced the Thirty-Year Rule for access to public documents to twenty years – gave the monarch, and the first and second in line to the throne, complete exemption from FoI.

In the case of Prince Charles, an eight-year battle to shed light on his behind-the-scenes lobbying resulted in three judges on the Information Tribunal ruling that the public should be allowed to see the contents of the twenty-seven letters because it was 'in the overall public interest for there to be transparency as to how and when Prince Charles seeks to influence government'.

At this point the Attorney General stepped in, exercising his ministerial veto to prevent publication of the letters and their 'particularly frank' contents on the grounds that to do so 'could damage the Prince of Wales's ability to perform his duties when he becomes king'.[54]

The matter ended up before Britain's most senior judge, the Lord Chief Justice, who ruled that while the Attorney General did have the power to veto the release of contents of the letters, the power that the Freedom of Information Act had given ministers to override the courts could be described only as 'a constitutional aberration', one that threatened to have a damaging effect on the rule of law.[55]

In March 2015, the Supreme Court finally ruled that the Attorney General had been wrong to apply the veto. The letters were released, showing how Prince Charles ignored the political neutrality that is the cornerstone of the monarchy, lobbying over matters as diverse as housing, homeopathy and international relations, and pushing to have his aides appointed to senior positions within Whitehall.

The government's attempts to suppress the letters had cost the taxpayer more than £400,000.[56]

In June 2015, the Secretary of State for Justice, Michael Gove – who, four years earlier, as Secretary of State for Education, had attempted to evade the Freedom of Information Act – announced that he would conduct a review of the law. He cited Tony Blair's misgivings as one of his reasons for doing so.[57] He then appointed to the Commission of Inquiry two people who had publicly criticised the Act – including Jack Straw, who had allegedly dismissed the committee that drafted the Act as 'crap fooey' – and a former leader of the Conservative Party, Michael Howard, whose expenses claims had been criticised when disclosed under FoI.

An FoI request seeking information about the way in which members of the commission were selected was rejected.

The Commission of Inquiry's slightly bizarre attitudes to transparency were on display when it held its first briefing for the British media on its work, at which it disclosed that it was considering the introduction of charges for FoI requests – and then asked the journalists not to disclose who was present, nor attribute anything they said.[58] *

At the time of writing, the Commission's report has yet to be published.

---

* The anonymous briefing was given by Lord Terry Burns, the chair of the commission.

6

The Vault

Secrecy and Northern Ireland's Dirty War

On the evening of Monday 8 January 1990, a group of British detectives decided that they had done enough for one day. It was getting late now, and some of the officers had been working for thirteen hours on a complex and politically fraught investigation that was being conducted against a backdrop of escalating violence.

Northern Ireland's savage little war had just entered its twenty-second year. Eighty-nine people had died the previous year. One, Pat Finucane, a lawyer, had been shot fourteen times after gunmen used sledgehammers to smash down his front door while he was having Sunday dinner with his wife and three children. Another was Loughlin Maginn, a father of four who was shot dead at his home in a village south of Belfast. It was the circumstances surrounding these murders, along with a string of others, that the police team led by John Stevens were investigating. At just past 9 p.m. they flicked off the lights of their incident room, locked up, and left the building.

The facility from which they were working was no ordinary police station. It was located beyond the chain-link fences, the razor wire and the CCTV that protected a seventeen-acre complex that the Royal Ulster Constabulary (RUC) operated on the outskirts of Carrickfergus, a coastal town twelve miles north of Belfast. Known as Seapark, the complex was home to forensic science laboratories, exhibit stores, a suite of offices and no end of confidential archives. It was one of the most secure policing facilities anywhere in the world.

Twenty minutes later, four members of Stevens' team who had been conducting inquiries elsewhere arrived back at the incident room, intending to lock some paperwork away for the night.

First they smelt the smoke. Then they saw the flames. The entire incident room was ablaze and they rushed to raise the alarm. Sarah Bynum, one of the detective constables, later recalled: 'There were a number of fire alarm points in the building and I went to one and I smashed it with the heel of my shoe and nothing happened. I ran down to another one and smashed that and again nothing happened.'

A heat-sensitive intruder alarm had also failed. Bynum raced to the guardhouse at the entrance to the complex, where an armed officer from the RUC was on duty. 'My first word to him was to call for the fire brigade and he replied that the phones were down. I then told him to get on his radio to call for help and his reaction was one of almost disinterest, of: "Well what do you expect me to do about it?"'[1] By the time the fire was eventually extinguished, the team's desktop computers had melted into pools of metal and plastic; steel filing cabinets had buckled, and the documents inside had incinerated.

Whoever started the fire clearly intended to destroy every scrap of documentary evidence that the police team had gathered.

The immediate suspects were not members of one of Northern Ireland's paramilitary groups, however, but British soldiers. Stevens and his team were convinced that the arsonists were from the Force Research Unit – a shadowy British Army Intelligence Corps body known as 'the FRU' that worked closely with MI5 and Special Branch, the intelligence wing of the RUC. They also suspected that detectives from Special Branch had helped the FRU to slip into the high-security complex and break into their office.

This remains their belief a quarter of a century later. While an RUC investigation concluded that the fire had been started by accident, John Stevens, now Lord Stevens, is of a different view: 'This incident, in my opinion, has never been adequately investigated and I believe it was a deliberate act of arson.'[2] Later, Stevens would look back on his investigation and lament that 'in almost thirty years as a policeman I had never found myself caught up in such an entanglement of lies and treachery'.[3]

It is unclear how much harm was caused to Stevens' investigation by the fire. Stevens says he had been warned that an attempt would be made to sabotage his inquiry, and had established a 'duplicate office' at the headquarters of the Cambridgeshire police. However, a senior member of his team, Detective Chief Superintendent Laurie Sherwood, says some written statements and exhibits could not be recovered.[4]

What is clear is that both the FRU and Special Branch would have been anxious to see an end to Stevens' investigation: they knew that if he pressed on it would be only a matter of time before he stumbled upon the true nature of the British government's role in the Northern Ireland conflict. A few hours after the incident room at Carrickfergus went up in flames, Stevens and his team had been due to arrest one of the men they believed to be behind the killing of Pat Finucane and Loughlin Maginn. That man, a former British soldier called Brian Nelson, was also known as Agent 6137: he was working for the British government.

Nelson had been placed on the payroll of MI5 and inserted, by the FRU, into the Ulster Defence Association, a loyalist paramilitary organisation. By the time Stevens and his team were about to come calling he had, by his own account, been involved in eight murders, two attempted murders, thirty-four conspiracies to murder and several other serious offences.[5]

In linking Nelson to the Finucane murder, Stevens' detectives were not merely solving a single crime – they were, in Stevens' words, about to uncover 'something extremely dangerous and difficult'[6] – namely, the evidence that the British state had been operating a death squad in Northern Ireland. It wasn't pulling the triggers of that squad's guns, perhaps, but, through Nelson – and others – it was pulling the strings of those who did.

For a generation, the overwhelming majority of the British people had regarded their armed forces as reluctant peacekeepers between two warring tribes in Northern Ireland, and had seen themselves as the innocent victims of a terrorist campaign. That narrative would be seriously undermined if it were to become clear that the British state was influencing, or even managing, the actions of the gunmen from one of those two tribes – if it were to emerge that elements within the British security forces had not merely begun to mirror the terrorists, but were in control of terrorism – and had been, almost from the beginning.

In a society as grievously divided as Northern Ireland, where two different communities have two different understandings of recent history – and where those differing perceptions are the reason they remain divided – any attempt to recover the truth about the past will always be a laborious and painful process. Accounts of the past differ enormously. There are different views on the rights and wrongs of the conflict and, as a consequence, different views about who should be praised and who should be blamed. There is no agreement on the causes of events, or even on the language that should be used to describe them. Was the conflict a civil war? Or was it a series of crimes?

In Northern Ireland today there is a contest for control of the narrative of the past. It can be a bitter struggle at times, in which historical research – and memory itself – fall under suspicion: they are seen not as neutral tools for exploring history, but as weapons in a fight for the future of a territory that has been claimed by two separate peoples.

In 2007, nine years after the Good Friday Agreement brought

the conflict largely to a close, the British government asked
Robin Eames, the senior Anglican clergyman in Ireland, and
Denis Bradley, a former priest and former vice chair of the
Northern Ireland Policing Board, to head a commission that
would examine ways in which Northern Ireland could find a
way forward out of its shadows.

Eames and Bradley concluded that any sustainable reconciliation must be centred upon an acknowledgement of the moral
dignity of each community's common humanity. Success, however, would require two other elements: 'A willingness for mutual
forgiveness and a willingness to address the truth of the matters
to which the mutual forgiveness is to apply.' It is not possible,
they warned, 'to complete an act of forgiveness unless a wrong
is acknowledged . . . only then is mutual forgiveness possible'.[7]

And there lies the rub.

The appalling acts of the paramilitaries were, with some notable
exceptions, acknowledged at the time they were committed,
even if some today insist they were committing 'political' rather
than 'criminal' offences. But some of the actions of soldiers and
the police continue to be concealed or denied, particularly those
acts that led to loss of life. Even more painstakingly hidden is the
extent to which the state, through its proxies like Agent 6137
Brian Nelson, was orchestrating acts of terror.

Attempts to investigate such crimes all too frequently face
obstruction, with the government failing to disclose material
it holds that would allow the truth to be established; inquests,
Ombudsman's inquiries, litigation and police reviews have
dragged on for decades.

There is a suspicion among some in Northern Ireland that the
British state is unable to contend with the past because it cannot
disclose the full truth, in all its intricacies.

The precise meaning of the noun *collusion* has been picked
over many times in Northern Ireland. Peter Cory, a Canadian

judge who examined the death of Finucane, concluded that when considering the need for public confidence in the army and police, the definition must be broad enough to include the turning of a blind eye. Stevens went further towards the end of his investigations, stating that collusion ranged 'from the wilful failure to keep records, the absence of accountability, the withholding of intelligence and evidence, through to the extreme of agents being involved in murder'.[8]

As the conflict ran its course, the relationship between elements of the British military and loyalist groups became so complex that the usual definition of collusion – secret understanding – is hardly sufficient to describe it.

When young British soldiers arrived in Northern Ireland in the early '70s, that relationship was founded on something quite simple: on their first patrols, they frequently encountered uniformed Protestant paramilitaries who were offering information and directions, and asking for telephone numbers that they could call if they had anything to report.[9]

Before long, mutual support morphed into collusion, with the Chief of the General Staff, General Michael Carver, candidly informing the Prime Minister, Edward Heath, that 'in general, the Army disliked having to operate in opposition to the Protestants'.[10] When the paramilitary Ulster Defence Association was formed in 1970, the British government decided that its members should face no bar to joining the locally recruited British Army unit, the Ulster Defence Regiment (UDR).[11]

The regiment had been raised to replace the almost exclusively Protestant and utterly discredited B-Specials, a quasi-military police reserve unit. Initially, more than a fifth of recruits to the new army unit were Catholic,[12] but before long many had departed, under threat from the IRA and disillusioned by the actions of the government, not least internment without trial. When the Ministry of Defence decided the following year that the regiment should be expanded, it did so in full knowledge that 'we will be largely arming one section of the community'.[13] The regiment continued to grow steadily, becoming the largest infantry regiment in the British Army. For most of the period of its existence, the majority of its soldiers were part time, performing their duties while also holding down other jobs.

Over the next twenty-seven years, the paramilitaries of the UDA were responsible for an estimated 408 murders[14] and would occasionally clash with British Army units. Yet the organisation was not banned until 1992, and some of its members – including men with serious terrorist convictions – played a full role in the operations of the British Army's Ulster Defence Regiment.

In one extraordinary episode in August 1974, the Secretary of State for Northern Ireland, Merlyn Rees, his two junior ministers and his highly influential Permanent-Under Secretary, Sir Frank Cooper, held a two-hour meeting with representatives of the UDA and the second major Protestant paramilitary group, the Ulster Volunteer Force (UVF), during which there was an exchange of views about the future of the regiment. Subsequently, the regiment was expanded into two full-time battalions, with the Northern Ireland Office acknowledging privately that this was being done in accordance with a suggestion put forward by the paramilitaries of the UDA.[15]

Repeatedly over the years, weapons disappeared from the Ulster Defence Regiment's barracks and found their way into the hands of the paramilitary UDA and the UVF, and soldiers serving with the regiment were involved in a great many terrorist attacks. These included the Miami Showband killings of July 1975, in which three members of a cabaret band were shot dead after their van was halted at a bogus Ulster Defence Regiment checkpoint, as well as, allegedly, the four coordinated car-bomb attacks in Dublin and Monaghan in May 1974 in which thirty-three people died and more than 300 were injured, making it the deadliest coordinated attack of the Troubles.

In mid-Ulster, soldiers serving with the regiment committed a series of terrorist offences alongside serving police officers. Up to twenty-five members and former members of the security forces are believed to have been members of the so-called Glenanne gang, which is estimated to have murdered up to 120 people between 1972 and 1977, many of them Catholics who were not involved in the conflict. Very often the murders were perpetrated shortly after the IRA had launched an attack on security forces in the area. One member of the gang, Robin Jackson, who had served with the Ulster Defence Regiment, is thought to have been involved in at least fifty murders, including the Showband shootings and the Dublin bombings. He never spent any significant time behind bars.

According to one estimate, over a twenty-year period, 320 of the regiment's soldiers were convicted of serious offences, including murder, kidnap and serious assault.[16] But this remains just that: an estimate. When a history of the regiment was being prepared on the twentieth anniversary of its foundation, its author was told that no records were kept of the number of members convicted of offences. It seemed that acts of collusion were bitterly regretted by many within the regiment, but that the facts about its members' involvement in loyalist terrorism had become 'a carefully protected official secret'.[17]

Parliament was also told that these statistics were not kept. This was not true. In the early 1990s, an Irish transparency group published a report based upon figures that had been extracted from the Northern Ireland Office. The group established that twenty-nine of the regiment's soldiers had been convicted of conflict-related offences between 1985 and 1989, compared with six police officers, eight soldiers from other regiments and 2,662 civilians. Seventeen of the regiment's soldiers had been convicted of murder. When these figures were weighted to assess the numbers of crimes per 10,000 people, the level of the regiment's criminality became clear: it had a rating of 9.1 per cent, compared with 5.9 per cent for the community as a whole: it was far more lawless than the population it was supposed to be policing and protecting.[18]

While it is undoubtedly the case that the vast majority of the men and women who served in the Ulster Defence Regiment were not involved in loyalist activities, the exact number who were British soldiers by day and terrorists by night will never be known – not just because many were never apprehended, but because they were frequently permitted to resign after they were arrested, or on the day they were to appear in court. On occasion, the resignations were backdated to the day of a murder they had committed; other times they would be discharged for 'poor attendance' after being charged with a terrorist offence.[19]

In 2005, a police unit called the Historical Enquiries Team was established under the command of a former Scotland Yard detective to review the thousands of unsolved murders from the Troubles. It found evidence that the security forces had altered the records of members of the Glenanne gang in order 'to remove the link between security force members and illegal activities, or to protect the name of the security force organisation'.[20]

It was not only the other ranks of the Ulster Defence Regiment who were involved with terrorism. An official review into the murder of Pat Finucane would discover that there had been 'reliable and repeated reports' from MI5 and military intelligence that senior officers of the regiment had been providing assistance to loyalists, as had comparatively senior RUC police officers.[21]

But no action had been taken and complaints about collusion had been dismissed. The Historical Enquiries Team would eventually reach the verdict that the Glenanne murder spree offered 'indisputable evidence of security forces' involvement with loyalist paramilitaries', and that while this evidence 'should have rung alarm bells all the way to the top of government', 'nothing was done; the murderous cycle continued'.[22]

It is difficult to avoid the conclusion that the murderous cycle was being permitted to continue; that the collusion between some members of this British Army unit and loyalist terrorism was officially sanctioned.

Members of the Ulster Defence Regiment were not the only British soldiers contributing to the terrorist bloodshed. For a short period in the early 1970s, a more shadowy group was also in operation.

One Friday night in May 1972, as people were spilling out of the pubs and clubs of Belfast to make their way home, two cars could be seen driving slowly around the Andersonstown district in the west of the city, darting into side streets, emerging moments later onto one of the main roads.

This was a time when much of the city had been carved up into no-go areas, with makeshift barriers erected across roads leading into residential areas, as both nationalists and unionists sought to protect their communities from deadly attack by outsiders. Andersonstown, a Catholic and nationalist area, was no exception.

A shade before midnight, two young men, Aidan McAloon and Eugene Devlin, climbed out of their taxi and walked towards one of the barricades. Just then one of the two prowling cars passed by and one of its passengers fired several shots from a machine gun, wounding both young men. 'I thought it was all over, I thought it was the end,' Devlin later recalled.[23] Within minutes, five more men standing by a barricade less than half a mile away were shot by an occupant of the second car. One of them, Patrick McVeigh, a father of six, was killed instantly.

The following day, the press office at army headquarters issued a statement saying that unknown gunmen had fired indiscriminately at civilians, and that McVeigh and the other men had been victims of 'an apparently motiveless crime'.[24] As all the victims had been Roman Catholic, this statement implied that it had been a sectarian attack by loyalists. It was a statement that could only heighten the friction between the two communities.

The statement was a lie. The two cars belonged to the British Army. All seven men had been gunned down by soldiers serving with a hitherto-unknown undercover British Army unit, the Military Reaction Force (MRF).

Formed during the summer of 1971, the MRF's operations appear to have been inspired by the ideas and writings of Brigadier Frank Kitson, who commanded the British Army in Belfast at that time.[25] A veteran of the end-of-Empire campaigns in Kenya, Malaya, Muscat and Cyprus, Kitson had come to see counter-insurgency operations as 'primarily concerned with the struggle for men's minds'.[26] He was also fresh from University College, Oxford, to which he had retreated for a year after being ordered by his superiors to prepare a report about the steps that might be needed to prepare the Army for dealing with future insurrections around the world. It is unclear whether Kitson was responsible for the formation of the MRF; the evidence is largely circumstantial: he has never commented on the matter. But clearly, some innovative military methods would be germinated by Kitson's campaign experience and campus contemplations, and a high degree of secrecy would be required to prevent the public from learning of the existence of these new tactics.

With its members recruited from across the British Army, the MRF was around forty-strong and based at a secret compound at Palace Barracks in Holywood, east of Belfast – a place that was off limits to other soldiers. Its members always operated in plain clothes, and never carried any item that could betray their identities. They eschewed military ranks, and their commanding officer, a captain, was known simply as 'the boss'.

One member wrote several years later: 'At times, we had a distinct feeling we were like trail blazing, Wild West pioneers flying by the seat of our pants. We were regularly reminded that we were operating outside the scope of the regular forces and we had very few restrictions imposed on us. We were a very small unit, often working out on a limb and we had to use maximum force when it was required, to survive. We really weren't too interested in rules and regulations.'[27]

Initially, the MRF was engaged largely in surveillance operations. On occasion these were conducted alongside paramilitaries, both republicans and loyalists, who had been 'turned' and were cooperating with the Army. Kitson had pioneered the use of such groups while serving in Kenya during the Mau Mau insurgency. It was in Kenya that Kitson had coined the term 'pseudo-gangs': state-run terror groups used to discredit the enemy.[28]

By mid-1972, the MRF was targeting men who were manning the barricades at the entrances to the Catholic no-go areas – whether they were armed or not – and then driving away towards Protestant districts. It seems the MRF had been given a new task: to inflame tensions in a way that would bring the IRA out to fight in the open, where its members could be seen, identified and killed. 'In the past, we would open fire at anyone seen to be carrying a weapon in the "hard areas",' one former member recalled. 'Now we would be going out on patrol, targeting selected groups and stirring up trouble in the street.'[29] This is how a number of men came to be shot in Andersonstown in May 1972.

In 2013, several former members of the MRF told BBC journalists that they had been unconcerned whether the men they were shooting at could be seen to be carrying weapons. They would open fire in any case, using weapons that were associated with paramilitaries rather than with the British Army. 'We used to just plod along [towards a barricade], assess the situation, then just move in and take a few targets out.' On occasion, one former soldier said, they would approach a barricade and 'give 'em a blast'. Another explained: 'We were not there to act like an army unit. We were there to act like a terror group.'

When it was put to one former member of the MRF that

individuals should not be killed on the basis that they may have an unseen weapon, he replied: 'Well you're not supposed to. But it all depends on where they are and what they're doing at the time. As far as we were concerned, people caught in a specific situation in a specific area were part and parcel of a terrorist organisation.'[30] Some police officers clearly knew what was happening. Six weeks after Patrick McVeigh was shot dead, an RUC detective tipped off his family that his killers had been British soldiers. There were other shootings by the MRF that year – it's unclear how many – and more Catholic men were killed and wounded.

Eventually, in June 1972, a sergeant serving in the MRF was arrested and charged with the attempted murder of three men he had shot in a street in west Belfast, and with the malicious wounding of a child who was injured when one of the rounds passed through the wall of a nearby house. He was acquitted the following May after telling the jury at Belfast City Commission that he had opened fire only after he was shot at.[31] By then, it appears that a decision had been taken in Whitehall that there was an unacceptable amateurishness about the MRF and its operations, and that it should appear to be wound up. By the end of the year the MRF was being reorganised as the Special Reconnaissance Unit, which was expected to take greater care to operate within the law.[32] This unit was rebadged as another surveillance outfit, the 14 Field Security and Intelligence Company.

But what became of the records of the MRF once the unit was disbanded? Every former MRF member who agreed to be interviewed by the BBC said that he routinely wrote reports at the end of each shift, and that these were passed to a military intelligence officer attached to the unit. More reports were compiled by the MRF commander, and others were generated by the army brigade to which the MRF was attached. The shift around 1972 from surveillance to offensive duties – to 'targeting

selected groups and stirring up trouble in the street', as one
member put it – must have been recorded in some way. And
if the MRF had been established by Kitson to test whether his
theories on counter-insurgency operations and pseudo-gangs
could have a practical application on the streets of west Belfast,
official conclusions about his experiment should also have been
recorded.

But the BBC journalists found that there was no trace of the
unit or its activities in the National Archives. Every record either
was being concealed by the Ministry of Defence or had been
destroyed: shredded – or double-shredded – and burned.

It was as though the Military Reaction Force – the British
Army's very own terror gang – had never officially existed.

In 1980, a major new initiative was launched in the secret
intelligence war against the IRA after Jack Hermon was
appointed Chief Constable of the RUC. Hermon was sworn in
on 2 January, amid carnage. The previous day, three people had
been killed. On the day of the ceremony a fourth died, and then
two more. By the end of the week the death toll had reached
nine, as three members of the Army's Ulster Defence Regiment,
one a twenty-one-year-old Catholic, were blown to pieces when
their Land Rover drove over a one-ton IRA bomb.[33]

Hermon had been a serving police officer for thirty years
and Deputy Chief Constable for almost four, time enough
to come to the conclusion that the RUC had become overly
reliant on interrogation. He was of the view that securing convictions by beating confessions out of suspects was a disastrously
counter-productive practice, as it had engendered deep hatred of
the security forces among nationalists, and may have prolonged
the conflict.[34] He was also concerned that the reports about
the brutality inside the police holding centres had damaged the
reputation of the force.[35]

Hermon believed that a subtle intelligence-gathering apparatus needed to be developed, in which information would be supplied not only by informants recruited from within the IRA and the other paramilitary groups, but also by agents inserted into their ranks. Senior British intelligence officers in the province, and Lieutenant General Sir Richard Lawson, the newly appointed Army commander, appear to have shared this view.

During the first week in his new job, Hermon asked the Irish Joint Section, the combined MI5 and MI6 organisation then operating in Belfast, to look into the issue and produce a report. The work was carried out by Patrick Walker, soon to become the most senior MI5 officer in the province and, by the end of the decade, Director General of the agency. Walker spent several months examining the options before producing a report which was to have far-reaching implications, both for the future shape of the British state's counter-insurgency operations in Northern Ireland, and for the relationship that some detectives and intelligence officers in the province would have with the rule of law.

Walker's recommendations have never been made public, but the confidential RUC memorandum that ordered their implementation has since surfaced. In February 1981, Assistant Chief Constable John Whiteside wrote to all officers between the rank of inspector and chief superintendent serving with the RUC's Criminal Investigation Department (CID) to inform them of the recommendations contained within what he termed the 'Walker Report'. Whiteside explained that these had been approved by Hermon and would come into force in one week's time.

The CID's detectives were responsible for detecting criminals; the Special Branch detectives were responsible for gathering intelligence. Whiteside's memo ordered that all informers providing information on 'subversive crime' and 'non-subversive crime' would henceforth be handled by Special Branch, whenever possible.

Critically, members of paramilitary groups who had been recruited as informants were not to be arrested – regardless of the crimes that they had committed – without consultation with Special Branch: 'All . . . planned arrests must be cleared with Regional Special Branch to ensure that no agents of either RUC or Army are involved.' Any decision to charge an agent with an offence 'must be the result of a conscious decision by both Special Branch and CID in which the balance of advantage has been carefully weighed.'[36] The Walker Report is said also to have stipulated that records should be destroyed after operations.[37]

The RUC's Chief Constable had decided, with the encouragement of MI5, that the gathering of intelligence would take priority over the apprehension and prosecution of people responsible for killings, kidnappings and bombings. And, on occasion, the people who were responsible for these acts would remain at liberty, if they were also working as informants for the police or the Army, and their usefulness to the state was assessed to outweigh the danger that they posed to the public.

This was just the beginning. As the decade progressed, informants were recruited *before* they joined paramilitary organisations. These individuals would then be given privileged access to selected police and Army intelligence material, which would enable those organisations to select targets for murder.

Police and Army agent-runners were effectively deciding who was to live and who was to die; and while such decisions were being taken, MI5 hovered nearby.

This presented the police with a legal dilemma, as outlined in the minutes of a meeting between senior RUC officers and Northern Ireland Office (NIO) officials from March 1987, which state: 'The RUC were to a large part dependent on intelligence if they were to be successful in combating terrorism. Such intelligence was obtained by placing/using informants in the middle ranks of terrorist groups. This meant they would have to become involved in terrorist activity and operate with a degree of immunity from prosecution.'[38]

The problem, as the RUC pointed out at this meeting, was that the only guidelines to police work of this nature had been written in 1969, before the conflict began, and 'were totally unrealistic/unworkable for dealing with terrorism'. In 1988, in a submission to the Northern Ireland Office, an Assistant Chief Constable spelled out the issue in the clearest possible terms: 'Taking the example of the terrorist informer who has been instructed to conceal munitions in his house to await their being used. Whatever instructions the informer's handler gives will be "wrong", in that if he directs the informer to refuse to comply, the latter will automatically become the subject of suspicion (and probable eventual death); if the handler tells the informer to assent, a breach of the guidelines (and probably the law) is involved.'[39] MI5's legal advisor, meanwhile, was warning that the fundamental problem with the guidelines was that 'in order to run a terrorist agent so as to gather intelligence or evidence, they must be continually breached'.[40]

The RUC's attempts to put its informer-handling operations on a legally sound footing came to nothing. In May 1987, an internal minute to the Permanent Under-Secretary at the NIO said: 'It would suit us if the process set in train by the RUC makes fairly slow progress. It would not be wise to take any steps at this juncture to halt it; we should simply desist from hastening it.'[41]

A short while later, Raymond White, the head of Special Branch, raised the problem with the Prime Minister, Margaret Thatcher. When she asked whether he needed anything else in order to combat terrorism, White replied that he regarded 'a sound legislative basis' as essential for such intelligence operations, rather than the 'grey area' in which he was obliged to work.

After some delay, government officials informed him eventually that 'the issue was too difficult to handle', and that Special

Branch should continue as before. White complained that the government's response was, in effect, to 'carry on doing what you're doing but don't tell us the details'.[42] The issue came to nothing because government lawyers knew that any guidelines that allowed serious crimes to be committed with impunity by police informers – agents of the state – could never be lawful.

The RUC's Special Branch was not the only force operating in a legal grey area. The Army's undercover Force Research Unit handled agents in an almost identical fashion. There were frequent tensions between the two organisations,[43] and some misunderstandings. Special Branch regarded the Army's sources as being 'rubbish and of a poor standard'.[44] But they shared this much in common: they were wings of the state that had been permitted to become *managers* of terrorism as part of a long-term counter-terrorism strategy. And behind both Special Branch and the FRU would stand MI5, offering a guiding hand,[45] a degree of political cover, and the cash to pay to informers.[46]

As a consequence of the implementation of the Walker Report, Special Branch would be compelled to impede some CID investigations – including murder inquiries – if key informers were to be kept out of prison. This no doubt explains why Alan Simpson, the detective who led the initial investigation into the murder of Pat Finucane, says that one of Hermon's assistant chief constables, Wilf Monahan, warned him at the outset to 'not get too deeply involved in this one'.[47] Although the Whiteside memo on the Walker Report was read by a great many CID detectives, some appeared not to immediately grasp its implications. Another Belfast detective was aghast to discover that Special Branch had tipped off a man he was planning to arrest for questioning about the murder of Finucane. 'They were obviously keen to protect someone,' he recalled. 'But who, and why?'[48]

These were the questions that John Stevens' team of detectives found themselves asking. Slowly, they discovered the answer. Without any public statement, the RUC had been transformed from a force that prioritised keeping communities safe through traditional policing practices, to one that aimed to win a secret intelligence war.

And one of the figures Stevens' team came to believe was at the centre of this intelligence war was also the prime suspect in the Pat Finucane murder: Brian Nelson.

A thin, nervous-looking man, a drinker and a chain smoker, Nelson was the most unlikely-looking terrorist and intelligence agent: 'not an inspiring specimen', according to Stevens. Born in 1947 in the loyalist Shankill district of west Belfast, he joined the Black Watch regiment of the British Army as a teenager, serving in Cyprus and Germany. But his disciplinary record was poor, marked by repeated periods when he was absent without leave, and in 1969 he was discharged.

Back in Belfast, Nelson joined the UDA, and in 1973 was sentenced to seven years in prison for his role in the kidnap and torture of a disabled Catholic man. He was released in 1977, and seven years after that he approached the Army and volunteered to become an informer. The Force Research Unit was put in charge of Nelson and asked him to rejoin the UDA. Over the next seventeen months, Nelson met his handlers around sixty times and was paid more than £2,000 in cash.[49]

Soon he was appointed as the intelligence officer for the UDA in west Belfast, playing a central role in selecting and locating targets for assassination. Although he occasionally kept this information to himself, Nelson would frequently pass details of these planned murders to the FRU. Over the years that followed, the FRU and the police took steps to prevent just two of the intended victims from dying. One of these individuals was Gerry Adams, the senior IRA commander. In the second case, the FRU appears to have intervened only because the UDA's plans involved Nelson driving the getaway car, which would have put him at risk of arrest.[50]

In June 1985, Nelson embarked upon the most extraordinary operation of his undercover Army career. The UDA's leadership asked him to help arrange a deal with Armscor, apartheid South Africa's arms corporation. A unionist from Armagh who had emigrated to Durban and was working for the company had been identified as a possible source of weaponry, and Nelson was asked to meet this man. The FRU not only encouraged him to do this, it paid for his airline tickets to South Africa and met his hotel bills.[51] One of Nelson's FRU handlers, a man whom he knew as Ronnie, had told him: 'You've really hit the big time here Brian.'[52] While some have claimed the FRU sponsored this arms-trafficking enterprise in order to intercept the weapons and prevent them from falling into loyalist paramilitaries' hands, others suspect that the FRU, and some of their political masters, were determined to help arm Ulster's loyalists.

In Durban, Nelson examined a number of weapons, and was particularly taken with an automatic shotgun called the Striker which 'could be used to devastating effect . . . in close-quarter combat'. Armscor made it clear that it would accept a cash sale, but also wanted to know whether the UDA could provide it with one of the latest generation of ground-to-air missiles that were under development at Shorts, an aircraft and armaments factory in east Belfast.[53] In the event, no weapons were purchased at that time, with Nelson being told that the UDA had insufficient funds.

A couple of years later, however, the connection Nelson had made with Armscor did bear fruit. Armscor provided weapons to loyalist paramilitaries in a trafficking operation that was financed by a £325,000 robbery from a bank in Portadown, thirty miles south-west of Belfast. The corporation's European agent, an American called Douglas Bernhardt, had learned that a large cache of arms held by a Lebanese militia in Beirut had come onto the market. Bernhardt arranged for the arms to be loaded into a container, which was shipped to Belfast via

Liverpool, accompanied with bills of lading and notes of origin that indicated it held ceramic floor tiles. 'There were at least a couple of hundred Czech-made AKs – the VZ-58,' recalls a former Armscor employee who helped to broker the deal. 'And 90-plus Browning-type handguns: Hungarian-made P9Ms. About 30,000 rounds of ammunition. Plus a dozen or so RPGs and a few hundred fragmentation grenades.' At every step of the operation, this source says, the UDA's intelligence officer was kept informed of its progress.[54] This was Nelson, the FRU's Agent 6137.

The weapons arrived at Belfast docks in late December, and were smuggled into the country undetected. Early the following month, at a farmhouse in County Armagh, the arsenal was divided three ways between the UDA, the UVF and a third loyalist paramilitary group, Ulster Resistance. The UDA lost its entire portion within minutes: its share of about 100 weapons was loaded into two hire cars, which were stopped and seized at a nearby police roadblock. Some of the UVF's weapons were also recovered over coming weeks, but most remained in the group's hands, and transformed the loyalists' firepower over the years that followed. The portion that went to Ulster Resistance was never captured, however. Nor were these weapons decommissioned during the peace process: they remain hidden today.[55]

There was an attempt to smuggle a further consignment of arms into Belfast the following year after three loyalists travelled to Paris with a stolen Shorts missile part. They were about to hand it over to Bernhardt and a South African intelligence officer, when all five men were arrested by the French security agency, the DST.

The loyalists and arms dealers involved in this operation are convinced that Nelson knew about both arms-smuggling operations, and assume that he must have informed the FRU. Noel Little, one of the loyalists detained in Paris, says: 'Brian Nelson was inserted into the UDA as an agent, he wasn't a recruited member. How could he know about it and not tell his handler?'[56]

Nelson himself would later confirm this, recounting in his journal how one handler, 'Ronnie', told him during discussions about his South African adventures that 'because of the deep suspicion a seizure would have aroused, to protect me it had been decided to let the first shipment into the country untouched'.[57]

As part of his investigation into the murder of Finucane, and the FRU's role in managing loyalist terrorism, Stevens attempted to discover more about this weapons consignment. Members of his team travelled to South Africa to interview former Armscor officials, but concluded eventually that evidence of a chain of responsibility would remain elusive. However, a senior member of the inquiry team says he believes it feasible that the UK government could have been involved in bringing the weapons into Belfast – or at least turned a blind eye. 'It's not at all far-fetched,' this senior police officer says.[58]

Whatever the truth about the FRU's role in the arms-smuggling operation, the consequence was that loyalists' access to high-calibre weapons – and their ability to slaughter both republicans and uninvolved Catholics – changed immediately. In the six years prior to the importation of the South African weapons, from January 1982 to December 1987, loyalists killed seventy-one people. In the seven years afterwards, from January 1988 to 1 September 1994, loyalists killed 229 people.[59] Today, loyalists boast that the IRA was forced eventually to 'sue for peace' because of the pressure it came under as the killings mounted in the aftermath of the largely successful South African smuggling operation.

By the end of 1985, a few months after his return from South Africa, Nelson had had enough. He resolved to break his links with both the UDA and the British Army's FRU,[60] and took his wife and three children to what was then West Germany. He found work in a small town north of Munich, fitting floors in new buildings.

In February 1987, however, the FRU phoned Nelson and asked if they could meet him. He was flown to Heathrow, where he spent several hours drinking in a hotel bar with a FRU agent handler and an MI5 officer, who persuaded him to return to Belfast and rejoin the UDA as a British agent.[61] He was promised a deposit to buy a new house, a car to enable him to work as a taxi driver, and £200 a week.[62] He would also receive generous bonuses. Even though he was earning more money in Germany, Nelson agreed.[63] From that point until his arrest in January 1990, Nelson was paid a total of £46,428 from FRU funds.[64] MI5 would later tell an official inquiry that it disapproved of Nelson's re-recruitment. In fact, however, the agency's own records show that it did want to see Nelson return to Belfast, as long as he could persuade the UDA to appoint him as its intelligence officer.[65]

With the help of the intelligence that was being passed to him by his Army handlers, Nelson quickly achieved this role, becoming the UDA's senior intelligence officer for the whole of the province. He went to work compiling a card index library detailing the home addresses, workplaces and haunts of suspected members of the IRA. Many of the cards had police photographs attached. Some of the material came from electoral registers and newspapers. Much of it came from montages of the names and photographs of terrorism suspects that were compiled by the police and issued to members of the security forces on checkpoint duty. Some information, such as car numbers, were supplied by his FRU handlers. At one point, the FRU helped him weed out material that was out of date.[66] Copies of the cards would be handed to UDA gunmen prior to an attack, and sometimes they were also supplied to the UVF. The FRU also kept its own copy of Nelson's entire card index library.[67]

After each of their meetings with Nelson, FRU handlers would complete contact forms detailing what he had said. During one meeting after another, Nelson would express his desire to see the UDA become more 'professional'; he was anxious to ensure that its violence was directed only towards the IRA. His handlers clearly approved. '6137 wants the UDA only to attack legitimate targets and not innocent Catholics,' they wrote on one contact form. Nelson 'wants to see an end purely to sectarian murders and to concentrate on specific targeting of legitimate republican terrorist targets', said another. Nelson's appointment as an intelligence officer 'enables him to make sure that sectarian killings are not carried out but that proper targeting of PIRA [Provisional IRA] members takes place prior to any shooting', noted a third.[68]

As well as the information supplied by the FRU, Nelson and other members of the UDA were receiving material from other soldiers and police officers. In the mid-1980s, MI5 estimated that eighty-five per cent of the organisation's intelligence was the result of security force leaks.[69] The largest single source was the Ulster Defence Regiment.[70]

Nelson did not see himself as a terrorist at this time, however, but as an undercover soldier – and, to an extent, so too did his handlers. As one of those handlers would later comment: 'He was a soldier not a tout. He saw himself as part of a team.'[71] But he was certainly being deployed to facilitate acts of terrorism.

A senior Army officer would eventually give a statement to the detectives of Stevens' team saying that Nelson had been used by the FRU to target individuals.[72] Through Nelson, the British Army was taking effective control of the UDA's death squads, and directing them towards known – or suspected – members of the IRA.

Inevitably, there were mistakes. In May 1988, Nelson selected a man called Terry McDaid for execution. McDaid and his wife Maura were settling down to watch the news on television at their home in north Belfast when there was an enormous crash at the front door. 'Terry and I just sat and stared at each other,' Maura recalled. 'The living room door flew back to the wall. Two men were standing at the door, they were completely clothed, there was no flesh to be seen. They ran in and just started firing.'[73]

McDaid, twenty-nine, was shot seven times, and died within minutes. The intended target had been his older brother Declan, who lived two streets away. The FRU had been aware of the plot to murder Declan McDaid for seven months by the time Terry was shot dead.[74] Nelson would later tell his solicitor, the police and a journalist that the FRU had provided the incorrect address, but later withdrew this claim.[75]

By early 1989, Nelson appears to have been coming under pressure from both the UDA and his handlers at the FRU, with each organisation complaining that he was insufficiently active. By 6 February, however, his main FRU handler was noting in her contact form, with evident satisfaction: 'Of late, Nelson has been more organised and he is currently running an operation against selected Republican personalities.'[76] One of these 'personalities' was the lawyer Pat Finucane.

Six days later, Pat Finucane was at his home in north Belfast, eating Sunday dinner with his wife Geraldine and their three children. On hearing a loud bang at the front door the couple leapt up, opened the kitchen door and looked down the hall. Striding towards them was a masked man wearing a green combat jacket that was belted at the waist. Large black gauntlets covered his forearms. He held a gun in his left hand. A second gunman was behind him.

The shooting began just as Geraldine reached out to press an alarm button. It was fast and furious at first, then slower, more deliberate. She curled up with her hands over her head, and was hit in the ankle by a ricocheting bullet.

Pat Finucane was thirty-nine. He was from a republican family: three brothers had been members of the IRA. As a solicitor, he had advised many members of the organisation, including the hunger striker Bobby Sands, and Gerry Adams. He also represented Protestants accused of terrorist offences.

Some within the British Army clearly believed Finucane to be a member of the IRA: he appeared within the records of the Northern Ireland headquarters as 'Patrick Finucane, RC, 21 Mar 49(D) PIRA P2327'.[77] MI5 also had little time for Finucane, and whether the agency believed him to be a terrorist or not, it wished others to believe that he was. For some time before that Sunday evening, MI5 had been spreading rumours about the lawyer. It was part of what the agency called a Counter-Action campaign that was being deployed against a number of prominent figures in the nationalist community at that time. The aim, the agency said, was to 'unnerve' these individuals. MI5 knew that the rumours about Finucane were reaching loyalist paramilitaries, yet it was not until after he had been shot dead that John Deverell, the head of MI5 in Northern Ireland, concluded that they had been 'on dangerous ground', and began to rein in the campaign. Even then, some MI5 officers wanted the Counter-Action activities to continue in order, as they put it, to ensure that 'Republican players feel that they, too, are as exposed as the members of the security forces who live daily under threat of the assassin's bomb or bullet'.[78]

The RUC also believed Finucane to have been too close to the IRA. In November 1988 four senior officers, including Jack Hermon and the deputy head of Special Branch, Brian Fitzsimons, complained during a meeting in Belfast with junior Home Office minister Douglas Hogg that some lawyers in the province were 'effectively in the pockets of terrorists'. When Hogg asked for more information, Special Branch provided him with documents identifying Finucane.[79]

A few weeks later, Hogg told the Commons: 'I have to state as a fact, but with great regret, that there are in Northern Ireland a number of solicitors who are unduly sympathetic to the cause of the IRA.' Nationalist MPs were appalled, with one, Seamus Mallon, immediately predicting that 'there are lawyers . . . who have become targets for assassins' bullets as a result of [Hogg's] statement'.[80] Less than four weeks later, the two gunmen were striding down the Finucanes' hallway, opening fire.

When the shooting stopped, Geraldine opened her eyes and saw her husband lying on his back beside her. His dining fork was still in his left hand. He had been shot six times in the head, three times in the neck and three times in the torso. One of the first detectives at the scene would later recall: 'I had attended the scenes of some two hundred murders, suicides and sudden deaths, but what lay before me was a picture of ferocity the likes of which I had encountered few times before.' The gunmen had downed Finucane with shots to the chest before standing over him and shooting him in the face. 'His face was heavily covered in powder burns, which indicated that he had been shot several times at a range not greater than 15 inches.'[81] Finucane's three young children had been watching.

Three inquiries would subsequently conclude that Finucane was not a member of the IRA, but a lawyer dedicated to defending his clients, who sometimes included members of the IRA. As part of the peace process, Peter Cory, a retired judge of the Canadian supreme court, was asked by the British and Irish governments to examine allegations of collusion between the security forces and paramilitaries. Cory concluded that in the case of Finucane, 'both military and police intelligence fundamentally misconstrued the role of solicitors and failed to draw the essential distinction that exists between lawyers' professional obligations, on the one hand, and their personal alliances, on the other'.[82]

A subsequent review by the former war crimes prosecutor Sir Desmond de Silva QC lamented that 'a lawyer could so callously and tragically be murdered as a result of discharging his professional legal duties'.[83] In addition, John Stevens would conclude that Hogg had been 'compromised' and that his comments were unjustified.[84]

Nelson was deeply involved in the murder of Finucane. He had passed the lawyer's photograph and address to the UDA, and may have been watching the house shortly before the attack. Cory concluded that he had seen 'strong evidence' of collusive acts by the FRU, Special Branch and MI5, but that the question of the FRU's advance knowledge of the attack could be resolved only through a public inquiry.

De Silva pointed out that during the period at which Nelson was being tasked with the targeting of members of the IRA, he was an employee of the Ministry of Defence.[85] 'The very nature of Nelson's re-recruitment from Germany and his subsequent handling leads me to the conclusion that by 1989 Nelson was, to all intents and purposes, a direct State employee,' he said. 'The FRU must, therefore, bear a degree of responsibility for whatever targeting activity Nelson carried out in his dual role as a UDA Intelligence Officer and a FRU agent during this period.' And while de Silva did not conclude that there had been 'an over-arching State conspiracy to murder Patrick Finucane', he did conclude that the lawyer would not have been murdered 'had it not been for the different strands of involvement by elements of the State'.[86]

Although the murder of Pat Finucane would become one of the major strands of Stevens' investigation, his team was originally brought over from England seven months after the lawyer's death to investigate the killing of a twenty-eight-year-old poultry processor called Loughlin Maginn.

Maginn had been mistakenly identified as a terrorist and his details placed on one of the montage cards of suspects' photographs used at security force checkpoints. In August 1989 a masked UDA gang fired several shots into his living room, then clambered through the shattered window to finish him off. Two of the UDA men had also been serving as soldiers with the Ulster Defence Regiment.

When Maginn's family remonstrated that he had had no connection with the IRA, the UDA attempted to justify its actions by producing a twenty-minute video, shot by soldiers from the UDR, which showed the wall of a police briefing room covered with photographs of IRA suspects. Maginn was among them. There was uproar among Northern Ireland's Catholic communities at this all too rare but irrefutable evidence of collusion between loyalist killers and the British state. An outside police investigation became unavoidable and John Stevens was appointed to run it.

Shortly after his arrival, senior military officers told Stevens that the Army never ran agents of any kind in Northern Ireland.[87] But it wasn't long before Stevens' team identified Nelson as one of the Army's key assets. It was the beginning of the end for the FRU's operations.

It was at this point that the mysterious fire broke out at the team's incident room, destroying their computers and incinerating the documents they were storing. Nelson was tipped off that he was about to be uncovered and fled to England, where arrangements were made for him to receive counter-interrogation training. He was arrested thirty-six hours later, however. The FRU immediately recovered his index cards of potential targets, which were concealed from the Stevens team for the next four months.[88]

Ignoring the FRU's advice, Nelson made a series of self-incriminatory statements to Stevens' team, and even agreed to their suggestions that he write a long account of his time as a British Army undercover agent. In spite of the fire, in time, Stevens sent a file detailing Nelson's involvement in several murders and other serious crimes to the Director of Public Prosecutions. At this point the Army and senior Ministry of Defence officials leapt into action to conceal the truth about the FRU's involvement in the management of terrorism.

After Stevens passed his file to the DPP, an officer on the Army's general staff sent a submission to the Defence Secretary, Tom King, which warned of the damage that could be caused should Nelson be put on trial. King recognised that Nelson was 'a terrorist, thug and hooligan' but also a 'productive source' who, he had been told, had saved lives. His initial view was that Nelson 'should not go near the courts'. He later questioned the accuracy of some of the information he had relied on and warned that Nelson could not be protected from prosecution if he had 'gone beyond the limit'. The general staff officer observed that although Nelson was now relying on the MoD to keep him alive – 'either in or out of prison' – and dependent on the department to protect the lives of his family, 'such protection would be conditional on his remaining silent about our covert operations'. The following month, arrangements were made to pay £1,650 a month to Nelson's wife. A few weeks later, a memo from the same staff officer to the MoD and the Army's Northern Ireland HQ said that Nelson should be reassured that his wife was being cared for and that his family would be resettled once he was released from prison, 'subject to his remaining silent about what he knows'.[89]

It is far from evident that government ministers had been in control of the events that had led to the death of Pat Finucane and the many others who were targeted by Nelson. It is possible that the FRU and Special Branch were permitted to operate under a system of political oversight that was so loose that the control that the state was exerting over loyalist paramilitaries could always be disavowed.

But regardless of how long the reins may have been, by late 1990 government ministers, senior civil servants and the Army's general staff were clearly concerned. They feared that the evidence of state-sponsored criminal violence – evidence that had been half-hidden for decades amid the confusion, the distrust and the daily recrimination of Northern Ireland's bloody little war – was about to be forced into the open.

There were Cabinet-level discussions about the impending prosecution, with King and Peter Brooke, the Secretary of State for Northern Ireland, both arguing that the case should quietly be shelved, and with David Waddington, the Home Secretary, expressing concern on behalf of MI5.

By this stage the entire Cabinet must have been fully aware that their security forces had been enabling a death squad. Brooke appears to have become slightly frantic, claiming that lives could be lost if Nelson appeared in court. The Prime Minister, John Major, described himself as conflicted, but indicated that charges should be brought if there was a chance of a successful prosecution.[90]

In Belfast, meanwhile, the Director of Public Prosecutions of the province was coming to the conclusion that it was in the public interest to bring charges. Along with the UK Attorney General, Patrick Mayhew, he withstood significant political pressure to drop the case against Nelson.[91] Eventually, the DPP decided that there was sufficient evidence to charge Nelson with two counts of murder, four of conspiracy to murder, one of attempted murder, and a number of lesser charges.[92]

At this point the Cabinet Secretary, Sir Robin Butler, became more engaged, sending a 'Top Secret' minute to Major in which he highlighted the public interest risks in taking Nelson to trial and attempted to persuade the Prime Minister to take steps to oppose it.[93] Not long afterwards, Major's principal private secretary was noting that the collapse of the prosecution would be 'a very good outcome', which appears to have reflected the prevalent view at the highest levels of government.[94]

By the time Nelson finally came to trial in January 1992, the murder charges had, without explanation, been dropped. Instead he was permitted to plead guilty to five charges of conspiracy to murder, and was sentenced to ten years' imprisonment. Previously, the DPP had appeared adamant that there should be no suggestion that he had accepted a plea bargain. It subsequently emerged, however, that the DPP had told the Attorney General that he was obliged to consider any approach by the defence, and that such an approach had been made.[95]

As a consequence, Brian Nelson, Agent 6137, was not cross-examined. Any light that he could have shed upon the role that the British state had played in the murder of its own citizens was quietly snuffed out.

Nelson served a little more than four years before being released. The Army was as good as its word – he had maintained his silence, after all – and he was given a new identity and a new life. His by-now-estranged wife and their children were provided with a new home in the north of England.

In April 2003 the MoD issued a brief statement announcing that Nelson had died of a brain haemorrhage, aged fifty-five. Journalists were briefed that he had been living in Canada. In fact, he had been living in Cardiff, under the name Brian Thompson. His death certificate listed his occupation as 'Army Officer (Retired)'.[96] Two weeks later, after more than thirteen years investigating collusion between the British state and the terrorists it was supposed to be combating, Stevens' third and final report was completed. By then, his work had led to the conviction of ninety-four people. None of them were from the Army's FRU, Special Branch or MI5. Instead, the FRU's commanding officer had been promoted, and Nelson's main handler had been promoted and decorated.

In the course of their investigation, Stevens' team had taken 9,256 statements and gathered 10,391 documents, totalling more than a million pages, not counting those lost in the fire at Seapark in Carrickfergus. His final report ran to several thousand pages.[97] Just nineteen of those pages were made public.

It would be another nine years before the full extent of the

British state's involvement in the murder of Pat Finucane would emerge. In 2012, de Silva's review of the case found that it went far beyond the control, through the Army, of the man who was feeding the names and locations of potential targets to the UDA's death squads.

Police officers had been urging loyalists to kill Finucane, while holding them for questioning about other offences.[98] The man who supplied the weapons used to kill Finucane had been a Special Branch informant for the previous eighteen months. He had warned his handlers that an attack was about to take place, but they took no action. The man who drove the getaway car later confessed to police, at which point he too was recruited as an agent and, in accordance with the provisions of the Walker Report, the case against him was dropped.[99] *

Nelson was the most notorious of the British agents operating within the loyalist paramilitaries' ranks, but he was far from alone. Long after his investigations into collusion in Northern Ireland were wound up, Stevens disclosed that of the 210 people his team arrested, only three were *not* agents of the British state. Some were working simultaneously for the police, the Army, MI5 and, he hinted, MI6. They were making handsome sums of money, frequently while fighting against each other, 'which was all against the public interest and creating mayhem in Northern Ireland'.[100]

These were agents within the ranks of the loyalist groups. Penetrating the IRA and the Irish National Liberation Army had been more problematic for Special Branch and the FRU, but not impossible. One FRU agent codenamed Stakeknife was Freddie Scappaticci, for many years one of the leaders of the IRA's internal security unit. Scappaticci was responsible for

---

* The case against this man, Ken Barrett, was revived following the Stevens Inquiries, and in 2004 he was jailed for life after admitting the murder of Finucane and twelve other charges. Under the terms of the Good Friday Agreement, he was released twenty months later.

the interrogation and, on occasion, torture and execution of others suspected of being informers. The former head of British forces in Northern Ireland has described him as 'our most important secret . . . a golden egg'.[101] Scappaticci is alleged to have engineered the murders of other informers – and even of a number of people who were not involved in the conflict – in order to save himself.

As the truth about collusion and agent-running operations seeped slowly into the open, elements of the security forces could be seen to have been embroiled in one cold-blooded murder after another. The official narrative – that the police and Army were attempting merely to defeat terrorism, within the law – appeared increasingly threadbare. But attempts to discover what actually happened have struggled and frequently failed.

The need to deal with what are described as 'legacy issues' – or sometimes it is simply referred to as 'the past' – is acknowledged by Northern Ireland's politicians, but while the issue is always on the agenda, it is never resolved.

Six years after the Good Friday Agreement was signed, a survey found that most people in Northern Ireland thought it important that a Truth Commission be established in order to lay bare the way in which the British state, and the republican and loyalist paramilitaries, had fought their wars. Younger people were particularly anxious that this should happen.

The results of the survey showed there was little confidence in a Truth Commission's prospects for success, however. Most people were sceptical that it could help provide 'a clean start' for the future, or help Northern Ireland to become a less divided society. There were even doubts about who could be trusted to run such a commission.

Ninety-nine per cent of people said that republicans could not be relied upon; almost a hundred per cent said the same of loyalists, as did ninety-two per cent about the British authorities. The people of both communities felt that Her Majesty's Government was little more trustworthy than the paramilitaries.[102] *

The British government has refused to convene any further public inquiries into specific events, blaming the length and cost of the thirteen-year inquiry into the fatal shootings of fourteen civilians by the Army on Bloody Sunday. David Cameron admitted that there were 'frankly shocking levels of state collusion' in the murder of Pat Finucane,[103] and one of his advisors told the Cabinet Secretary that the Prime Minister 'shares the view that this is an awful case, and as bad as it gets: far worse than any post 9/11 allegation'.[104]

Nevertheless, Cameron's government reneged on a supposedly binding international agreement to hold a public inquiry. Meeting Geraldine Finucane at Downing Street to explain his decision, Cameron raised one finger in the air, according to a number of those present, drew a circle, and said that there were 'people in buildings all around here who won't let it happen'.[105]

Other mechanisms for establishing the truths about deaths – such as inquests, litigation, Police Ombudsman's inquiries or detectives' cold case reviews – have proved largely ineffective for an assortment of reasons.

The coronial inquest system, which has been recovering the truth about sudden or unnatural deaths in England and Wales for 800 years, appeared in Northern Ireland during the Troubles to have bowed to the more pressing requirements of a counter-terrorism campaign. Coroners were unable in law to record unlawful killing verdicts, and were reluctant at times to probe too deeply into possible criminal conduct on the part of the security forces.

Since the conflict came largely to an end, the inquest system appears to have been unable to reassert its independence: it is

---

* In a sign of the depth of the distrust that pervades Northern Ireland, when asked whether 'ordinary people' could be trusted to run a Truth Commission, seventy-six per cent of respondents said no.

not unusual to see inquests suffer one delay after another as a consequence of the failure of the police or Ministry of Defence to produce relevant files. And these delays are measured not in months, or even years, but in decades.

As of 2014, inquests had yet to be concluded into seventy-four killings during the conflict in Northern Ireland. Around half were inquests that the Attorney General had ordered to be reopened after finding that the original hearings were flawed; half were cases that had been adjourned shortly after the death, and never completed.

By April that year, the average time that families had been waiting for an adjourned inquest to be concluded was twenty years and seven months. Almost all concerned killings by police officers or soldiers, or by loyalist paramilitaries who were suspected of being state agents.[106]

The Historical Enquiries Team (HET), the police unit set up in 2005 to re-examine unsolved murders, knew nothing about the two vast warehouses of documents that the MoD maintained at Swadlincote in Derbyshire, and nobody at the MoD saw fit to inform the team of their existence. When this archive was reported in the media, a senior HET investigator said: 'There could potentially be documentation about every case we are interested in.'[107]

The HET was already facing questions about its independence after it had emerged that former Special Branch officers were among the gatekeepers who were deciding what intelligence material held in Northern Ireland it would be permitted to see.[108] The HET unit was shut down after a highly critical report by Her Majesty's Inspectorate of Constabulary concluded that it was investigating killings by soldiers and police with less rigour than it was investigating killings by paramilitaries.

At the time of writing, the Police Ombudsman for Northern Ireland was attempting to investigate around 300 allegations of serious wrongdoing by officers during the Troubles, including collusion in murder. These included the Glenanne gang killings, and the question of whether police failed to prevent Stakeknife's killings. As a consequence of budget cuts, the Ombudsman has warned that some investigations will take twelve years to complete.[109]

Like the coroners and the HET, the Ombudsman's investigators have experienced enormous difficulty in accessing the intelligence documents that they need to complete their inquiries. In 2014 the Ombudsman was compelled to bring judicial review proceedings against the Chief Constable over his refusal to hand over papers concerning the role of agents of the state in around sixty murders, including that of a police officer who was killed in 1992.[110]

Official documents, of course, can provide a key to understanding the official mind. As a consequence, in Northern Ireland not all have survived. Many were destroyed the moment they were no longer required, as stipulated by the Walker Report. Others vanished as peace began to be established. Like those colonial officials who lit the global end-of-Empire conflagration that became known as Operation Legacy, some senior RUC officers saw little reason to risk the eventual disclosure of their most sensitive records.

In 2011, police admitted that files that had been held at Gough Barracks, their regional headquarters in County Armagh, had been destroyed within weeks of the 1998 Good Friday Agreement. The papers included incident reports dating back to the 1970s and notes of interviews of murder suspects who had been questioned at the barracks between 1985 and 1993. This was a period when there is alleged to have been collusion between a number of police officers and loyalist gunmen who were killing local Catholics.

The destruction operation was made public only after the family of a young Catholic man shot dead by loyalists in 1991

discovered that none of the police records relating to his unsolved murder any longer existed.[111] The reason given for their
destruction was identical to that given by the Ministry of Defence
for the non-disclosure of some of its most sensitive papers – they
had been stored in an area where asbestos had been found.

What the announcement did not mention is that contractors
brought in to deal with the asbestos problem had warned that it
would be unsafe to burn or shred the documents, and suggested
that they should be dumped either in a landfill site or at sea.[112]
One particular minute, echoing the dumping of the most
damning documentation of Kenya's brutal conflict into the 'very
deep and current free waters' of the Indian Ocean, recorded
that a senior officer said he favoured dumping the papers in
Beaufort's Dyke, a deep underwater trench between Northern
Ireland and Scotland. The officer explained that this would be an
advisable course of action because 'the action of the sea water on
the paper would over time pulp it and destroy the information
held thereon'. He eventually decided on cost grounds that they
should be buried in a landfill site.[113]

Despite the warnings they had received, senior RUC officers
ruled that the papers should be shredded before being secretly
removed to the landfill site. Much to the alarm of the contractor
carrying out the work, a police officer was stationed inside the
room to watch the shredding being completed. So concerned
was the contractor that he contacted the Police Authority, requesting indemnity against legal action should the officer
become contaminated.[114]

Today, the shredded remains of the Gough Barracks archives,
and the secrets that they held, are buried fifteen metres beneath
an old landfill site in north Belfast that is due to be turned into
a park.

By the time Stevens' three inquiries in Northern Ireland came to
a conclusion in 2003, the documents that his team had amassed

were estimated to weigh around 100 tonnes. Following the fire at his incident room, he had been taking very good care of them: before he left Belfast they were loaded into Ford Transit vans and driven to an airport where a Hercules transport aircraft was waiting. The vans drove straight up a ramp and into the aircraft, which took off immediately for a secure location in England.[115]

In 2007, members of the Stevens' team complained that the MoD and MI5 were pressing Scotland Yard for the return of the documents. 'There are calls from certain agencies for their documents to be returned,' said one officer. 'In some cases we have handed them back and they have been shredded. The pressure on us is growing and it has got to the stage where we have told them what part of the word "no" don't you understand?'[116]

In 2011, the Stevens archive was handed to the police in Northern Ireland, although Scotland Yard says it kept a copy in electronic format. Three years later, this author asked the Yard whether it considered this copy of the archive to be subject to the provisions of the Public Records Acts, to be preserved and handed eventually to the National Archives at Kew. The Yard spent two months contemplating whether the Freedom of Information Act gave it a reason to not answer the question.[117] Eventually, the Yard said that it did not believe this copy was subject to the Public Records Act, but that it was 'likely to be considered for permanent preservation'.[118]

So it was likely that the archive wouldn't be destroyed, but there was no guarantee.

The copies of the Stevens papers that were handed over to the police in Northern Ireland were sent to an equally secure location: Seapark, the high-security police facility at Carrickfergus where the Army's arsonists staged their desperate attempt to bring Stevens' inquiries to a halt in January 1990. They sit there today, unreachable, alongside the documents that the coroners have been unable to get their hands on, and the files the Police Ombudsman was permitted to read only once he had won a courtroom battle with the Chief Constable. Nearby are stored the secret reports written by two other English detectives, John Stalker and Colin Sampson, after they were drafted in to investigate the RUC's so-called shoot-to-kill policy of the early 1980s. Doubtless there are also police files on acts of collusion by soldiers of the Ulster Defence Regiment, and on the murderous activities of the MRF. All these papers, and many others, are held together: the annals of the dirty war that the United Kingdom fought within its own borders for more than thirty years.

The gatekeepers to the archive at Seapark – the men and women who decide what is made public, what is redacted, what is withheld – are the officers of the 'Legacy Support Unit' of the Police Service of Northern Ireland. Many of them are former Special Branch detectives, brought out of retirement specifically to perform this task.[119]

In 2015, George Hamilton, the Chief Constable of Northern Ireland, used the term 'The Vault' to describe this archive while giving a television interview. 'It's a colourful metaphor – "Vault" – but let's use that,' he said. 'If The Vault was to be opened, I know there will be literally millions of documents. I'm not just talking about intelligence documents, I'm talking about plans for covert operations, I'm talking about minutes of meetings.

'My understanding is that the IRA, the UVF and the other players in this didn't keep notes or minutes of meetings or records of decisions. We did. And I think all of that has left us somewhat exposed.'

Police records in the UK are subject to the Freedom of Information Act, but they are not subject to the Public Records Acts, or to the Thirty-Year Rule – soon to become a Twenty-Year-rule – of those Acts.

There's another reason why the Vault may remain locked for ever, however. Hamilton made it clear that his repository contained papers that would be enormously troublesome for people other than police and intelligence officers, civil servants and ministers. 'Other people have stories to tell and questions to answer,' he said. When the door to The Vault is opened up, there should be no doubt that 'out of that will pour material that will present challenges for other people in the system'.

The implication was that the Vault contains material that all sides engaged in the conflict would wish to remain buried, and for a very long time. Furthermore, while many of those who waged that war have since passed away, others are now in government, in both Westminster and Stormont.

'If we're sitting on millions of pages of intelligence documents from a very busy time, when there were killings happening almost on a daily basis, and some sort of atrocity happening on a regular basis, you would expect that there will be material there that will present challenges for individuals,' Hamilton said. It would also, he made clear, provide opportunities for investigators.

'That's the way it works.'[120]

7

Bodyguards of Lies

The Battle to Conceal the Secret State

Deception is an essential tool of the intelligence agent's trade. At times of conflict, it becomes a tool of statecraft, and the suppression, dissemination and fabrication of information become weapons – part of the armoury with which war is fought. Deception operations do not merely create false impressions that exist fleetingly while war is being fought, however: they can colour our view of history.

The Second World War saw perhaps the greatest ever feat of disinformation, when a fusion of modern science, mathematics and the tightest possible security at Bletchley Park enabled the creation of a masterpiece of strategic deception.

The story of the master code-breakers of Bletchley has been told many times. What has not been so closely explored is the way in which the hall of mirrors that both protected their work and materialised from it was erected with such stealth and guile that successive generations gazed into the glass for years, unaware that what they saw was not what it seemed.

Nor has there been close examination of the way in which the secrecy that enshrouded Bletchley during the war laid the foundation for the concealment of the mass surveillance programmes of today.

The nineteenth-century mansion and grounds of Bletchley Park, fifty miles north of London, were bought by MI6 in 1938. The following summer the estate became the home of the Government Code and Cypher School, an organisation that operated under MI6 supervision, and which had grown out of a First World War code-breaking unit at the Admiralty known as Room 40 OB.

Even before the Second World War broke out, senior GC&CS staff had toured leading universities on the lookout for young academics who might be recruited as code-breakers. Initially, mathematicians, classicists and linguists were favoured. These recruits were never quite certain where they were going: they were told that they should wait for a telegram informing them that 'Auntie Flo is unwell', and should then make their way to somewhere called 'Station X'* at Bletchley Park.[1]

Initially, few background checks appear to have been made. Jean Campbell-Harris, later Baroness Trumpington, who was hired as a German speaker, later recalled: 'Despite the importance of the work and the need for great secrecy, there was no vetting. It was because they were snobs. With us Foreign Office people, they assumed that if you spoke the Queen's [sic] English and had been to the right schools, you were a reliable person, which is absolute rubbish, of course.'[2]

New staff were ordered to 'sign-on' – to the Official Secrets Act – the moment they arrived. Often, the officer watching over this ritual would place his revolver on the table while they signed the form. Recruits were then given a sharp lecture, in which they were warned that they must *never* divulge anything that they would see, hear or learn once inside the gates.

They were usually allocated to one of the compound's huts when they joined a unit – units that were much greater in size

---

* Other wartime cover-names for the GC&CS included the London Signals Intelligence Centre and the Government Communications Headquarters.

than a single hut by the end of the war – and told that they must not discuss their work with anyone from any other hut. A few were assigned to outstations at Eastcote and Stanmore, on the north-west outskirts of London, or to the discreet offices in Berkeley Street in London's Mayfair, from which GC&CS had, since the pre-war years, been attacking the diplomatic and commercial signals traffic of friend and foe alike.[3]

At first, fewer than 100 people worked at Bletchley Park, but they were engaged in the most vital intelligence operation of the war: deciphering high-level Axis communications. Some of the country's most brilliant minds laboured around the clock, by hand, by brain, and by operating what was known as 'specialised analytic machinery'. The word computer was rarely used at this time, although one of the machines, the Colossus, developed in 1943, was the world's first programmable electronic computer. Famously, the staff at Bletchley used these machines to crack the German Enigma and Lorenz ciphers.

Contrary to the impression given in some popular representations of Bletchley Park, most of the work was not carried out by pipe-smoking young men in tweeds who cracked codes in between completing *The Times* crossword. Most of the recruits were women, for the pragmatic reasons that they were cheaper to employ and less likely to be required by the armed forces. And the labour was relentless. Staff operated like factory workers, on three shifts a day: nine to six, four to midnight, midnight to nine. 'You could never get a sleep pattern,' Trumpington recalled. 'I was tired all the time.' The intellectual pressure was also enormous; some suffered breakdowns. Staff nicknamed Bletchley Park 'the Nut House'.[4]

These efforts enabled the Allies to gain vital tactical advantages: knowing where German U-boats were being dispatched, for example, or where and when some German air raids were to be mounted. Critically, by giving an insight into the enemy's strategic intentions and his intelligence operations, Allied signals intelligence – or sigint – informed and underpinned the Allies' use of strategic deception: the war-long policy to mislead the enemy's high command.

At no time was this more important than during preparations for the invasion of France, when sigint helped the Allies to understand the extent to which they were successfully deceiving German commanders into making faulty strategic dispositions of their forces. Six months before the invasion, while discussing this deception with Stalin, Churchill commented: 'In wartime, truth is so precious that she should always be attended by a bodyguard of lies.' Stalin apparently found this hilarious. 'Upon this note,' Churchill recorded, 'our formal conference ended gaily.'[5] Henceforth, the deception was given a new codename: Operation Bodyguard.[6]

The intelligence gathered through sigint was so highly prized, and so sensitive, that the top security classification of that time – 'Most Secret' – was considered no longer to be adequate. In the summer of 1941, a new classification was created: 'Ultra'. After the war, the word Ultra began to be synonymous with high-level wartime signals intelligence. This vital source of information could exist only so long as the enemy was given no cause to suspect that its communications were not entirely secure. The work at Bletchley Park was to be protected by unprecedented levels of secrecy.

All around the mansion and the huts, posters warned: 'Careless Talk Costs Lives'. In addition, in May 1942, members of staff were handed a notice that read: 'Month after month instances have occurred where workers at BP have been casually heard saying outside BP things that are dangerous. It must be uppermost in your mind every hour that you do not speak to outsiders. Do not talk at meals: there are waitresses and others who may not be in the know regarding your own particular work. Do not talk in the transport: there are drivers who should not be in the know. Do not talk in the billet: why expect your hosts, who are not pledged to secrecy, to be more discreet than you? Do not talk by your own fireside. If you are indiscreet and tell your own folks, they may see no reason why they should not do likewise.'[7]

In the early hours of 7 May 1945, shortly before dawn began to break over Bletchley, the decryption staff working the night shift at Hut 6 received a copy of a telegram that had been transmitted a short time before.

The message had been sent by Grand Admiral Karl Dönitz, Commander-in-Chief of the German Navy and, following Hitler's suicide a week earlier, the country's *Reichspräsident*. The message was remarkable for two reasons. The first was that it had been transmitted *en clair*: no attempt had been made to encode it. The second was that Dönitz was instructing senior military commanders to agree to Germany's unconditional surrender. The war against Germany was over.

The man who was handed the message was Asa Briggs, who thirty years later would be ennobled as Baron Briggs of Lewes, one of the country's most distinguished historians. On this day – his twenty-fourth birthday – Briggs was a slightly breathless conscript in the Intelligence Corps. He took the message to the translation staff at Hut 3, and later recalled: 'I felt that I was participating in history as I passed it on with a mingled sense of excitement and relief.'[8]

What followed was even more remarkable. The news rapidly spread around the men and women on the night shift at Hut 6, but the head of the section, Stuart Milner-Barry – who in peacetime had been the chess correspondent of *The Times* – issued an instruction that they should not utter a word to any of the members of the day shift who were about to replace them. The code of silence that governed every waking moment at Bletchley Park was still to be observed.

'My appeal . . . was honoured in full,' Milner-Barry recorded many years later, with evident satisfaction. The day shift learned of the end of the war against Germany only when it was officially announced on the radio several hours later.[9]

By the time of Germany's surrender, Victor Cavendish-Bentinck, an aristocratic diplomat with the sharpest of minds, had spent almost six years at the very heart of Britain's intelligence war as chairman of the Joint Intelligence Committee (JIC), the Cabinet body that coordinates intelligence operations. That summer, Cavendish-Bentinck had time to look back and contemplate his country's intelligence successes, and its future intelligence requirements.

On 20 July, in a paper marked 'Top Secret', the JIC warned that the work carried out at Bletchley Park must remain hidden, for two reasons: '(i) Other enemies may arise in the future. Were they to know what successes were achieved in the war as a result of this special source, they could ensure that this source would not be available to us. (ii) No possible excuse must be given to the Germans or Japanese to explain away their complete defeat by force of arms. Knowledge that this source of information was available to us would provide such an excuse.' The JIC concluded at the end of its paper: 'It is imperative that the fact that such intelligence was available should NEVER be disclosed.'[10]

Looking back at these conclusions after the passage of seventy years, it may be difficult to appreciate just how anxious Britain's military and intelligence chiefs would have been at the prospect of their defeated foes discovering that they had not been beaten fair and square on the field of battle. But in 1945, these men would have recalled all too clearly how an embryonic Nazi party had seized upon the so-called *Dolchstoßlegende* myth, the conspiracy theory that the Germany army had not lost the First World War on the battlefield, but had been stabbed in the back at home. Cavendish-Bentinck and his colleagues were determined that there should be no future need for yet another generation of young Britons to go to war with Germany.

The first point is easy to understand, however: anyone who grasped the nature of the work carried out at Bletchley Park during the war would realise that espionage had undergone a technological revolution. They would also see that such work was highly unlikely to have come to an end with the cessation of hostilities. They may even have seen that it opened up almost boundless new opportunities for mass surveillance.

This was the third, unspoken, reason for keeping the wartime work of the Government Code and Cypher School concealed from view: it was going to continue operating in peacetime.

At Bletchley Park, Sir Edward Travis, the head of the GC&CS, had already taken the precaution of issuing a special order to all staff, thanking them for their discipline and discretion, and warning them to resist 'the temptation now to "own up" to our friends and families'. It was vital, he explained, that 'nothing we do now shall hinder the efforts of our successors'.[11]

By this time, there were more than 10,000 people serving with the GC&CS. One of them was Sir Harry Hinsley, who served as a code-breaker at Bletchley before editing the official British history of Second World War intelligence operations. Hinsley later concluded that the work had shortened the war in the Atlantic, Mediterranean and Europe 'by not less than two years and probably by four', and that without it, the outcome would have been uncertain.[12]

The question of the extent to which the code-breakers influenced the course of the war is one that is likely to preoccupy historians for generations to come. It is clear, however, that what happened at Bletchley Park was one of the greatest intelligence coups of all time. That so many people should be involved in such vital work, and that their work remained a secret for the next three decades, is something of a miracle.

Following the surrender of Japan, many of the staff were given a week's pay and told they were no longer required. Before leaving they were hauled before a senior military officer to be warned that if they ever breathed a word about what they had seen they would face thirty years in jail, or a firing squad.[13]

Some not only remained silent, refusing to discuss their wartime service with spouses or children, they became deeply secretive people. 'I used to be terrified that I would say something in my sleep,' one says. 'There were women who refused operations in case they said something under anaesthetic.'[14]

Churchill was to comment that Bletchley Park was home to 'the geese that laid the golden eggs and never cackled'.[15] Departing staff were told that once hostilities had ended, Churchill had ordered the destruction of the 'specialised analytic machinery' that had helped to crack the German and Japanese codes. Many appear to have believed this to be true, and decades later would speak of how the computers had been broken down into pieces the size of a man's fist, and the designs incinerated.

In fact, senior staff at the GC&CS had been giving great thought to the future of British sigint operations, and as early as July 1943 had concluded that it would be 'desirable to take the long view'.[16] During the summer of 1945, Travis asked his aides to indicate which of the machines needed to be preserved for the 'computing machine research units' that were being planned. He was advised that six machines, including the latest two of the ten Colossus machines, should be 'retained for research work'.[17]

However, neither the threats of prosecution under the Official Secrets Act nor the canard about the destruction of the computers at Bletchley Park would be sufficient to protect what was to be United Kingdom's greatest secret of the post-war years. An act of history theft would be called for.

It appears to have been Victor Cavendish-Bentinck who first understood that British intelligence had something of a history problem. During that summer, he realised that any historians who studied closely the actions of the Axis forces throughout the war, and the Allies' responses to those actions, would notice, sooner or later, something rather curious: the Allies responded remarkably quickly to events.

An examination of the war in the Western Desert, for example, would show that whenever German and Italian convoys began to cross the Mediterranean to resupply Erwin Rommel's *Afrika Corps*, the RAF and Royal Navy quickly located the enemy ships and inflicted heavy damage. Similarly, any study of the movements of U-boat packs during the Battle of the Atlantic, and the manner in which Allied convoys subsequently changed course, would suggest something equally uncanny had been happening.

Many other examples would soon be found in the archives, and it would not be long before historians began to consider that the Allies had reacted on occasion with such rapidity, and to such profound effect, that they appeared almost to have some forewarning of the enemy's intentions . . .

Both the JIC and the London Signals Intelligence Board, Whitehall's supreme sigint decision-making body, considered this complex problem.* Both concluded that there was little point in attempting to dismiss the evidence that would emerge from the archives as mere coincidence.[18] They also considered whether some effort should be made to suppress the German archives, but decided that this was not feasible: the British did not have possession of all of the Nazi regime's documents.

Instead, a body called the Advisory Panel on Official Histories was established. It was later renamed the Committee for the Control of Official Histories. Historians were to be employed directly by the government and would be encouraged to examine an entirely different aspect of Britain's wartime intelligence operations: the work of the Special Operations Executive, which conducted espionage and sabotage operations in occupied Europe and Southeast Asia. This would serve two purposes – it would distract attention away from sigint, and it would counter

---

* Not all the Board's conclusions are known: seventy years later, some of the papers are still withheld under Section 3(4) of the Public Records Act.

the widely held view that the most effective anti-Nazi resistance within occupied Europe had been organised by Communists.

Furthermore, these official historians would be informed discreetly about the decisive role that sigint had played in the Allied victory, and then warned that they must never talk or write about it. Ultra was to be airbrushed from history.

To reinforce the point, they were required to sign a form, classified 'Ultra Secret', in which they gave the following undertaking: 'I hereby declare that I am fully aware of the responsibilities which I have now assumed concerning the security of the source of Special Intelligence. I will ensure that this source of intelligence is adequately protected by me at all times. I will abide by any of the Provisions of the Special Security Regulations which may be brought to my attention now or in the future. I am aware of the implications of the Official Secrets Act with special reference to safeguarding this vital source of information.'

The form was to be signed in the presence of a military officer who was known, for the purposes of this ritual, as 'the Indoctrinating Officer'. The historians were also expected to sign a second undertaking, in which they pledged never to disclose the code word Ultra, and never to attempt to gain access to sigint material once their service as official historians had come to an end.[19] The United States government and Commonwealth counties agreed that they would take similar steps to hide the role that sigint had played in securing victory.

The first book to be written under the terms of this carrot-and-stick approach was M. R. D. Foot's *SOE in France*, which was followed by a tranche of further official Special Operations Executive histories. Retiring generals, diplomats and ministers were persuaded that they should erase all trace of Ultra from their memoirs. Even Churchill agreed, over dinner with Sir Stewart Menzies, the head of MI6, that he would ensure nothing appeared in his own account of the war.[20]

An elaborate peacetime deception operation was developed in order to conceal a wartime deception operation. And the truth would remain hidden for decades.

Having taken steps to conceal the role sigint had played in the war, Cavendish-Bentinck and the JIC began to consider the scope of future operations. With the Soviet Union consolidating its hold over Eastern and Central Europe, it was clear, even during the summer of 1945, that another major conflict could not be discounted. Moreover, the achievements of Bletchley Park showed that sigint could be deployed not only in support of strategic deception, but to leverage enormous diplomatic and commercial advantages.

The JIC quickly reached the conclusion that future sigint operations should be very ambitious indeed. The committee produced a report making five recommendations for the post-war organisation of British intelligence; one was that 'its collecting agencies must cover the world'.[21]

Faithful allies, neutral countries and potential enemies were all to be targeted, and not only for militarily useful intelligence. According to an August 1945 assessment of sigint operations that were likely to be required in the Far East after the war, the capture of diplomatic signals and economic intelligence would take priority.[22]

Some remaining Bletchley Park staff were outraged when told that they were to start work on the decryption of intercepted French traffic. One recalls that there was 'almost a mutiny' in the huts. 'We were lectured about this. There was a definite revulsion about spying on our former allies [but] there was nothing for it, if we didn't want to do this we had to go.'[23]

The British opened talks with the Canadian and Australian governments, and with the colonial authorities in India, with a view to establishing intercept stations across the Empire. While the Canadian military was enthusiastic, New Zealand expressed little initial interest, and the JIC decided that the South Africans should definitely not be involved. Locations for the stations were selected in Egypt, Malta, Gibraltar, Delhi, Ceylon, Malaya, Hong Kong, the Gold Coast in West Africa, Australia and Canada.

In the UK, intercept bases known as Y Stations were to be maintained at Brora and Hawklaw in the north and west of Scotland, Sandridge and Knockholt in the Home Counties, and Wincombe in Dorset. The Home Office was asked to ensure that no amateur radio enthusiasts in those areas were granted licences, to avoid any interference with signals, while orders were issued that German prisoners of war – thousands of whom were still working on farms across the country – were to be barred from coming within 400 yards.[24]

The London Signals Intelligence Board, chaired by Menzies and attended by Travis and the Chiefs of Staff, was given responsibility for the 'world-wide problem' of gathering sigint. A charter was drawn up to clarify that these responsibilities would entail 'carrying out within the British Empire, and in collaboration with other nations when authorised, the Chiefs of Staff policy in respect of the interception of *all** communications and radio transmissions of other nations'. This would have meant intercepting US signals too. But the United Kingdom, utterly bankrupt after six years of total war, was about to rely heavily upon the United States' largesse, not least to guarantee future European security. Eyebrows would have been raised across Whitehall at this proposal, and it seems certain that Churchill would have opposed any plan to read the Americans' traffic.

Instead, the close wartime intelligence collaboration, which had seen the UK share almost all of its technical knowledge with the United States, was to continue in peacetime. The UK needed the Americans' money. And for the Americans, there were pragmatic reasons for extending this alliance: unlike the United States, the UK controlled territory around the globe.

---

* Emphasis added.

President Roosevelt was complaining to his Secretary of State Edward Stettinius at this time that 'the British would take any land anywhere in the world, even if it were only a rock or sandbar'.[25] Nevertheless, the US Army Security Agency – forerunner of the National Security Agency – needed access to intelligence that could be plucked from the airwaves over these rocks and sandbars.

By the time the London Signals Intelligence Board's charter was formally adopted in late July 1945 it had been amended, so that the Board was now responsible to the Chiefs of Staff 'for instituting and carrying out, both within the British Commonwealth of Nations and, in conjunction with our Allies throughout the world, their policy in respect of the interception of all enemy and neutral communications and radio transmissions of other nations'.[26]

But the imperative was clear: Bletchley Park's post-war successor intended to hoover up as much signals intelligence as was politically permissible, and technically possible, everywhere in the world.

On 5 March the following year, in the small town of Fulton, Missouri, Winston Churchill, by now no longer Prime Minister, gave his famous speech in which he declared that 'from Stettin in the Baltic to Trieste in the Adriatic, an iron curtain has descended' across Europe, and that the east of the continent was now under Soviet domination.

At exactly the same moment, in a heavily guarded office in Washington, DC, representatives of the London Signals Intelligence Board and their counterparts from the US State–Army–Navy Communication Intelligence Board were signing a seven-page intelligence-sharing agreement, stamped 'Top Secret'.

This document superseded and expanded a 1943 sigint-sharing pact known as the BRUSA Agreement, and has been described as the most important and longest-lasting agreement between two foreign intelligence services that has ever been conceived.[27] It established the free exchange of signals intelligence between the two nations, and provided specifically for joint efforts to target Soviet and French ciphers. Canada, Australia and New Zealand were referenced as British Dominions whose sigint operations were to be conducted under British direction.

One passage was intended to ensure that the post-war sigint activities of the UK and United States remained enshrouded in official secrecy: 'It will be contrary to this agreement to reveal its existence to any third party whatever.'[28]

Shortly afterwards, the US Air Force opened its own Y Station in the UK at an airfield at Kirknewton, west of Edinburgh. The agreement was extended to include Canada in 1948, and Australia and New Zealand in 1956. Classified documents referring to this anglophone intelligence-sharing arrangement were marked 'AUS/CAN/NZ/UK/US EYES ONLY', and in time the pact would become known as the Five Eyes alliance.

Three weeks after Churchill's iron curtain speech, the GC&CS left Bletchley Park and moved to its former outstation at Eastcote. That year it also shed its name and adopted one of its wartime cover-names: the Government Communications Headquarters: GCHQ. The two Colossus machines also went to Eastcote, along with an array of material from a laboratory at Bletchley known as the Robinson Research Unit.

The facilities at Eastcote were considered to be cramped: there was room for 2,000 people, but Travis, now the director of GCHQ, believed it would need to expand to 6,000 on the outbreak of any future war.[29] Cherry Lavell, who was recruited as a seventeen-year-old clerk at Eastcote, and who later became a Colossus operator, recalls entering a compound with cartoon posters on the walls warning that 'Walls Have Ears!' The lecture that she and half a dozen other new entrants received was no joking affair. 'It was a very solemn moment. We were told about the work there, and we understood that we simply couldn't talk about it. People were a lot more restrained in those days any way, there was much more discipline. But there was also this tremendous feeling about the work that had been done to defeat Hitler.'[30]

By 1947, the Foreign Office had agreed that GCHQ should move once more, and a site was chosen at Cheltenham, in the west of England, which was considered to be far enough from London that it would be untouched by any nuclear strikes on the South-East.* In the event, the agency did not move until the early '50s, in part because so many new homes needed to be built to accommodate the staff and their families. Locally, it was acknowledged to be a sensitive 'Foreign Office facility' but, as at Bletchley, few people asked any questions, and even fewer answers were given.

From time to time, however, hints of what had happened at Bletchley, and was continuing at Cheltenham, did seep out.

In 1950, Duff Cooper, who had been a member of Churchill's war cabinet, lifted the lid on one wartime disinformation operation when he penned a lightly fictionalised account of Operation Mincemeat, the now-famous episode in which the body of a man in a British military uniform was deposited off the coast of Spain, bearing misleading plans for an invasion of Europe. As a consequence, Ewen Montagu, the naval intelligence officer who had concocted the operation, pressed successfully for permission to make public his own account, which was published as *The Man Who Never Was*, and made into a film with the same title.

---

* Other locations for the UK's post-war sigint headquarters that were considered, then rejected, included Cambridge and Norwich. Liverpool was also contemplated, but dismissed for what one senior Foreign Office civil servant described in a memorandum as 'the obvious reasons'. He did not elaborate. The Foreign Office also considered briefly whether GCHQ should be based in Canada, to place it further from the Soviet Union's nuclear arsenal. GCHQ was being concealed from the public, but Whitehall accepted that Moscow knew about its activities.

Then, ten years after the Second World War came to an end, the Cambridge historian Herbert Butterfield – who had been denied the opportunity to join the privileged ranks of the post-conflict official historians, but who appears to have known about Ultra – wrote an essay which offered some clues about what had been happening. In the essay, entitled 'Official History: Its Pitfalls and Criteria', Butterfield pointed out that governments which wished to be honest with the public could open their archives 'to the free play of scholarship' if they wished, but added: 'I do not personally believe there is a government in Europe which wants the public to know all the truth.'

Butterfield was an original and unorthodox historian, and he was deeply sceptical of collections of official documents, which he considered to be designed to mislead as much as to enlighten. He called on the British government to make public the rules governing official historians at that time. This was something that did not happen until almost fifty years later, when the undertakings that the official historians had been obliged to sign, classified Ultra Top Secret, were quietly deposited at the National Archives.

He also expressed concern that the post-war government of Clement Attlee, having secured the silence of the official historians in order to conceal the Ultra secret, appeared to have developed a taste for history theft: he wrote that the government was attempting to rewrite the history of some of Britain's most calamitous wartime defeats by permitting the generals who had commanded garrisons in Singapore and Greece to alter, in retrospect, the dispatches they had sent during the war, prior to their post-war release to historians.

Butterfield offered two maxims to guide historians – and the wider public – when dealing with governments that were attempting to control the past: 'First, that governments try to press upon the historian the key to all the drawers but one, and are very anxious to spread the belief that this single one contains no secret of importance; secondly, that if the historian can only find out the thing which government does not want him to know, he will lay his hand upon something that is likely to be significant.'[31]

The first people from outside Britain's secret world to attempt to unlock the British government's sigint drawer were the two Oxford students, William Miller and Paul Thompson, who earned three-month jail sentences for their 1958 article in *Isis* magazine in which they hinted at the work of the 'statistical analysers at Cheltenham'.

By now, Cheltenham's work had expanded from sigint – the capture and decryption of signals communications – to the all-embracing comint* – the capture of all forms of electronic communications. The British public learned nothing about this until 1967, when the *Daily Express* published the scoop that Chapman Pincher had persuaded the somewhat inebriated D-Notice committee secretary, Sammy Lohan, to confirm over lunch at the much-bugged À l'Ecu de France. But Pincher's story, which revealed that British government, in cooperation with the United States, was routinely intercepting every cable and telegram that entered or left the UK, was describing just one aspect of the much larger comint operations conducted by GCHQ and the NSA.

Although the British public remained in the dark, by this time the Soviet Union and its Eastern European allies were aware of the existence of these operations and their scope, and they also knew the details of what had been happening at Bletchley Park during the Secord World War. The first book to describe the cracking of the Enigma code was published in Poland in 1967, under a title that translates as 'Battle of Secrets'.[32] Few in the West appeared to notice its publication.

---

* By 2008, this had been supplemented by socmint: social media intelligence. By 2012, MI5 was using the term Digint to describe its own collection and analysis of digital communications.

The American public was kept in similar ignorance about the activities of the NSA. The agency's name appeared for the first time in unclassified government documents in the late 1950s, but its functions were still a complete mystery more than a decade later. The first hint that the US government possessed a vast, worldwide signals interception and decryption capacity came in June 1971, after Daniel Ellsberg, a military analyst, leaked to the *New York Times* the US Defense Department's encyclopaedic history of the country's involvement with Vietnam: the so-called Pentagon Papers.

Two years later a second book about Enigma, written by Gustave Bertrand, a French wartime military intelligence officer, was published in Paris.[33] Bertrand detailed the way in which Polish code-breakers had developed the machines that first cracked German codes, and how Polish and French intelligence officers – himself included – decrypted thousands of German messages at Vignolles near Paris, before the fall of France. His book spilled most of the secrets, but since it was published in French, it made as little impact on the anglophone world as the Polish publication.[34]

It wasn't until 1974 that the English-speaking public was able to read about the code-breaking work that had been performed around the clock at Bletchley Park. That year, Group Captain Frederick Winterbotham, who had served as a security officer at Bletchley, was given permission to publish *The Ultra Secret*, which detailed exploits he described as the 'near miracle' of Allied signals intelligence.

It was an enthralling moment. 'It undoubtedly produced the most sweeping sensation thus far created by an historical revelation,' one historian wrote, adding that 'immediate and wholesale revisions' would be required of the assumptions about the war in the western hemisphere.[36]

It was also a profoundly disturbing moment. Historians who had not been indoctrinated into the Ultra secret began to reflect on how little they had speculated about the extent of Allied code-breaking during the war, and how they had, for so long, failed to ask the right questions.

The wider public, meanwhile, began to realise that the Allies' victory that had been, for many, the most significant event in their lives, had not been won in the manner in which they had been led to believe for the previous three decades. Victory had been secured not merely through force of arms, and through the blood, toil, tears and sweat of which Churchill spoke in 1940, but through the exploitation of a secret science. The public began also to see how effortlessly their governments could manipulate and distort their perception of the past and the times through which they had lived.

Two years later there was another shock.

Until the mid-1970s, the acronym GCHQ had never appeared in any newspaper. Duncan Campbell, a twenty-four-year-old Scotsman who had taken up journalism after studying physics at Oxford, and Mark Hosenball, a twenty-five-year-old American reporter based in London, were about to change that

Campbell's mother had served at Bletchley P   g the war, and he had long held a fascination for t'   rk of microwave towers that littered both the English   de and the remote outposts of Empire. In May 197   )ut, London's left-leaning listings magazine, published   that he and Hosenball had researched and written, w'   lp of Philip Agee, a former CIA officer living in Lonc   lined 'The Eavesdroppers', and running over two pa'   orted: 'Britain's largest spy network organisation is not   I6 but an electronic intelligence network controlled from a country town in the Cotswolds. With the huge US National Security Agency as partner, it intercepts and decodes communications throughout the world.'

The article went on to name GCHQ, disclose the existence of

the Five Eyes alliance, identify the locations of British listening posts around the world, detail some of the contracts that the agency awarded to suppliers and describe the way in which it could interfere with the IRA's remote control bomb detonation technology.[36]

It was a seminal piece of post-war British journalism. It was ignored completely by Fleet Street and the BBC. But not by MI5, and not by the residents and workers of Cheltenham.

The article caused uproar, and not only among GCHQ's senior management. Most of the spouses of the agency's staff had only a faint idea of what their husbands and wives were doing all day; word soon went around that a small magazine in London was alleging that they had been operating a global electronic espionage network. When copies of the magazine began to arrive in the town, posted by friends in the capital, their astonishment was complete.

The Home Office moved quickly against Hosenball and Agee. The two men were served with deportation orders. Hosenball, who had played a minor role in researching and writing the article, went to court to demand an explanation, but won nothing more than a brief appearance before the members of a secretive deportation tribunal, a trio known informally as the Three Wise Men, who convened in an oak-panelled room at the United Service Club in Pall Mall. A few weeks later the Home Secretary confirmed that the presence of the two men was no longer 'conducive to the public good', and that they were to be kicked out of the country.

Dealing with Campbell took a little longer.

Nine months after publication of 'The Eavesdroppers', the government seized its chance. John Berry, a former soldier, had made contact with a committee that had been established to protest against the deportation of Hosenball and Agee. Berry explained that he had served at GCHQ's intercept station at

Ayios Nikolaos on Cyprus, and wanted to help. Crispin Aubrey, a *Time Out* journalist, made arrangements to see him at his flat in north London. He took along Campbell and a tape recorder.

Campbell was under surveillance by MI5 and Special Branch,[37] and thirteen Branch detectives arrested the three men just as the meeting ended. They were charged under Section 1 of the Official Secrets Act, which put the collection of information by a journalist on a par with spying. The Attorney General, Sam Silkin, was making history: it was the first time that journalists had been charged under Section 1. All three men were also charged under Section 2. The array of charges that they faced could have earned each of them sentences of thirty-two years' imprisonment if they were convicted.

However, the case began to descend into farce even before it reached the Old Bailey. The Foreign Secretary of the day, David Owen, had been promised that the trial would be heard in secret.[38] It was not, and senior intelligence officials were terrified at the prospect of details of sigint operations being 'bandied about in open court'.[39] One of the prosecution witnesses who gave evidence at the committal hearing at the magistrates' court insisted that he could be identified in open court only as 'Colonel B'. Campbell knew Colonel B to be Hugh Johnstone, commanding officer of the army signallers at Ayios Nikolaos, and in due course his name appeared in two left-wing magazines, *The Leveller* and *Peace News*. Each magazine was fined for contempt of court.

As a result of this fiasco, a number of MPs asked questions about Johnstone in the House of Commons. Reports of parliamentary proceedings are privileged; nobody can be prosecuted for publishing them. When Silkin threatened to prosecute regardless, every national newspaper and broadcaster protested. The hapless Colonel Johnstone was on his way to becoming a household name.

By the time the trial opened in September 1978 it was known

as the ABC case, after the initials of the defendants' surnames. Thanks to the government's mishandling of the case, it was probably the most widely reported Official Secrets trial of the century.

The defence informed the jury that much of the material that the prosecution alleged to be highly secret could be found in open sources such as the *Civil Service Yearbook* and regimental magazines. When Lord Hutchinson QC, counsel for Campbell, asked Johnstone how secrets were classified as such when they were already in the public domain, the colonel replied: 'What remains secret is what is designated secret by whoever makes the designation.'

Hutchinson: 'You mean the rules that are laid down for what is and what is not secret are themselves secret?'

Johnstone: 'Yes.'

After a heavy hint from the judge, the Section 1 charges were withdrawn.[40] The trial on the remaining Section 2 charges was a protracted affair. Before the judge started his summing up, he took the highly unusual step of telling all three defendants that he had no intention of jailing them if they were convicted. After sixty-eight hours of deliberations, the jury found all three guilty: Berry was given a six-month suspended prison sentence and ordered to pay £250 costs, while Aubrey and Campbell were both conditionally discharged and ordered to pay a proportion of the costs.

The case lasted forty-two days. It resulted in far more people reading 'The Eavesdroppers' than would otherwise have been the case, and brought GCHQ and its activities a great deal of publicity, much to the discomfort of the agency and its political masters.

Outside the Old Bailey, the trio cracked open a bottle of champagne.*

---

* A large part of the MoD file on the case remains withheld from the public under the 'any other special reason' clause of the Public Records Acts.

Despite the worldwide attention that the trial had brought to the activities of both GCHQ and MI5, the British government persisted with a curious attitude to its intelligence agencies: it pretended that they simply did not exist. The names of these agencies appeared regularly in the press; they employed thousands of people and occupied several office blocks across central London. Nevertheless, for seventy years, the position of Her Majesty's Governments was that there were no such organisations.

This policy, known within Whitehall – confidentially, of course – as 'disavowal', meant that there could be no official statement about the agencies' operations or their personnel. It also meant that Parliament could exercise no control over them. The system of oversight was hidden within the executive branch of government, an arrangement that was supported by a bipartisan consensus.

It was not only Parliament that turned a blind eye to MI5, MI6 and GCHQ and their activities: so too did the courts. As there was no statutory basis for MI5 and GCHQ to be involved within the UK in what were known within the secret state as the Three Bs – bugging, burglary and blackmail – it was important that this fiction of non-existence was maintained.

Disavowal also granted MI6 officers de facto immunity from prosecution in the UK for any crimes they committed overseas. The 1948 Criminal Justice Act had extended the reach of English law to Crown servants in whichever country they served. As a result, an MI6 officer who offered a bribe in Moscow would be committing an offence under English law unless it could be pretended that that officer was not a Crown servant, because he or she did not officially exist.

Disavowal meant that the agencies did not exist within UK law, and could therefore operate beyond its reach. The policy of disavowal also buttressed the barricade of secrecy surrounding their activities. There could be no acknowledgement of those actions, no explanation and no complaint. Even the names of the heads of each agency were official secrets.

One of the few heads of MI5 to be named publicly was Percy Sillitoe, an ex-policeman who, on his appointment in 1946, was infuriated to find that secrecy was so pervasive within the agency that he could make neither head nor tail of what was happening around him. Senior staff talked to each other in Latin, apparently so that he could not understand them. 'When I joined,' Sillitoe later wrote, 'I found it so extremely difficult to find out precisely what everyone was doing.'[41]

Many years later, when MI5 and MI6 began to advertise for new recruits, the adverts would give no hint of the identity of the employer. One advert which appeared in the *Guardian* in 1987, for example, offered opportunities for people with 'an imaginative approach to problem solving', who would be rewarded with 'a London-based career in a congenial environment, job security . . . and occasional travel', but omitted to mention anything about intelligence work.[42]

It was not unknown for some recruits to be unaware that they had joined MI5 until some time after they began their employment. Jonathan Evans, who was Director General for six years until 2013, later recalled how MI5 used 'a discreet cover as some opaque government department' when it recruited him straight from university in 1980. 'It says something about the secret nature of the Service in those days, and my own naivety that I did not fully realise that I was working for MI5 until a few days after I had joined.'[43]

But while the policy of disavowal may have helped to conceal the work of the UK's intelligence agencies from Parliament, the courts and the public, it could not always conceal that work from the nation's enemies.

The Foreign Office and both MI5 and MI6 were successfully penetrated by Soviet intelligence, most notoriously through the recruitment of the Cambridge spies who passed on classified material between the 1940s and the 1950s. Official secrecy also failed dismally to prevent the Soviets from learning almost all it wished to know about the development of Britain's nuclear weapons. The official historian of the JIC has commented on the remarkable number of British scientists, spies and civil servants who supplied information to the Soviets about the UK's nuclear secrets, and on Whitehall's slow comprehension of what was happening.[44]

The MI6 officer George Blake, who had been a double agent for eight years by the time he was unmasked in 1961, had told his KGB handlers all that he knew about Five Eyes sigint operations. Moreover, the Soviets had for several years been enjoying the services of a well-placed source within GCHQ's headquarters at Cheltenham.

With each breach, the agencies appear to have become even more obsessive about secrecy. The default position, as Sir Martin Furnival Jones told the committee compiling the Franks Report, was: 'It is an official secret if it is in an official file.'

This became most obvious in the attitude to documentation generated within the agencies – it was either stored with the greatest possible security, or instantly destroyed. Among the documents routinely destroyed were the reports that MI5 prepared for government ministers and senior civil servants.

Stella Rimington, who was Director General of MI5 for four years until 1996, recalls what happened when one of these reports was misplaced during the 1980s. 'I remember the panic, exacerbated by the general hysteria of those days, when a minister at the Department for Energy lost one. People were sent down to Thames House, where his office was, to search down the sides of chairs and sofas, but when he casually remarked that he thought it might have blown away while he was reading it in his garden, we gave up and waited for the furore to start when it turned up. As far as I know it has never been seen again. When MI5 moved into Thames House and the whole place was gutted, I wondered whether the report would turn up behind the panelling, but it never did.'[45]

To reinforce the secrecy surrounding sensitive official documents, these papers are currently given four levels of protective marking, or classification: Restricted; Confidential; Secret; and Top Secret, the latter being reserved for material which it is believed would be 'likely to threaten the internal security of the UK or friendly countries' if disclosed, or which could cause severe long-term damage to the UK economy, or widespread loss of life.

In addition, there are what are known as National Caveats, such as UK EYES ONLY; separate code-word-based classifications for specific material, such as ATOMIC; and a complementary system of classification known as STRAP. This is a code word for three further layers of secrecy that are intended to restrict the dissemination of documentation within the secret state. Such is the passion for protective security at the Ministry of Defence that the department expects its security staff to be familiar with no less than 128 different acronyms for secrecy-related protocols, such as BTR (British TEMPEST Regulation), SyOPS (Security Operating Procedures) and TSCO (a Top Secret Control Officer).[46]

Against this background, it is unsurprising to find that the agencies have little enthusiasm for the disclosure of historical documentation for which the Public Records Acts provide. After the 1967 Act reduced the period of protective embargo from fifty to thirty years, British governments began to operate the system of 'blanket' Lord Chancellors' Instruments for the retention of security and intelligence documents. These blanket approvals enabled not only the agencies, but also the government departments such as the Foreign Office and the Ministry of Defence, to withhold entire classes of documents without the need to provide a specific rationale.

In 1983, when a House of Commons committee took evidence on the government's position on intelligence records, the Cabinet Secretary, Sir Robert Armstrong, informed it that although some Bletchley Park records had been made public, records about sigint operations between 1918 and 1939 would remain closed because they were far more sensitive than the operations mounted against Nazi Germany.[47]

Another former Director General of MI5, Stephen Lander, would eventually conclude that the nervousness following the espionage coups of the Cambridge and atomic spies led to the growth of a culture of secrecy within the agencies that was deeply harmful. 'Sorting out the consequences of those two blows,' he said, 'was to take two decades and, in my view, to leave the UK [intelligence] community with a defensiveness, introspection and damagingly strict need-to-know culture that it only finally shook off during the 1980s and 1990s under the pressures of responding to terrorism with new generations of staff.'[48]

This process of recovery would actually start with another humiliating espionage scandal. The revelations about the Cambridge and atomic spies had been damaging enough, but the next major security breach would not only dent the agencies' confidence in their ability to keep secrets, it would force their very existence out into the open.

One morning in early January 1968, on the road corridor that ran through East Germany to the enclosed city of Berlin, a car had slowed to a halt at a checkpoint. The driver had wound down his window and handed his passport to the Russian soldier manning the checkpoint, and then he did something completely unexpected: he threw a small object through the glass hatch of the sentry post.

In his alarm, the soldier quickly picked up the object and threw it back into the car – so quickly that he did not see that it was a small stone, wrapped in paper. The driver, by means of a few words and some frantic sign language, made it clear that he was passing on a message. He tossed the stone back into the sentry post, took his passport, and accelerated away.

The man who would betray the deepest secrets of GCHQ – and, quite inadvertently, put the UK's intelligence agencies on the road to ending the policy of disavowal – had just made his first contact with the Russians.

Geoffrey Prime was a sergeant in the Royal Air Force, based at RAF Gatow in south-western Berlin, where he served as a wireless operator with a sigint unit. He was a talented linguist who had taught himself Swahili while previously serving in Kenya, and who had been taught Russian at the Joint Services School for Linguists at Tangmere in Sussex.

Prime was a few weeks short of his thirtieth birthday. Partly as a consequence of the poverty he had witnessed in post-colonial East Africa, and in part as a result of his bruising encounters with the English class system while training as an RAF linguist, he was also a committed Communist.[49]

In the note he had thrown into the Soviet sentry post, Prime stated simply that he wished to make contact. Two months later he returned to his parked car to find a small magnetised metal cylinder attached to the door, beneath the handle. Inside was a handwritten note that directed him to the Friedrichstraße S-Bahn station. As he stepped off the train, an attractive woman in her early twenties approached him and introduced him to her older colleague, who was standing nearby.

Valya and Igor became Prime's handlers, and over the next six months the trio would meet every other Wednesday afternoon at a flat in the Soviet sector of the city. Prime was given a miniature Minox camera and shown how to photograph documents. He told his handlers which communications were being monitored at Gatow, and which codes had, and had not, been broken. He was told that he would be known as 'Mr Rowlands', and that if approached by anyone who said,

'I believe we met in Pittsburgh in 1968,' he should reply: 'No, at that time I was in Berlin.'

Knowing that Prime's posting at Gatow was about to come to an end, Igor suggested he apply for a post with GCHQ. The agency's existence had still not been acknowledged to the British public, but the KGB was well aware of its importance. Prime agreed to do so, and was recruited to one of the agency's outposts, the Joint Technical Language Service (JTLS) in the City of London.[50] Prime continued to communicate with his handlers through encrypted messages sent on a shortwave radio, and via dead letter drops at Abbey Wood in south-east London and Banstead railway station in Surrey. Occasionally he would fly to meet them in Italy, Ireland or Cyprus.

In March 1976, Prime joined the other members of the JTLS in a move to Cheltenham, where he joined J Division, which handled Soviet traffic. His delighted handlers arranged to meet him in Vienna, and handed over £800.[51]

The following year Prime married his landlady, Rhona Ratcliffe. A lively and sociable woman, Rhona was attracted to Prime despite his shy and slightly anxious manner. She knew that he was prone to bouts of depression. What she did not know was that, perhaps as a consequence of the sexual abuse he had suffered during his unhappy childhood in Staffordshire, Prime had also developed into a paedophile. It was a trait that would eventually lead to his exposure and arrest, but not before he had spent a decade spying for the Soviets.

Such were the pressures of his life of deception that he began to fear for his sanity and considered defecting to the Soviet Union. Instead, he quit GCHQ and found work as a minicab driver. Before long, the minicab office began to receive calls from a woman who said she was ringing from London, and was anxious to speak to Prime. He would return the calls from a nearby phone box. After his sister received a call from a man with a foreign accent who said he was an old friend from Berlin,

Prime boarded a plane to Vienna. There, he was approached by a man who called himself Mike, and who said: 'I believe we met in Pittsburgh in 1968 . . .'

Prime spent several days in the company of KGB agent-runners, who attempted to pressurise him into returning to GCHQ. On his return to the UK, his depression deepened. He had already joined an underground organisation called the Paedophile Information Exchange, and went on to build up a card index of 2,287 young girls, whose names and addresses he gleaned by scouring the photographs published in local news-papers. He made obscene telephone calls to a number of these girls, and subjected two to serious sexual assaults in their own homes.

After police called at Prime's home, explaining that a car resembling his distinctive brown and white Ford Cortina had been seen near the scene of one of the attacks, he confessed all to Rhona. She was astonished by his paedophilia, but was not so surprised by his admission that he was also a Soviet spy. 'In a funny sort of way, I could cope with that easier,' she said later.[52]

Rhona called the police, and Prime was arrested. He quickly confessed. On 10 November 1982, at Court One of the Old Bailey, he pleaded guilty to seven breaches of the Official Secrets Act and was sentenced to thirty-eight years' imprisonment: thirty-five for betraying GCHQ's secrets and three for the sexual assaults on the young girls. It was the second-longest prison sentence in UK legal history, after the forty-two years that had been given to the double agent George Blake in 1961. Prime would eventually be released in March 2001, after serving half his sentence.

The Attorney General, Sir Michael Havers, who led the pros-ecution, was careful not to disclose in open court any details of the information Prime had passed to his handlers, other than to say that it had caused 'exceptionally grave damage and had threatened NATO plans for defending Western Europe'. The court sat in secret while MI5 presented an assessment of the damage that Prime had inflicted on the country's most sensitive espionage operations.[53]

For many months, GCHQ refused to give its American counterparts at the NSA a frank account of the damage caused by Prime; requests for a copy of MI5's damage assessment were met with evasive responses. Before long, the NSA was telling journalists that it believed GCHQ and its international outposts to be 'as leaky as an old scow'.[54] Relations between the two agencies reached the lowest point in their joint history.

After the Old Bailey trial, disavowal of the UK's sigint agency became meaningless. The day after Prime pleaded guilty, an incandescent Margaret Thatcher made a statement to the House of Commons. She acknowledged that Prime had been engaged in highly classified work at the agency, and said that his espionage on behalf of the Soviet Union had damaged both British and US interests, and NATO as a whole.[55]

Thatcher remained opposed to the avowal of MI5 and MI6, however, apparently declaring in 1984 that 'too much has been said and written about intelligence and less should be in future'.[56] The following year she began to relent, and agreed to the publication of an official history of Britain's wartime strategic deception operations, which had been researched and written during the 1970s by the military historian Sir Michael Howard.*

In 1987, there was renewed pressure to extend the policy of avowal as a consequence of the government's shambolic attempts to prevent a former senior MI5 officer, Peter Wright, from publishing his memoir, *Spycatcher*, in Australia, in breach of the Official Secrets Act.

Wright's book was enormously embarrassing, and not only because of his much-quoted declaration that he and his MI5

---

* It was to be a further five years before Howard's book saw the light of day.

colleagues had 'bugged and burgled our way across London at the State's behest, while pompous bowler-hatted civil servants in Whitehall pretended to look the other way'. Here was a retired Assistant Director of the Security Service painting a picture of an agency that was out of control and stuffed with colonial relics and gung-ho amateurs, and which all-too frequently found itself to be hopelessly lost in the wilderness of Cold War espionage and counter-espionage – a wilderness that was partly of its own making.

Wright's description was widely believed to be accurate. MI5 was exposed to an unprecedented level of public ridicule, and at the conclusion of an action against newspapers which had published some of the allegations within the book, the Master of the Rolls, Sir John Donaldson, suggested that 'it may be that the time has come when Parliament should regularise the position of the Security Service'. MI5 is said to have agreed, its Annual Report for 1987–8 apparently concluding that there was 'complete acceptance among staff of the desirability of legislation for the Security Service'.[57]

Ministers initially disagreed, but were overtaken by events at the European Court of Human Rights. In 1987, in a case brought by a Swedish national, the court had indicated that European security services should be placed on a statutory footing. There was also a pending case from the UK, brought by Patricia Hewitt and Harriet Harman, civil liberties campaigners – and future Cabinet ministers – who had discovered that they had been under lengthy surveillance. Eventually, MI5 would be found to have breached Hewitt and Harman's human rights. The pressure to avow the agencies and place them on a statutory basis became irresistible.

MI5 was first, in 1989, with the passing of legislation that set out its functions. Three years later, when Stella Rimington was appointed Director General, she was told she was going to be publicly named. Rimington objected, but was told that because the agency was now on a statutory footing, the public would consider itself to be entitled to know who was in charge.[58]

By this time, the Soviet Union was breaking apart, and the UK's intelligence agencies needed to show their faces because they were also casting about for new roles. In 1992, Prime Minister John Major told MPs that the government also believed 'that the time has come to acknowledge publicly the continuing existence of the Secret Intelligence Service'. Having thus avowed MI6, Major also named its chief, Sir Colin McColl,* saying it was time to 'sweep away some of the cobwebs of secrecy which needlessly veil too much of government business'.[59] In 1994, MI6 and GCHQ were also placed on a statutory basis with the Intelligence Services Act, which codifies the relationship between the agencies and the Foreign Secretary, defines their functions and provides for a degree of oversight by parliamentarians.

As MI6 officers were now avowed as Crown servants, steps were taken to ensure that they could not face prosecution or civil claims in the UK after committing crimes overseas. The new Act contained a clause that is said to 'disapply' UK law, as long as any crime they commit has been authorised in writing by a Secretary of State. The architects of this piece of legislation, who included the former Master of the Rolls, Lord Denning, did not have only the Three Bs in mind: they intended that it should cover any crime, including murder. 'We needed to do this because, of course, we had no idea what the future might hold,' said one of those architects.[60] It was James Bond's licence to kill.

With the British state no longer pretending that its intelligence agencies did not exist, it was inevitable that there would be growing calls from historians and members of the public for the release of those agencies' historical documents. The end of the Cold War reduced the sensitivity of many British government

---

* Even today, the names of the deputy heads of the agencies are kept from the public.

files, and when the Soviet Union embarked on a policy of *glasnost* – literally, publicity – there were many in Westminster who believed that the UK would need to demonstrate a superior attitude to transparency.

By then, however, the intelligence agencies had destroyed large parts of their archives. Some of the oldest MI6 files are said to have been destroyed in the 1920s.[61] More went up in smoke when the agency moved headquarters in the early '60s.[62] Large numbers of MI5 documents were destroyed at the end of each of the world wars: according to a Home Office estimate in the 1990s, around 175,000 MI5 files had been destroyed between 1909 and the early 1970s.[63] It was later reported that the agency's incinerators had again been active in the early '90s, despite its obligations under the Public Records Acts. This was around the same time that the Foreign Office had been destroying the contents of the 170 Top Secret boxes that contained its most humiliating decolonisation files. By the time this purge had been completed, it was estimated that around forty per cent of MI5's historical archive no longer existed.[64]

In 1998, several years after the incinerators had done their work, the Lord Chancellor's advisory council made recommendations on the sort of MI5 records that should be preserved, and in 2001 the first batch of the agency's historical files was passed to Kew.* By this time MI5 was acknowledging that 290,000 of the 440,000 files that it held were on individuals, and that it was continuing to use or update around 13,000 files that it held on UK citizens.[65]

At the time of writing, around 4,000 MI5 files have been passed to Kew, representing around one per cent of its archive. All the released papers predate 1959.[66] Most of the files that have been released were created during wartime operations or

---

* At this point, the KGB and its successor organisations enjoyed greater access to MI5's historical documentation than did the British public: the double agent Anthony Blunt had handed over 1,771 documents in the 1940s.

the Cold War, giving the impression that the agency has been concerned largely with the monitoring of enemies: the released papers contain little information about espionage aimed at allied and neutral governments, or about the surveillance of British citizens. They present a carefully sculpted image of the history of British intelligence: MI5 fully grasps the importance of the politics of archives.

Files from Bletchley Park and its predecessor, Room 40 OB, have also been passed to Kew, but GCHQ has yet to release any files created after 1948.

At least MI5 and GCHQ are making some of their files available, however. MI6 is not. It has released some of the records of the Special Operations Executive, whose archive it inherited in 1946. From 2005 the Foreign Office began also to release selected pre-war papers from the Permanent Under-Secretary's Department, the point of liaison between the Foreign Office and MI6. And in 2013, another set of secret papers concerning the intelligence agencies, known as the 'Cabinet Secretaries' miscellaneous papers', began to be made public. But MI6 refuses to disclose any of its own historical records. The Public Records Acts obliges it to preserve these papers, but the blanket exemption that has been signed off by successive Lords Chancellor has absolved it of any obligation to make them public. Only one official historian has been permitted to scrutinise the historical papers of MI6, for a book that examines the agency's first forty years.

MI6 insists that this secrecy is required to safeguard the identities of its sources. The risk of retribution, according to the agency, can extend beyond a single generation. MI6 also maintains that many of its records consist principally of information relating to agents and sources, and that there is no body of records containing assessments of intelligence or foreign policy, a preposterous claim that has nevertheless been accepted by some historians. Furthermore, MI6 is concerned not only that its own papers should be concealed for ever – it runs a dedicated team of sensitivity reviewers which vets the files of other government departments on a daily basis to decide whether their transfer to Kew could jeopardise the agencies' secrets.[67]

Some of the papers that remain hidden from view are now so old that the claim that they need to remain closed to protect sources – and sources' descendants – stretches credulity. MI6 files on the Agadir Crisis of 1911, for example, remain inaccessible. So too do any pre–First World War papers that it holds on Germany's naval ambitions, or on the armies of the Austro-Hungarian Empire. Documents that describe the way in which MI6 enlisted the assistance of American private detectives to spy on Irish and Indian revolutionaries in the United States during those pre–First World War years may also still exist. If so, they too remain out of bounds.

At the moment when GCHQ was agreeing to join MI5 in making selected papers from its historical archive available to the public, electronic communications were expanding rapidly. Cables, satellites and the Internet were becoming increasingly rich sources of information, so the agency's opportunities and responsibilities were expanding at a near-exponential rate.

Because no GCHQ documents created since 1948 have yet been released, the official disclosures about the history of Britain's signals intelligence operations remain frozen in the Bletchley Park era, with its computers the size of minibuses, its patriotic debutantes and brilliant young men in tweeds, and, of course, its stunningly successful attacks on the Nazis' encrypted traffic. They exclude almost all of the documentation created after that moment, in the summer of 1945, when the London Signals Intelligence Board and its political masters decided that the Government Code and Cypher School should attempt to achieve 'the interception of all communications and radio transmissions of other nations'.

By releasing only those documents that are more than sixty-five years old, three key aspects of modern British signals intelligence remained hidden from view: the extent to which GCHQ's operations are shaped by the priorities of its close partners at the NSA; the industrial pace and scale of those operations; and the manner in which the electronic communications of Britain's own law-abiding citizens are routinely captured.

The intimacy of the relationship between GCHQ and the NSA in the post-war years – politically, technically and operationally – cannot be exaggerated. In 1969, Leonard Hooper, the Bletchley veteran who had risen through the ranks to become Director of GCHQ, wrote to Marshall Carter, his opposite number at the NSA, to say: 'Between us we have ensured that the blankets and sheets are more tightly tucked around the bed in which our two sets of people lie and, like you, I like it that way.'[68]

During the 1950s and '60s, GCHQ relied heavily on its US partner for technical supplies, and by the 1980s the NSA was partially funding many of the UK's listening posts around the globe, in return for US access to large numbers of British dependent territories.

Each agency was also able to assist the other in its attempts to sidestep the regulatory and legal framework in which it was expected to operate. At the GCHQ post at Morwenstow on the north coast of Cornwall, for example – a facility that was constructed and equipped largely with funds from the NSA – British staff were by the 1980s intercepting the transatlantic communications of American citizens, while NSA staff working alongside them were intercepting the communications of British citizens. The contents of these intercepts would then be exchanged.[69]

It was always an unequal relationship, however, and one to which the UK side clung with a degree of nervousness, fearful of losing access to its senior partner's resources and intelligence produce. In 1994, an in-house GCHQ manual entitled *Strategic*

Direction Summary warned that the agency's contribution must be 'of sufficient scale and of the right kind to make a continuation of the Sigint alliance worthwhile to our partners'. It also admitted: 'This may entail on occasion the applying of UK resources to the meeting of US requirements.'[70]

With the support of its senior partner, GCHQ expanded steadily, and in 2004 it moved into its enormous new headquarters on a 166-acre site in the suburbs of Cheltenham. Nicknamed the Doughnut, the building houses 5,500 staff and is so large that London's Royal Albert Hall could fit comfortably within its central courtyard.

By 2013, GCHQ was receiving around £30 million a year from the NSA, giving the US government considerable hold over the UK's largest intelligence agency. In return for the finance, the NSA sets GCHQ a series of minimum expectations. In 2010, according to one internal GCHQ briefing paper, the United States had 'raised a number of issues with regards to meeting NSA's minimum expectations', adding that the British agency 'still remains short of the full NSA ask'. It added: 'GCHQ must pull its weight and be seen to pull its weight.'[71]

The 'Eavesdroppers' article published by *Time Out* in 1976 described a global signals intelligence operation on an industrial scale, but over the next few years, the pace at which the Five Eyes agencies were capturing communications was utterly transformed. By the early 1980s, they were jointly operating a computer network codenamed Platform and a borderless software package codenamed Echelon.* This allowed the partners to submit targets to each other's listening posts, and to share the results. By the turn of the century, Echelon was drawing in billions of intercepts every day and storing them in a near-bottomless storage facility at NSA's headquarters at Fort Meade in Maryland, which each of the Five Eyes agencies

---

* While Echelon was originally the codename for the software package, it was later used to describe the entire collection and analysis network.

could access, and from which they could retrieve whatever they wished.[72]

The expansion of sigint operations had a major advantage for the politicians whom the Five Eyes agencies served: an enormous number of secrets could be accessed quickly and with comparatively little risk. Meanwhile, as it concentrated more on terrorism and organised crime, the distinction between overseas and domestic communications became less meaningful to GCHQ. Furthermore, its expanding operations against the IRA showed that it could intercept the communications of large numbers of British and Irish citizens without the populations of either country being aware.

It was not entirely risk free, however, and many European governments – particularly the French – were furious when they learned about Echelon. A series of investigations by the European Parliament concluded that this enormous sigint vacuum cleaner was sucking up not only military, intelligence and diplomatic signals, but also personal and commercial communications.[73]

The implications of Echelon for personal privacy were enormous: no individual could know whether information about them was being captured and stored; nor could they be permitted to have any understanding of how that information was being used or abused. Therefore, the state's seemingly boundless capacity to gather personal data needed to be kept secret.

The al-Qaida attacks of 9/11 resulted in GCHQ and the NSA being granted the increased finance that was required to develop new surveillance capabilities, and the political backing to operate at the very outer limits of the law. Within two weeks of the attacks, the NSA had developed a programme codenamed Stellar Wind that enabled it to mine vast amounts of its citizens' communications data without the court-approved warrants ordinarily required.[74] It would be another four years before the American public would learn what had been happening.[75] One former NSA official would later condemn the agency for becoming a form of 'dystopian Stasi on steroids that just wants to "know everything" about anybody, anytime, anywhere – regardless of any and all constraints'.[76]

But while the finance and political support may have become available as a consequence of the 9/11 attacks, the desire to 'capture everything' can be traced back to the summer of 1945, when Victor Cavendish-Bentinck, the Joint Intelligence Committee and the London Signals Board realised that it might one day be technically possible to acquire every electronic communication in the world – and were determined to do so.

This ambition is implicit in the name of a programme for which GCHQ received £1 billion in funding over three years from October 2007, and which enabled the agency to embed interception probes inside communication providers' networks. Within GCHQ and among its private-sector contractors, this programme was known as MTI: Mastering the Internet.[77]

In the UK, GCHQ was already operating under the lightest of legal and regulatory frameworks. The Regulation of Investigatory Powers Act (RIPA), which came into force a year before the attacks, gives ministers the power to issue warrants authorising electronic or human surveillance following requests from the intelligence agencies, senior police officers or customs officers. In the decade after RIPA came into force, 20,000 interception warrants were issued to authorise the tapping of phones or reading of emails, there had been more than 30,000 authorisations for directed surveillance, such as following someone in public, and there were more than 2.7 million requests for communications data. Of these three million surveillance operations, fewer than 5,000 appear to have been approved by a judge.[78]

While RIPA is a piece of legislation of notoriously Byzantine complexity, one section, at least, is perfectly clear: Section 19 imposes a duty on every person involved with any warrant, or involved with the surveillance that it authorises, to remain forever silent. 'A person who makes a disclosure to another of anything that he is required to keep secret under this section shall be guilty of an offence' and will face up to five years in jail, the Act says.

The judges who oversee the regime invariably conclude that any interception is lawful as long as the warrants have been issued. RIPA and the relaxed system of oversight give GCHQ the power to spy on the world. They are, the agency has acknowledged privately, an important 'selling point' in its dealings with the NSA.[79]

What this means in practice became clear in the summer of 2013.

Every post-war generation has had its own sigint whistle-blower, an individual who has taken considerable risks to inform the public about the extent to which their communications are being monitored by their governments. Some of their disclosures have caused a sensation. Others have been barely noticed.

In the summer of 1958, it was William Miller and Paul Thompson, the idealistic Oxford undergraduates who were jailed for publishing an article in their student magazine about the western 'spy boats' and the 'statistical analysers at Cheltenham'. In 1967, it was Robert Lawson, the telegraphist who tipped off Chapman Pincher of the *Daily Express* about the way in which telegrams were being intercepted as they entered and left the UK. In the 1970s, and again in the '80s, it was Duncan Campbell's sources, many of them former NSA officials.

Each of these people had different motives, and the consequences for each varied greatly. After release from prison, Miller became a successful publisher and literary agent, while Thompson eventually became a professor of history. Lawson escaped prosecution, for reasons that remain obscure. On seeing the sensation that his disclosure provoked, he asked the *Express* for £1,000, but was told he would not be receiving a penny.[80] After the ABC trial, John Berry moved to the south-west of England, where he worked as a social worker. Another of Campbell's sources, Philip Agee, was forced to move from one country to another before settling in Cuba, where he died in 2008.

In 2013, it was Edward Snowden's turn. Snowden was a twenty-nine-year-old computer infrastructure contractor at the NSA's facility in Hawaii. On 19 May that year he asked his employers for leave of absence for medical treatment, and flew to Hong Kong, carrying with him a massive cache of secret Five Eyes data. The exact number of documents has never been confirmed: the NSA put the figure at between 50,000 and 200,000,[81] while the US Department of Defense later put the figure as high as 1.7 million.[82]

The first news report based upon the cache – about the US government obtaining a secret court order that obliged a telecoms company, Verizon, to hand over its customers' records – was published in the *Guardian* on 6 June that year.* Over the months that followed, there was a deluge of disclosures about Five Eyes operations. Many of the news reports were based upon documents that showed how the US and UK governments had been capturing and storing vast amounts of data, not just on possible terrorists or criminals, but on everyone. For a global audience that had largely forgotten about Echelon – or had been unaware of that programme's existence – these were startling disclosures.

Both governments said that Snowden and the journalists to whom he handed the material had failed to grasp the distinction between the bulk collection of data and mass surveillance – that is, that the mere storage of communications data was very different from the selected reading of some elements of those data. It's like searching for a needle in a haystack, the public was told: we need to gather the public's hay before we can locate the terrorist's needle.

---

* The day after the first disclosure in the *Guardian*, the DA-Notice Committee issued an email asking the UK media not to repeat the contents of the report, or anything similar that might appear in the future.

However, many documents within Snowden's cache revealed operations that could not be defended by the haystack argument. GCHQ's Operation Optic Nerve, for example, intercepted and stored the webcam images of millions of Yahoo! users around the world; between three and eleven per cent of the images contained sexually explicit communications. An in-house guide warned staff about 'undesirable nudity', adding: 'Users who may feel uncomfortable about such material are advised not to open them.' This was not a blanket collection of data, but a selection. The targets were selected at random. None were suspected of wrongdoing.[83]

The documents showed that some GCHQ staff working on one particularly sensitive programme expressed concern about 'the morality and ethics of their operational work, particularly given the level of deception involved'.[84] Had any of those staff expressed their concerns in public, however, or revealed that the agency was spying on deeply personal communications through Operation Optic Nerve, they would have faced prosecution under the Official Secrets Act.

All of the Five Eyes agencies were found to have been spying on foreign heads of state, while GCHQ had set up fake Internet cafés to enable it to spy on delegates to the G20 summit in London in 2009.[85] Furthermore, the archive showed that the NSA had obtained direct access to the systems of major Internet companies, such as Facebook, Yahoo!, Apple and Microsoft.[86]

While there was outrage across much of the world at the programmes that the leaked documents disclosed, in the UK the public's reaction was more muted. The government decided that the time was right to bring forward its draft Investigatory Powers Bill, in order to put on a statutory footing the surveillance practices that the agencies had always denied, until exposed by Snowden.

When introducing the Bill, the government made a surprising admission: that MI5 and GCHQ had been not only intercepting vast amounts of the telephone and email records of the British public for the previous fourteen years, they had also been storing them.[87]

Prominent within the draft Bill were the provisions designed to conceal from the public the details of the surveillance operations that the new law is intended to authorise: anyone who discloses them will be punished by imprisonment or a fine, or both.

What was not made clear with publication of the Bill was the scale of the data-collection operations that were already under way. At the heart of GCHQ's headquarters at Cheltenham is a data store that holds the Internet browsing records, search engine requests and instant messenger records of people around the globe. Between August 2007 and March 2009 this facility stored 1.1 trillion pieces of such data.

By 2010, the agency was storing thirty billion such pieces of data each day. Two years later it had increased the data stores capacity so that it could accept fifty billion, and work was under way to double that to 100 billion each day.[88]

The agency has a particularly apt code name for this vast repository: it is called Black Hole.

8

Beyond Kafka

When Justice Cannot Be Seen to Be Done

The open justice principle – the axiom that for justice to be done, it must be seen to be done – is said to be a fundamental feature of the rule of law in a modern democratic society. Hailed in the mid-seventeenth century as 'the first fundamental liberty of any Englishman', it became integral to the British constitution in 1913 with a ruling by the House of Lords that 'every court in the land is open to every subject of the King'.

'Trials derive their legitimacy from being conducted in public,' the authors of a classic study of media law proclaimed in the 1980s. 'The judge presides as a surrogate for the people, who are entitled to see and approve the power exercised on their behalf. No matter how fair, justice must still be seen before it can be said to be done.'[1]

In practice, much of the business of the courts in the UK remains closed to public scrutiny even when the courtrooms are themselves open to the public and the press. There are more than sixty separate statutes covering the activities of the press, for example, and a significant number of these feature restrictions on what may be reported from a hearing or a trial.[2]

Furthermore, that which is said in open court represents only a small part of each case, much of which is committed to documentation that is not readily available to the public or the media. One American journalist, accustomed to the US media's automatic right to inspect what is known as 'the court record', was dismayed to be confronted by what she described as a 'barrage of obscure, illogical and mercurially enforced rules' when she began reporting on court proceedings in the UK. 'Trying to obtain court documents is about as easy and affordable as circumnavigating the globe,' she concluded.[3]

There are also a number of circumstances in which the court can sit in secret, or in camera. Judges have the power under both common law and the 1981 Contempt of Court Act to withhold evidence from the public, or to ban reports of court proceedings, 'where it appears to be necessary for avoiding a substantial risk of prejudice to the administration of justice'. Anyone breaching such a ban can be jailed for up to two years.

Courts routinely sit behind closed doors in cases involving the adoption of children, for example, and during cases concerning divorce, eviction or applications for injunctions. In recent years the courts have granted so-called super-injunctions, court orders whose very existence could not be disclosed. There is provision in the 1920 Official Secrets Act for trials under those Acts to be heard in secret.

Under the principle of English law known as Public Interest Immunity (PII), which has developed over decades through case law, the courts can allow one party to a case – almost invariably the government – to withhold potential evidence if its disclosure would not be in the public interest. After a government minister has certified that the public interest favoured non-disclosure of relevant material, it is up to the judge in the case to conduct his or her own balancing exercise. In practice, the request is often made by senior civil servants rather than ministers, sometimes applying a definition of 'public interest' that is highly elastic.

Finally, a series of judgments by Law Lords has determined that while national security considerations will not, by themselves, justify a departure from the open justice principle, courts may sit in camera if the case would not otherwise go ahead: the requirement for justice to be seen to be done must, in exceptional cases, give way to the yet more fundamental principle that the paramount objective of the court is to *do* justice.

It is perhaps unsurprising that the open justice principle should be set to one side to protect the administration of justice in times of national emergency. One Law Lord declared that while in theory the scales of justice should be unaffected by dangerous times, 'in practice the flame of individual right and justice must burn more palely when it is ringed by the more dramatic light of bombed buildings'.[4]

But there are occasions when the principle has been abandoned in a manner that has concealed from the public some of the less savoury actions of the state; there have been occasions, during times of emergency, when the flame of individual right and justice has been almost snuffed out.

One of these occasions was the summer of 1940. When Churchill succeeded Neville Chamberlain as Prime Minister on 10 May that year, German forces had captured Denmark and seized much of Norway, and were about to invade France, Belgium and Holland. The new Prime Minister was convinced that the enemy's breathtaking military successes could be explained only by the presence of a network of spies behind the Allies' lines – rather than by their superior weaponry, tactics and fighting spirit – and assumed that a legion of foreign fifth columnists must also be at work in Britain.

Churchill demanded that his law officers explain how the legal system would deal with such individuals. But while British subjects could be tried for treason, it was far from clear that Germans, or other foreigners, could be prosecuted in the same way. The Lord Chancellor, Lord Simon, explained to the Lords that it was 'a very doubtful question indeed whether under the existing law of treason you could proceed against an alien who has come here suddenly, surreptitiously by air or otherwise, for the purposes of wreaking clandestine destruction or doing other acts against the safety of the realm'.[5]

A new law was required. Lawyers at the Admiralty were instructed urgently to consider the problem, and within a few days had drafted a piece of legislation called the Assistance to the Enemy Bill.[6] By the time it was introduced to Parliament, it had become the Treachery Bill, under which any person attempting to carry out any act 'designed or likely to give assistance to the naval, military or air operations of the enemy . . . shall be guilty of a felony'. Death by hanging was the only penalty for those convicted under the Act.

The Treachery Act received royal assent on 23 May, just thirteen days after Churchill became Prime Minister. The daily morale report recorded that day by the social research organisation Mass-Observation consisted of just one sentence: 'Outwardly calm, inwardly anxious.' At Buckingham Palace, King George VI was confiding in his diary that he feared the country's servicemen in France were about to suffer immense loss of life.[7]

It would not be long before this draconian piece of legislation would be put to work.

Shortly before midnight on 2 September, a pair of German minesweepers put out from Boulogne, each towing an old fishing smack. When they were five miles from the coast of England, the boats were let loose. Two men clambered from each smack into two small dinghies, and rowed the final few hundred yards to the shore.

The four were: Carl Meier, twenty-three, a Dutch-born Nazi Party member who had spent some time in Birmingham before the war; Charles van den Kieboom, twenty-five, a Dutch-Japanese dual national; Sjoerd Pons, twenty-eight, a Dutchman; and a twenty-five-year-old who described himself as German and called himself Jose Waldberg.

All four were agents of the Abwehr, the German military intelligence service, and their mission was to reconnoitre beaches for the invasion that was, they were told, just weeks away. Officially, they were part of Operation Lena, which was the codename for the Abwehr's contribution to Hitler's invasion plan. Unofficially, their spymasters considered the mission to be so perilous that they called it the *Himmelfahrt*: the ascension to heaven.[8]

All four were discovered within hours. During six weeks at MI5's wartime interrogation centre, Camp 020, they were persuaded to make lengthy statements and charged under the Treachery Act. On October 24 they were brought before a magistrate at Bow Street in central London under conditions of complete secrecy, and sent to stand trial at the Old Bailey the following month.[9]

When the trial opened on 19 November, the Solicitor General, Sir William Jowitt, asked the judge, Sir Frederic Wrottesley, to make an order under Section 6 of the Emergency Powers (Defence) Act banning 'disclosure of any information with regard to any part of the proceedings'. This Act, which had been passed the previous year, gave courts the power to sit in secret whenever they were 'satisfied that it is expedient', in the interests of the safety of the public or the defence of the realm. 'There are very obvious reasons for which I think it is necessary,' said Jowitt.*

It was the first such order to be made for a Treachery Act trial. And it would lead directly to a terrible miscarriage of justice.

Waldberg surprised the court by admitting the offence. Meier, Kieboom and Pons pleaded not guilty. Pons told the court that

---

* Parts of the transcript of the trial, and some of the judge's notes, remain secret. The Home Office plans to withhold this material until the year 2041, by applying the exemption within the Freedom of Information Act that is intended to protect personal data, although the Data Protection Act applies only to the living, and all those present in court are now deceased.

he had assisted the Abwehr under duress: he had been threatened with incarceration in a concentration camp after being caught smuggling gems from Holland to Germany, and he insisted that he had no intention of doing anything to assist the Germans on his arrival in England.

After a trial that lasted four days, the jury took just eighty-three minutes to convict Meier and Kieboom. They, along with Waldberg, were sentenced to death. The jury accepted Pons' defence, however, and acquitted him. He was promptly rearrested as an enemy alien and taken back to Camp 020, where he remained for the rest of the war under Defence Regulation 18b, the power that was deployed to keep 'enemy aliens' and British fascists locked away.

In due course Waldberg and Meier were informed that they were to be hanged at Pentonville Prison in north London, and that the execution would take place at 9 a.m. on the morning of 10 December. Kieboom was to hang on 17 December.

A week before the first executions, Sir Alexander Maxwell, Permanent Under-Secretary at the Home Office, began to have serious misgivings about the way in which the three men had been sentenced to death in complete secrecy, and sent a confidential letter to Lord Swinton, the head of the Security Executive, a committee established by Churchill to manage MI5.

'It is of course as a general proposition wrong that a sentence of death should be passed and executed without the public knowing anything about it,' Maxwell wrote. 'Public opinion and public criticism is the most important safeguard for the proper administration of justice, and to carry out sentences of this kind in secrecy is contrary to all our traditions.'

Not that Maxwell was going to call for the practice to be discontinued. On the contrary, he explained: 'I do not of course for a moment suggest that there may not be very good reasons for departing from these general principles in an exceptional case.' But if the secret spy trials were to return to haunt anyone in the future, Maxwell wanted to be sure that it would be Swinton and MI5 who would carry the can, and not the Home Office or the Home Secretary, Herbert Morrison. 'The Home Secretary . . . may at any time be asked by his colleagues or perhaps by the Lord Chief Justice whether he is satisfied that these unusual steps are really necessary in the interests of the defence of the realm, and I think he ought to have on the Home Office records a letter from you on the subject.' If there were good reasons for abandoning the open justice principle, then 'the Home Secretary should be safeguarded by a full statement from the Security Service of these reasons'.[10]

Swinton's reply two days later, in a letter marked 'Most Secret', hinted at the manner in which British intelligence was beginning to develop its highly elaborate strategic deception operation. This was based largely on the code-breaking work at Bletchley Park, and supported also by the use of enemy agents who had been 'turned' after interrogation at Camp 020, an operation that would become known as the Double Cross System.

Swinton suggested to Maxwell that MI5 could prepare carefully worded communiqués about the prosecution, conviction and execution of spies, which would be handed to the BBC and the Fleet Street press. But the trials – even the sentencing hearings – must be kept secret: 'Something may slip out which it is most desirable to keep hidden; even in passing sentence, a judge may inadvertently err.'

Going into some of the operational detail of Double Cross, Swinton said that 'in some cases it is both possible and necessary to use the man and his equipment'. In others, where a recalcitrant spy was to be imprisoned, or prosecuted and hanged, 'the enemy should believe him to be still at large'. Finally, he warned: 'The combined work of all the Services has built up, and is continually adding to, a great structure of intelligence and counter-espionage; and a single disclosure, affecting one individual, might send the whole building toppling.'[11]

However, by the time Maxwell received Swinton's letter, both MI5 and the Home Office had become aware that there was a serious problem with one of the Old Bailey convictions.

At Pentonville Prison, Jose Waldberg had asked for permission to write a number of final letters to his family. Once he began writing, it became clear that Waldberg was not his name; nor was he German. The condemned man's real name was Henri Lassudry, and he was Belgian. He was undoubtedly an Abwehr agent, and had actually carried out some spying – he had sent three brief radio messages from the Kent coast before his capture – but, like the acquitted Pons, he had been acting under duress. He had reluctantly agreed to work for German intelligence after spending time in a Gestapo prison, where he had been informed that his father – also a prisoner of the Gestapo – would be killed if he did not cooperate. His false identity had been created by the Abwehr. Unlike Pons, however, he had not denied the offence and had thrown himself at the mercy of the jury, because he had assumed that this trial in an English court would be open to the press and the public, and he had been petrified that mounting such a defence would put his father at greater risk.

In a series of letters, Lassudry explained to his mother, as well as to his uncle Pierre and his fiancée, how his lawyer at the Old Bailey had advised him through an interpreter that he should plead guilty. This man, a barrister called Blundell, appears not to have informed Lassudry that he was pleading guilty to an offence that carried a mandatory death sentence. The hapless young spy explained to his family that he had planned to confess all to the judge when he went on trial. He had not understood that there would be no examination by the judge after he had entered his guilty plea.

Instead of attempting to dispatch Lassudry's letters to his family, the Home Office sent them to MI5. Attached to them was a note, pointing out that the condemned man was complaining that 'English Justice failed him at his trial . . . he alleges that, *inter alia*, he was deceived into pleading guilty and that his trial only took three minutes'. The Home Office did not wish to see this complaint see the light of day. 'These passages, of course, would prejudice the letters from our point of view, if there is any question of forwarding them to their destinations.'[12]

MI5's files on the case show that Lassudry had made an identical complaint to its own officers. On 5 December, the agency had dispatched one of its most senior men, Lieutenant Colonel William Hinchley Cooke, to the Attorney General, Sir Donald Somervell. Hinchley Cooke wanted to enquire whether the belated discovery of the true name, nationality and motivation of one of the men who was due to die in five days' time might in any way call for a stay of his execution.

Hinchley Cooke, who was half German and a fluent German speaker, had interrogated the four men at Camp 020, yet had failed to establish the true identity of 'Waldberg'. Somervell, meanwhile, had been a pupil of Sir William Jowitt, who had prosecuted the four men at the Old Bailey. Returning to MI5, Hinchley Cooke said that he had asked Somervell whether 'the legal position had changed' in any way. 'I gather,' he said, 'that he thinks it does not.'[13]

In his final letter to his mother, written from one of the condemned prisoners' cells at Pentonville less than forty-eight hours before he was due to die, Lassudry once again complained about his treatment at court: 'I didn't have a trial . . . only three minutes to hear the sentence through the interpreter, and it was over.' He apologised once more for what he said might be regarded as a 'long and cruel silence', but reiterated that he had been a prisoner first of the Gestapo, and then of the British. He also begged his family to attempt to repatriate his body to Belgium once the war was over. 'God knows when you will get this letter,' he wrote. 'Maybe in a year, or even two.'

There was a postscript: 'I shall die on Tuesday December 10th at 9 o'clock. Your loving Henri.'[14]

Meier died first, followed by Lassudry, who went to the gallows under the name Jose Waldberg. At 9.25 a.m., a two-paragraph communiqué written by MI5 informed the media that the two men had been 'apprehended shortly after their surreptitious arrival in this country', with a wireless set and a large sum of money; that they had been tried and convicted, and hanged that morning. The communiqué added: 'Editors are asked not to press for any additional facts or to institute inquiries.' A week later an identical note announced the execution of Kieboom. No mention was made of Pons.[15]

Lassudry's mother never did receive his final letters. Nor did his fiancée or uncle. They were not sent, and instead remained buried within MI5's archives, until they were quietly transferred to Kew in 2005. By then, a number of semi-official chronicles of the era had recounted the capture and conviction of a seasoned German spy called Waldberg. Lassudry was lost to history, along with the manner in which he had been persuaded to plead guilty, and sentenced to die.

Over the next three-and-a-half years a further thirteen enemy spies were prosecuted in secret in London and executed,* while in Gibraltar two Spanish saboteurs were similarly dealt with. Four of the spies were British, the others Belgian, Dutch and German.

Decisions about which captured agents should be prosecuted were taken by a group of interrogators at Camp 020. Such was the certainty that the men selected would be convicted that the group was known as the Hanging Committee. The committee chose men who were refusing to cooperate or whose assistance was no longer required by the Double Cross System, as well

---

* A fourteenth spy, a junior official at the Portuguese embassy in London, was convicted and sentenced to hang in April 1943, but was granted a reprieve by King George VI after the Portuguese government pledged to help dismantle the Abwehr's network in Lisbon.

as spies whose apprehension had been witnessed by too many members of the public.[16]

By mid-1941, friction was growing between the Fleet Street editors who sought more information about the trials for their readers, and the architects of Double Cross, who were continually anxious that their opposite numbers in the ranks of the Abwehr would stumble across some small detail that would expose the truth about the enormous hoax.

MI5 was concerned that the in camera procedure deployed at the Old Bailey was too insecure. 'It is generally known to journalists in Fleet Street within a few hours of the trial having started,' complained Brigadier Oswald Harker, the Deputy Director General. Furthermore, the law required that notices of execution be posted on prison gates for twenty-four hours before any hanging, and that a coroner conduct an inquest into the death of the hanged man, with a jury.

The remedy, Harker suggested, would be to court-martial spies at military establishments, and then shoot them. There would be no prying journalists, no need for execution notices, and no coroner's juries – although MI5 would still need to consider how a death certificate could be issued in secret.[17]

The Home Office was distinctly queasy about the prospect of mounting courts martial for foreign nationals who were not members of any armed forces, and resisted the idea. MI5 did get its way with one spy, however, after he was discovered to be a former soldier and a reservist.

Josef Jakobs, a forty-two-year-old German dentist, had agreed to work for the Abwehr in return for his release from the concentration camp to which he had been consigned after he was caught selling adulterated gold for dental work. After training in Hamburg and The Hague, Jakobs was dropped by parachute into Huntingdonshire, but had broken his leg on landing and was immediately captured. He decided to cooperate with his MI5 interrogators at Camp 020 in an attempt to save his life, but was charged under the Treachery Act and, because he was an army reservist, prosecuted at a court martial. After a two-day hearing at Chelsea Barracks in west London he was found guilty, and nine days later he was taken to the Tower of London.

There, Jakobs was marched to an indoor shooting range beneath the Tower's eastern wall. An eight-man firing squad from the Scots Guards was waiting. Jakobs was tied to a small wooden chair and a circular piece of white lint was pinned over his heart. At exactly twelve minutes past twelve midday, the officer commanding the squad gave the order to fire.[18]

Later that day a brief communiqué from the War Office to the press disclosed Jakob's court martial and execution at the Tower. It was so uninformative that the press began to rebel. 'The announcement gave a minimum of information and had a very bad reception in Fleet Street,' one Home Office official subsequently reported. A number of newspapers began making their own inquiries about the spy's capture. Reporters from one paper, the *Daily Express*, located and interviewed a number of people in Huntingdonshire who had spoken with the spy before he had been taken into police custody. The *Express* informed the official censor at the Ministry of Information that it planned to publish and be damned.

At a crisis meeting, Swinton, Harker, Maxwell and Somervell agreed that while it was preferable that journalists were told as little as possible about the secret prosecutions, this course of action could lead to more, rather than fewer, disclosures in the press. Somervell, meanwhile, agreed to explain the communiqué arrangement to the Lord Chief Justice, who had been complaining that the release of *any* information about a trial that had been conducted in secret – even by the government – was a serious contempt of court.[19]

At the end of the war, steps were taken to suspend and then repeal the Treachery Act, which Parliament had been promised would remain on the statute books only as long as the conflict continued.

There was time, however, for one final prosecution. In September 1945, Theodore Schurch, a former member of the British Union of Fascists who had been supplying information to Italian intelligence officers since the mid-1930s, was found guilty of nine separate charges under the Act after a court martial at Chelsea. He went to the gallows at Pentonville Prison on 4 January 1946.[20]

Secrecy was applied more sparingly during the post-war years, but was found to be a useful means of limiting the public's knowledge of the extent to which the Soviets had penetrated the country's intelligence apparatus.

In 1961, a Soviet defector exposed George Blake, an MI6 officer, as a KGB double agent. The Prime Minister, Harold Macmillan, was horrified – so horrified, in fact, that his first instinct was to grant Blake complete immunity and hush the whole matter up.

The problem was not only the Americans, who would be furious that the transatlantic intelligence alliance had been betrayed by yet another British double agent: Macmillan was also confounded by the policy of disavowal. 'Naturally we can say nothing,' he wrote in his diary. 'The public do not know and cannot be told that he belonged to MI6 – an organisation which does not theoretically exist.'[21]

MI6 knew that its American allies would never accept such a course of action, and would demand to see Blake severely punished. So he was charged under Section 1 of the Official Secrets Act and an arrangement was made for him to be offered 'a good and helpful solicitor' who had previously worked for the agency and could be relied upon to persuade his client to sign a confession.[22]

The secretary of the D-Notice Committee, Rear Admiral

George Thomson, sent a series of letters to editors, informing them that Blake was an MI6 officer, but asking them not to publish this fact. The committee's records show that initially, at least, 'every editor played ball'.[23]

In advance of Blake's first appearance before magistrates, Bow Street Magistrates' Court in central London was cleared of members of the public and the press. Four policemen stood guard at the entrance and, after three days of secret proceedings, a note was pinned outside, stating that the defendant had been sent for trial at Crown Court.[24]

The Attorney General, Sir Reginald Manningham-Buller, informed Blake's counsel, Jeremy Hutchinson,* that he wanted no mention of MI6 made in open court. Hutchinson then decided it was better for the trial to be held in secret,** so that he could present mitigating evidence to the judge in full.[25] Hutchinson was unaware that Macmillan had informed Manningham-Buller that he wished to see Blake hit 'with the biggest hammer possible', to assuage American anger, or that Manningham-Buller had passed information about the case covertly to Lord Parker, the Lord Chief Justice, who was to preside over the secret trial.[26]

At the end of the hearing, members of the press were permitted into Court One of the Old Bailey to witness Parker sentence Blake to forty-two years in jail. As a consequence of the secrecy surrounding the case, Macmillan felt able to make a seriously misleading statement to Parliament in which he said that 'Blake was never an established member of the Foreign Service', and that 'he did not have access to secret information on defence, nuclear or atomic matters'.[27]

On this occasion, the deception was short-lived. The following

---

* This is same Jeremy Hutchinson who would defend Duncan Campbell at the ABC trial at the Old Bailey seventeen years later.

** Similar measures were in place at the Old Bailey in 1984 for most of the six-day trial of Michael Bettaney, an MI5 officer who had attempted to spy for the KGB.

day the *New York Times* reported the embarrassing fact which the D-Notice and the courtroom secrecy had been intended to conceal from the British public: that Blake had been an MI6 officer.[28] This key fact was widely reported outside the UK. Despite this, the government repeated its request that the British press refrain from reporting on Blake's occupation even though it was, of course, known to the Soviets.[29]

Not all periods of heightened threats to the state have led to heightened levels of courtroom secrecy.

At the end of the '60s, when violence erupted on the streets of Northern Ireland, and during the years that followed, when the lawlessness began to spiral out of control, it was not considered necessary to introduce secret court procedure. Very occasionally, the criminal courts would draw upon their powers to sit in camera and, from time to time, Public Interest Immunity was used to exclude evidence from civil cases. A new statute was also introduced to create non-jury courts. But no attempt was made to introduce new law that would extend the degree to which the courts shrouded their work in secrecy.

A small number of secret tribunals were held in Northern Ireland, however, from November 1972, after the British government decided that steps needed to be taken to counter the widespread international criticism of the introduction of internment without trial the previous year.

At Long Kesh, the camp south-west of Belfast where hundreds of men were being held, each of the internees was offered a hearing. Police and Army officers gave evidence while standing behind a curtain, and the prisoner and his lawyers were excluded when evidence from informers was being discussed. The only part of the process that resembled a normal criminal trial was that in which the prisoner, and any witnesses called on his behalf, faced cross-examination.[30]

These procedures were actually borrowed from an earlier

era of executive detention, during the Second World War. The Home Office advisory committee had followed a similar process when reviewing the internment of supposed Nazi sympathizers under Defence Regulation 18b.[31] It had used this power to hold people like Sjoerd Pons, the Dutch Abwehr spy, even after he had been acquitted by an Old Bailey jury.

After internment came to an end in Northern Ireland in December 1975, the secret tribunal system found a new lease of life in London. A procedure that was said to be an exceptional response to an emergency was to become a norm.

At the Home Office, a three-person panel, chaired by a former appeal court judge, was established to review decisions by the Home Secretary to deport individuals on the grounds of national security. At this time, there was no right of appeal against such decisions, but the panel – whose members came to be known as the Three Wise Men – could review the evidence available to the Home Secretary and make recommendations.[32] The Three Wise Men would hold their tribunals in the United Service Club, the gentlemen's club in Pall Mall. It was here that the journalist Mark Hosenball and former CIA officer Philip Agee were called for questioning about their role in exposing the existence of GCHQ, before being deported.

This cosy arrangement began to unravel in 1990, however, after a Sikh separatist, Karamjit Singh Chahal, who had been refused asylum and was facing deportation on the basis of information he could not see, turned to the European Court of Human Rights in Strasbourg. There, judges ruled that Chahal had been denied a fair trial. The Chahal case appeared initially to represent a severe setback for the British government. It was an adversity that it turned to its advantage, however, in a manner that was to have legal and political repercussions for many years.

The European Court recommended that the Three Wise Men system be replaced by a procedure similar to that used in Canada, which would permit the government to introduce evidence in secret. While appellants such as Chahal and their lawyers would not be able to see or challenge it, this evidence could be tested by specially vetted advocates, appointed by the courts.[33]

So-called Special Advocates would be able to take instructions from the appellant prior to the start of the procedure. They could then see the secret evidence, and cross-examine government witnesses. But once they had done so, they could no longer communicate with the appellants or their lawyers; they could take no further instructions.

This suggestion led to the creation in 1997 of the Special Immigration Appeals Commission, or SIAC, where secret evidence – or 'closed material', to use the Commission's terminology – is deployed by government lawyers. It would not be long before closed material procedures would seep into many other areas of UK law.

Today, SIAC is located in the windowless basement of an anonymous building in a street off London's Chancery Lane. Few journalists and even fewer members of the public are seen at SIAC. There is little point: as a result of the secrecy that surrounds its proceedings, it is extraordinarily difficult to make head or tail of what's going on there.

The appellants, who are usually people said to have terrorist links and who are fighting deportation, are equally in the dark. They are not informed about what is being alleged against them behind the Commission's closed doors. And the court's rulings are never fully revealed to the press or the public.

One journalist who occasionally attends SIAC explains: 'It's the only court I can think of where I can be told there is a case of national importance – only to find the doors locked and no clear indication of when they are going to open. A reporter can spend literally days at SIAC and come back with very few reportable facts because secrecy is the key part of the court's business. As a consequence, its press seats are often empty.'[34]

When SIAC was being created, Parliament was told that ministers believed that these special measures would be used no more than five times a year to deal with complex immigration cases.[35] Before long, almost a dozen other tribunals were using closed material procedures. They include employment tribunals, the Northern Ireland Sentences Review Commission, the slightly Orwellian-sounding Pathogens Access Appeal Commission, and the Parole Board. The secret evidence sessions became so common that they were known simply as CMPs.

Finally, in October 2015, the senior judge who was head of the family courts in England and Wales ruled that CMPs could be used during applications to have children made wards of court. This was to be permitted if there were concerns that the children, or their families, were planning to travel to areas of Syria controlled by the Islamic State.[36] This meant that courts could remove children from their parents on the basis of secret MI5 evidence that those parents would have no opportunity to rebut. With the double layer of secrecy that would envelop any such case – a hearing concerning not only the welfare of children, but national security concerns – it was unclear, at the time of writing, whether any procedures of this kind have happened or not.

From the moment SIAC and the other commissions were established, there were concerns that CMPs constituted a departure not only from open justice, but from natural – or real – justice. There were complaints that they fell far short of the common-law tradition of fairness: that it was not possible to have an effective adversarial trial when one party did not know the whole of the case that was being mounted against them. It was perhaps telling that the greatest critics were the Special Advocates – the vetted barristers who were permitted behind the closed doors, and who could see how the system was working.

There have been complaints too that CMPs are not only

fundamentally unfair, they may also result in the courts being misinformed. One critic, Lord Kerr, a Justice of the UK Supreme Court, has observed that 'evidence which has been insulated from challenge may positively mislead'.[37]

One example of this happening at SIAC concerned a man who was alleged to have been a terrorist, and who was accused of using another man's passport in an attempt to travel to the Netherlands on a particular date. On reading the secret evidence, his Special Advocate realised that in another case before SIAC in which he was instructed, an entirely different man had been accused of using the same passport, on the same date, to enter the same country.[38]

Another example arose after the Parole Board used closed material to deny parole to Harry Roberts, one of Britain's most notorious murderers, who was seeking release after serving almost forty years behind bars for the murder of three police officers in west London in 1966.

The Parole Board considered evidence from the Home Secretary's lawyers in secret, and then informed Roberts that he was going nowhere. At this point, some of the secret evidence was leaked to Roberts in prison. The allegation against him was that he had attacked a number of animals while working at an animal sanctuary while on day release. Once these allegations had been leaked to Roberts, his lawyers were able to demonstrate that he could not possibly have been responsible, as he was locked up in prison at the times of the attacks.

Roberts had been represented by experienced Special Advocates, but once they had seen the 'evidence' of his involvement in the attacks, they could not talk to him about it, or consult his lawyers, to establish whether the allegations were true or false.*

At SIAC, much of the evidence heard in secret is based upon intelligence supplied by the security and intelligence agencies;

---

* Roberts' application for parole was rejected in any event, but for different reasons. He was freed in 2014.

this, in turn, is often supplied by overseas intelligence agencies, many of them in North Africa and the Middle East. There was some argument about whether SIAC could rely on evidence that might have been extracted under torture and, eventually, the House of Lords ruled that it could not.

In 2003 and 2004, however, during a period of rapprochement between the British government and the Gaddafi regime in Libya, a dozen Libyan opposition activists who had been living in the UK were detained pending deportation to their homeland. Their appeals were heard at SIAC, with MI5 officers giving evidence in secret.

When Gaddafi was toppled in 2011, documentation recovered from government offices in Tripoli showed that evidence to have been based upon information extracted from two leading opposition figures who had been kidnapped with the assistance of MI6, flown to Libya, and tortured. One had made clear that he was being tortured when two British intelligence officers visited him in prison in Tripoli.[39] Despite this, MI5 had sent more than 1,600 questions to be put to the two men, and the Gaddafi regime was told that the answers were required by SIAC.[40]

The use of evidence extracted under torture had been banned in England in the mid-seventeenth century; CMPs had enabled its return, by stealth.

Once SIAC had been operating for a few years, and with CMPs being deployed across a sweep of civil tribunals and at immigration appeals hearings, it was perhaps inevitable that greater secrecy should begin to spread to other corners of the legal system too.

In 2004 Peter Cory, the Canadian Supreme Court judge, completed his inquiry into the murder of the Northern Irish lawyer Pat Finucane. Three years earlier the British government, while entering into a binding international agreement with the Irish government as part of the peace process, had given an undertaking that it would hold a public inquiry into Finucane's murder if Cory recommended that this should happen. Cory not only found that there was sufficient evidence of state collusion in the solicitor's murder to warrant such an inquiry, he warned that any failure to hold one 'could be seen as a cynical breach of faith' which could undermine the peace process.[41]

The government's response came a few months later, while Parliament was closed and MPs were enjoying their summer break: the inquiry would be held only after new legislation established a different regime for tribunals of inquiry. Section 19 of the new law, the Inquiries Act of 2005, gave ministers the power to order that parts or even all of a 'public' inquiry should be held in secret; it also gave ministers the power to censor inquiries' final reports.

Cory was contemptuous of the move, saying the new law created 'an intolerable Alice in Wonderland situation' in which government ministers could thwart all attempts to inquire into the actions of their own departments. 'I cannot contemplate any self-respecting Canadian judge accepting an appointment to an inquiry constituted under the new proposed Act,' he said.[42]

With a number of tribunals making use of closed material procedures, and a new regime for 'public inquiries' which ensured that government ministers could decide what would, and would not, be aired in public, it was only a matter of time before criminal trials became the focus for the government's more imaginative lawyers.

The opportunity arose during a murder investigation that seemed, at first glance, to be more of a whodunit than a national security case.

Downshire Hill is a picturesque road that cuts through the heart of one of north London's most affluent neighbourhoods, coming to a gentle halt at the edge of Hampstead Heath. For years, however, the neglected four-storey house at Number 9 had been sorely out of place among the stuccoed Regency mansions: through the wild trees and masses of brambles outside, the building could be seen to be falling apart.

Allan Chappelow, a reclusive photographer and writer, had lived at Number 9 since he was a boy. In the early summer of 2006, he was eighty-six years old, and had not been seen by neighbours for some time. In June that year police went to the house, having been alerted by Chappelow's bank in the wake of a number of suspicious transactions, and his failure to respond to their inquiries. The writer's body was found buried beneath an enormous pile of book proofs. He had been beaten to death about five weeks earlier, after being tormented by having molten wax poured on his body.

It was not long before police inquiries focused on Wang Yam, a Chinese nuclear scientist who had left Beijing after the Tiananmen Square demonstrations of 1989, and who had been living two streets away from Chappelow. Wang was from an influential Chinese family with strong links to the leadership of the Communist Party. His grandfather was Ren Bi-Shi, a comrade of Chairman Mao. After settling in the UK, Wang carried out a string of frauds, tricking members of the Chinese community in Britain out of money with fake mortgage and insurance deals. While projecting an image of success, wearing Armani suits and Rolex watches, Wang had been declared bankrupt with debts of £1.1 million, and he and his pregnant girlfriend were facing eviction.[43]

Wang had fled Britain shortly before Chappelow's body was discovered, and he was later found to have been accessing the dead man's bank accounts by impersonating him over the Internet and telephone. Eventually Wang was traced to Switzerland, arrested and deported back to the UK. When he came to trial, the Crown's case was that he had stolen Chappelow's mail in order to access his bank accounts, and had possibly been caught red-handed by Chappelow, whom he had then beaten to death.

Much of the trial was held in secret, however, after the Home Secretary signed PII certificates that asserted this to be necessary on the grounds of national security. Asked by the judge whether the case would be dropped if it was not heard behind closed doors, prosecuting counsel replied: 'There is a serious possibility the Crown may not proceed in this case.'

The jury – which had been vetted by MI5 – convicted Wang of theft and fraud, but failed to reach a verdict on the murder charge. A retrial was held, during which the entire defence case was heard in camera. This time Wang was convicted and jailed for life with a recommendation that he serve a minimum of twenty years.

At this point, the reason for the secrecy became partly clear: much to the outrage of the trial judge, *The Times* newspaper reported that Wang had been working for MI6, that part of his defence rested on his activities as an informant, and that it had been the agency that had wanted the case heard largely in camera.[44]

The judge referred *The Times* article to the Attorney General as a 'serious and urgent matter', clearly believing that the newspaper and its journalists should be prosecuted for contempt of court. He even claimed that journalists could be committing a criminal offence if they were to speculate about what might have been happening behind closed doors at the trial. 'Speculation . . . whether accurate or inaccurate, which purports to reveal the matters which were considered in camera . . . may itself be a contempt of court,' he said.[45]

In the event, the newspaper escaped prosecution by demonstrating that information about Wang's involvement with MI6 had entered the public domain before the judge had issued his order. *The Times* was not alone in reporting on Wang's links to MI6. A few years later Lord Phillips, the former President of the Supreme Court, published an article in which he described how he cycled along Downshire Hill each day, and had always been puzzled by the poor state of disrepair of Number 9. Phillips explained how the man convicted of the murder 'had some link with the security services, which he wished to rely on by way of defence'.[46]

In 2015, the Supreme Court refused Wang permission to take his case into the open at the European Court of Human Rights. A key part of his defence remains hidden, and any attempt to make it public would constitute a criminal offence.

By the time Wang was convicted, the intelligence agencies, the Home Office and the police were encouraging government legal advisors to explore the possibility of extending courtroom secrecy to terrorism cases.

As it had been so often in the past, the Official Secrets Act was regarded as a legal blunderbuss with a dangerous tendency to backfire: it could not be trusted as a means of keeping the state's secrets. Instead, the state relied upon the courts' common-law power to sit in camera, and upon the 1981 Contempt of Court Act, which contains criminal penalties to discourage anyone from disclosing evidence heard in secret, or which the judge has ordered should not be published.

Before long the Contempt of Court Act was being deployed during the prosecution of Islamist terrorists, in a manner that concealed evidence that horrendous crimes were being committed not only by al-Qaida and its affiliates, but also by the very law enforcement and intelligence agencies that were bringing those terrorists to justice.

At the Old Bailey in 2007, and the following year at Manchester Crown Court, two young British Muslims who were accused of being terrorists – and who would eventually be convicted of very serious terrorist offences – alleged that MI5 and MI6 had effectively orchestrated their torture at the hands of Pakistan's notorious intelligence agencies.

The government's responses to the allegations were given after the courts were cleared of press and the public. At Manchester Crown Court, police erected a metal detector at the door of the courtroom and prevented journalists from entering not only when the court was sitting in camera but also, on occasion, when it was supposed to be sitting openly. At one point, lawyers for the Greater Manchester Police attempted to prevent the media from publishing a picture that showed that three of the defendant's fingernails had been removed after he was detained in Pakistan at the suggestion of MI6. The police argued, unsuccessfully, that publication would be a breach of copyright.[47]

The details of what had emerged behind closed doors at Manchester Crown Court became public only as a result of the legal immunity enjoyed by Members of Parliament. David Davis, the Conservative MP and former Shadow Home Secretary, used parliamentary privilege to declare that the evidence that was being heard in secret, during legal argument ahead of the trial, showed the detention and interrogation of the defendant to have been 'an evidential showcase for the policy of complicity in torture'.[48]

The defendant's lawyers argued that the manner in which he had been treated was so outrageous that the court should not permit his prosecution to proceed any further. At the end of the legal arguments, the judge ruled that it should go ahead. There are two versions of his judgment, however: one 'open', or public, and one 'closed', or secret. After the two judgments were handed down, a government official arrived at the court and, without identifying himself, took the closed judgment, locked it inside a briefcase, turned on his heel, and walked out.

As a result of Davis' intervention, key facts contained within the closed judgment are known. But the judge's wider conclusions are not. Nor is it clear whether his secret judgment, and others like it, will be made public at some point in the future, so that historians may have a more complete picture of the way in which the UK sought to combat terrorism in the years after 9/11.

★

Such was the depth of the UK's involvement in the so-called rendition programme after 9/11 – and so cogent was the evidence that the country's intelligence agencies had embarked on their own kidnap and torture operations after a brief period of immersion in the CIA's enterprise – that it was inevitable that a number of compensation claims would reach the courts.

There were dozens of such claims, each of which threatened not only to severely tarnish the reputation of the agencies, but also to undermine the cherished British notion that torture was in some way alien, a crime perpetrated only by others.

Perhaps the best-known case was that brought by Binyam Mohamed, a British resident and terrorism suspect, over the role that MI5 had played in his interrogation at a time when he was being tortured in Pakistan in 2002.

The Court of Appeal concluded that MI5 knew Mohamed was being tortured before it sent one of its officers to Karachi to interrogate him. Further, there was evidence to suggest that MI5 also knew that Mohamed was about to be 'rendered' to Morocco, where he suffered months of barbaric abuse.

The government's lawyers battled for months to persuade the Court of Appeal to excise from its judgment all reference to the evidence that MI5 had been complicit in Mohamed's torture. They also asked that the judges expunge their condemnation of MI5 as being dishonest, devious and failing to respect human rights.[49] They failed, the judgment was made public, and Mohamed received around £1 million in compensation.

A second case, which also caused the government great discomfort, was brought by a group of former inmates of the US detention and interrogation facility at Guantánamo Bay. These men sued the UK government and its intelligence agencies over their involvement in their 'rendition' and mistreatment.

When the Guantánamo case came to court, government lawyers mounted a series of delaying tactics, claiming at one point that the process of assessing material prior to a PII application could take three years.

A small number of documents did trickle into the public domain, however, and they could not have been more damning. They showed, for example, that Jack Straw, as Foreign Secretary, had consigned British citizens to Guantánamo, and that these individuals had been rendered to the US detention facility after Tony Blair had been made aware that the Americans were torturing their prisoners. The government quickly negotiated compensation payments amounting to many millions of pounds, striking a deal before more troublesome documentation could see the light of day.

Against this background, the legal advisors of MI5 and MI6 had an inspired idea: why not argue that the closed material procedures being used in SIAC and elsewhere could be used in civil trials? The trial judge in the Guantánamo case had concluded that this was permissible, but the Court of Appeal rejected the notion. The Supreme Court agreed to rule upon the matter. Phillips, who was president of the court at the time, later rued that decision: 'On reflection I am not sure we were wise to do so.'[50]

The Supreme Court could not agree. But the majority of Justices believed that only Parliament, and not the courts, could introduce CMPs into civil litigation. The government's response was immediate: it brought forward proposals for legislation that would introduce secret evidence into civil trials in which the government was itself the defendant.

The government was planning to codify the cover-up.

So far-reaching were the new proposals, and so great the likelihood of protest, that the government prepared the ground carefully for its Green Paper. Its first step was to brief selected sections of the media, telling journalists that the new law was urgently required as a response to the 'public outrage' at compensation payments to the former Guantánamo inmates, whom officials dismissed as terrorists. 'Secret Courts to Shut Down £1m Cash-point for Terror Suspects', read the headline in one newspaper.[51]

Far from the proposed legislation being designed to safeguard the public purse, it was being introduced at a time when the courts were showing an increased willingness to hold the UK's intelligence agencies to account.

The Green Paper made clear that the proposed legislation was a response both to the agencies' failure to persuade the courts to permit CMPs in the Guantánamo case, and to the UK intelligence community's deep discomfort over the disclosure of the evidence in the Binyam Mohamed case, which the paper described not as evidence of torture and of MI5's involvement in that torture, but as 'sensitive US intelligence material'.[52]

The head of MI5 was reported to be lobbying personally for a change in the law, as a direct result of the damage that the disclosures in the Mohamed case had inflicted upon his agency's reputation, and because revelations in the courts had assisted journalists who were investigating the UK's involvement in the kidnap and torture of terrorism suspects.[53]

The Green Paper proposed a radical reduction in the degree to which judges could use their discretion to decide what material should be made public, and what should be excluded under PII. Instead, ministers could apply to courts for evidence to be heard in secret, and judges' ability to refuse the application would be limited.

Hundreds of lawyers signed a petition in which they deplored the proposed departure from openness, fairness and equality under the law. Concern spread beyond the UK: civil liberties groups from Egypt, Argentina, Canada, Ireland, South Africa, Hungary and the United States warned in a joint statement: 'If the UK Parliament passes this proposal into law it will be a huge setback for those of us fighting to secure truth and fairness from our own governments and within our own justice systems across the world.'

The law also faced vociferous opposition in both the House of Commons and the House of Lords. But after a tumultuous passage through both houses, the Justice and Security Act became law in April 2013. Ministers were not slow to use the Act, and just months later, the consequences of its secret evidence provisions were becoming clear.

Over the next year, government ministers and chief constables made five applications for the use of CMPs in the civil courts.* The following year the number of applications more than doubled, to eleven.[54] Many of the cases concerned claims brought in the courts in Northern Ireland; others revolved around allegations of government complicity in kidnap and mistreatment in Somaliland, Thailand and Libya.

The Justice and Security Act enabled the government to use secret evidence in civil cases in which it was itself the defendant, and during the course of which the reputation of the UK's intelligence agencies might be at risk, but it was difficult to imagine how any further damage could be inflicted upon the open justice principle.

Six months later, a black E-Class Mercedes saloon was driving near Tower Bridge in central London with two young men inside. A few yards from the bridge three unmarked police cars positioned themselves in front of, behind and alongside the Mercedes and forced it to a halt. Armed officers leapt out and ordered the men to get out of the car. When the Mercedes edged forward a few inches, the police blew out its tyres with shotgun rounds. The two occupants of the car were pulled out and searched. Both men were found to have small SD memory cards, wrapped in tape, concealed inside their iPhone cases.

Stored on the cards were a number of documents, including a five-page bomb-making manual. A listening device had been

---

* The Ministry of Justice discloses the total numbers, but will not identify the cases concerned.

installed in the car thirteen days earlier, and had picked up conversations in which the two men, Erol Incedal and Mounir Rarmoul-Bouhadjar, had discussed a recent trip to Syria, and talked about their plans to buy a firearm. Incedal's email communications with a man in Syria, in which he agreed to carry out a terrorist attack in London, had also been intercepted.

Both men were charged with possession of a document likely to be useful to a person preparing an act of terrorism, while Incedal was also charged with the more serious offence of preparing acts of terrorism over a twenty-month period.

When the two men were brought before the courts, Crown prosecutors said they needed the entire case to be heard in secret, with the defendants anonymised as AB and CD. Were this not agreed, they said, there was a possibility that others – who remained, at that point, unidentified – may not cooperate with the prosecution.

The trial judge, Andrew Nicol, was the lawyer who, a few years earlier, had written that 'trials derive their legitimacy from being conducted in public', and that 'no matter how fair, justice must still be seen before it can be said to be done'. He was also the former Special Advocate who had spotted the government's attempts to rely on evidence at SIAC that involved different people using the same passport to enter the same country, the Netherlands, on the same day. In this case, however, he believed he needed to accede to the Crown's demand.

The application was supported by ministerial certificates, obscure legal devices that are not founded in either common law or statute, but which are drawn up on behalf of the Home Secretary or Foreign Secretary, to impress upon judges the need to protect national security.

In the event, as a consequence of a challenge by lawyers representing the media, the Court of Appeal made unique arrangements for the trial. The evidence would be heard at the Old Bailey in three parts. Some parts of the case would be held in open court, with any member of the public or the press free to attend. Other evidence would be heard in secret, but a small number of journalists would be permitted to be present. They would not immediately be allowed to report what they saw and heard, and at the end of the trial, Nicol could decide whether or not to lift the reporting restrictions. The third, most secret parts of the trial would be heard without any members of the press being present. The jury would hear the entire case.

Throughout each of the secret sessions that some journalists would be permitted to attend, those journalists would be expected to surrender their mobile phones, which would be locked in soundproof boxes. At the end of each session, the journalists were expected to hand their notebooks to a police officer, to be locked in a safe at the back of the court. The police watched closely to ensure the journalists did not attempt to remove any notes from the court. There was a comic moment when a detective accused the man from the *Daily Express* of surreptitiously making a second set of notes and attempting to smuggle them out. The journalist handed over the crossword he had been completing during lulls in the proceedings. Less amusingly, a reporter from the *Daily Mirror* was threatened with arrest at his home for allegedly removing notes, when he had not even been in court.[55]

To reinforce this secrecy, Nicol handed down an order that prohibited the journalists from making any notes outside court from memory. The order also stated that if any of the journalists wanted to discuss the case with their own lawyers, this must be done in a confidential meeting, which was defined as one that would take place in a room 'in which the door is closed and it is clear that no one can overhear from outside the room what is being said during the meeting'. The order added that 'no part of the meeting can be recorded and no notes made'. A proposal that the order should also decree that the door to the meeting room should be locked and that there should be no CCTV in the vicinity was considered, but abandoned. It was to be the most secret Old Bailey trial since the prosecutions of the double agent George Blake in 1961 and the would-be double agent Michael Bettaney in 1984.

Shortly before the trial began, Rarmoul-Bouhadjar pleaded guilty to possessing the bomb-making manual. Incedal, a twenty-seven-year-old law student from south London, denied both counts. As Incedal's trial began, Nicol warned the jury that they could be prosecuted for contempt of court – an offence that carries a penalty of up to two years' imprisonment – if they divulged to anyone what they were about to hear.

It was also made clear to the journalists that they would be in contempt of court if they attempted to tell the public what was being hidden from them. Whenever the court went into a fully secret session, one of the police officers would lock the doors from the inside. Nicol told the jury that the evidence heard during these sessions would never, in any circumstances, be made public.

At the end of the four-week trial, Incedal was convicted of committing a crime by possessing the bomb-making manual, but the jury could not agree a verdict on the charge of plotting a terrorist attack. A second jury was sworn in for a retrial, and the warnings about contempt of court were issued over again.

After the second jury retired to consider its verdict, the journalists were told that if Incedal was convicted they would be permitted to remove their notebooks from court, but only once certain words were 'completely excised' from their pages. They were also informed that the identity of the people making this demand should not be disclosed.

Incedal was acquitted. The jury's decision was no great surprise to the journalists who had been permitted to hear some of the secret evidence, but they were unable to explain that decision to their readers and viewers. Nor were they able to report on the single most important matter at the heart of the case.

At the end of this bizarre and disturbing trial, Nicol ruled that the reporting restrictions would not be lifted. He handed down his decision in two judgments: one was open, and the other, of course, was secret. At this point, the police officers in court told the reporters that they would never see their notebooks again.

Nicol's refusal to lift the reporting restrictions led to a further appeal by lawyers representing the media. At this point, the Lord Chief Justice, Lord Thomas, let part of the cat out of the bag when he made clear, in open court, that the representations that had been made to Crown prosecutors – and that had led to the demands for complete secrecy – had been made by MI5 and MI6.

Having previously lobbied for the introduction of the Justice and Security Act, which extended CMPs to civil trials in which they were themselves the defendants, the security and intelligence agencies were now attempting to undermine the open justice principle in criminal trials.

Lord Chief Justice Thomas was furious. 'One thing the security services cannot do is to say they will not hand over material to the prosecution,' he said. 'That is absolutely impermissible. It cannot be for the security services to say: "Well we may not cooperate", because that would suggest that they are not subject to the rule of law.'[56]

Thomas rejected the media's second appeal, with the result that the reporting restrictions remain in place. However, he warned MI5 and MI6 that they must never again threaten to withhold evidence in a bid to secure courtroom secrecy. 'It is a significant, important and proper part of the duties of the security services that they act in accordance with the law,' he said.[57]

Needless to say, Thomas had further comments to make while the Court of Appeal was sitting behind closed doors. But disclosing what he said would be a criminal offence.

If members of the public are concerned that the security services have not acted in accordance with the law – and believe that they have suffered as a result – they are entitled to lodge a complaint with the UK's most secretive court: the Investigatory Powers Tribunal.

The IPT is a court that has proclaimed itself to be completely independent of government. It was established in October 2000 under the Regulation of Investigatory Powers Act, the legislation that gives ministers the power to issue warrants authorising electronic or human surveillance. Its president is a High Court judge, and its other members are judges, practising barristers or academic lawyers. Its role is to investigate complaints about the UK's intelligence agencies, as well as other public bodies with the power to conduct covert surveillance, such as the police and some military units and, occasionally, local authorities. It is the court to which members of the public may complain if they believe their phone has been bugged, they have been placed under surveillance or their home has been searched, without lawful authority.

Anyone who wishes to lodge a complaint about the activities of MI5, MI6 or GCHQ, or any other public body, is expected to make that complaint to the IPT by writing to a Post Office box number – 33220 – and using the postcode of the sorting office: SW1H 9ZQ. In time, their letter will be delivered to a two-storey sorting office at the far corner of an industrial estate in Battersea, south London. Where their letter goes from there is intended to be a mystery. The Royal Mail refuses to discuss this PO box number. 'Unfortunately we are unable to supply any details relating to this PO box,' a spokesperson says. Asked why not, her reply is as terse as it is uninformative: 'Because it's confidential.'

The location of the IPT is an official secret.

The enigma does not end there. Individuals who lodge complaints with the IPT are not entitled to attend any hearings into their complaint. Indeed, they are rarely told if there has been a hearing. A handful of hearings are in public, and from early 2014 the IPT began giving public notice of when it was planning to have an open hearing. Before this, nobody would know that they were sitting in open court. But the overwhelming majority of hearings are not open. Usually, complainants have no opportunity to see or challenge the evidence that the intelligence agencies submit in their defence. Instead, in due course they will receive a letter from the IPT, with the mysterious PO Box number and the south London postcode at its head. In theory, if the IPT concludes that the complainant has been the subject of unlawful actions by one of the agencies, the individual concerned will be informed of this.

In practice, however, this almost never happens. During the first ten years of its operation, the IPT received more than 1,100 complaints, and upheld nine, five of them from members of one family who had all lodged complaints about surveillance by their local council. It did not uphold a single complaint against any of the UK's intelligence agencies.

In almost every other case, the IPT concluded either that the complainant was not being spied upon, or that they were, but that this was not unlawful. When this happens, the complainant is not told of the tribunal's conclusion. Instead, in order to conceal evidence of lawful surveillance operations, the complainant receives a letter that simply states: 'No determination has been made in your favour.' There is no right of appeal.

In defence of these statistics, one of the High Court judges who has acted as president of the tribunal says that many of the complaints that it receives are of a 'frivolous, vexatious' nature; they are lodged, he said, by the sort of individual who becomes convinced that MI5 has implanted listening devices in their teeth.[58]

But as a result of the secrecy, it has not been possible to know with what rigour the IPT investigates the complaints that it receives. Because justice is not seen to be done, it is not clear whether, or to what extent, justice is being done.

And secrecy is not the only serious problem with the tribunal, according to a number of lawyers who have lodged complaints on behalf of clients: its procedures appear to be stacked very heavily in favour of whichever body is said to be carrying out the espionage operation, and against the complainant. There is no legal aid for complainants, for example: if they hire lawyers, they must do so at their own expense, and it is unlikely that those lawyers will be permitted to attend a hearing. Indeed, there are very often no hearings at all. Instead, a number of the eight-strong panel of senior lawyers who sit on the IPT will meet to read a number of documents provided by whichever public body is the subject of the complaint, and then reach a decision.

In 2014, under pressure from complainants' lawyers, the IPT began to hold an occasional public hearing. Finally, in February 2015, it found against one of the intelligence agencies for the first time, ruling that GCHQ had been breaking the European Convention on Human Rights for seven years by sharing with the US National Security Agency the electronic communications that it had been capturing in bulk from people around the globe.[59]

But perhaps the most extraordinary aspect of the IPT has concerned the attempts that were made to conceal the location from which it operates. The reason for these efforts became clear once the tribunal's whereabouts was discovered.

For fifteen years, the hundreds of letters of complaint that were sent each week to the sorting office in Battersea were immediately redirected and driven a mile-and-a-half across the Thames to Marsham Street in Westminster. There, they were delivered to the IPT's offices, inside the headquarters of the Home Office.

The entire staff of the supposedly independent tribunal is based at the Home Office. The department funds its £296,000 annual budget. At the time of writing, the senior member of its secretariat is an individual who served previously with the Office for Security and Counter-Terrorism, which is a division of the Home Office, and who before that was a member of the Home Office's covert investigation policy team.[60]

The 'independent' IPT was attempting to conceal the fact that it was part of the machinery of government.

After the author discovered this in March 2014, and reported on it for the *Guardian*, the IPT responded by rewriting its website: it no longer described itself as 'independent'. Within a few months it had moved to another location. Its new address is also an official secret.

The extraordinary level of secrecy that surrounds the IPT has been described frequently as Kafkaesque. But when Franz Kafka wrote *The Trial*, his story of Josef K, a young man who finds himself subjected to a legal process that he will never be able to understand or influence, the writer at least ensured that his protagonist was provided with the name of the street where the court was located. Josef K could at least find the court that was dealing with his case, and attend the first hearing.

Kafka did not conceal from his protagonist the location of the tribunal that was to decide his case, nor prevent him from learning whether or not there had been a hearing. That, perhaps, would have been a little too surreal.

One of the many problems with secret justice is that it creates secret case law. It is a conundrum that some MPs and peers identified as the Justice and Security Bill was being debated, but it was not resolved before it became law. As a consequence, a whole body of legal precedents will be created over time to which the government's lawyers may have access, but others – such as claimants in civil cases, defendants in criminal trials, and even judges – may not.

It is a problem that was identified by the Lord Chief Justice, Lord Thomas, in the judgment in which he ruled that the reporting restrictions in the Erol Incedal case should remain in place. Recommending that a working party should examine the issue, Thomas said that courts ought to be able to refer to previous decisions, and 'closed' judgments need not remain secret for ever.[61]

Another problem that has arisen is the question of when 'closed' judgments will be opened to historians. Will they, like other official papers, be preserved and eventually transferred to the National Archives when the need for secrecy is no longer justifiable, or will they remain hidden from sight in perpetuity?

No inclination has been shown by either Parliament or the courts to implement mechanisms that would ensure there is a review of the closed status of court judgments. The government's current position is that 'closed' court judgments are not subject to the thirty-year disclosure rule, and that it is up to the court itself to decide whether to make them public. 'It is open to any person to approach the court to ask them to open up a closed judgment in whole or in part,' the government said.

In practice, however, approaching the court means asking the judge. If the judge has retired – or died – 'the court' cannot release the closed judgment. And, as the government added, 'because the final decision to release a closed judgment rests with the court, any decision to transfer a closed judgment to the National Archives without permission from the court would be considered to be a Contempt of Court . . .'[62]

As matters stand, judgments from cases in which there have been secret evidence sessions – and the hidden historical truths that these documents could tell us about the nature and conduct of the British state – are to be buried with the judges who write them.

Epilogue

While researching and writing this book, I came across many examples of state secrecy that went far beyond the understandable and expected precaution of national security. From the destruction of historical documents to the refusal to comply with Freedom of Information requests, and from the extraordinary secrecy surrounding the Investigatory Powers Tribunal to the concealment of entire military campaigns, I became convinced that secrecy in the government was not just an occasional necessity but the fiercely-protected norm.

In the middle of the last century, the American social philosopher Edward Shils spent some time considering this British phenomenon, which he first encountered when he arrived at the London School of Economics with a Fulbright Fellowship.

'The British ruling class is unequalled in secretiveness and taciturnity,' he wrote. 'Perhaps no ruling class in the Western world, certainly no ruling class in any democratic society, is as close-mouthed as the British ruling class.'

This is a class, Shils concluded, whose members are extraordinarily comfortable in the company of each other, and 'this feeling of proximity . . . restrains the tendency to fear hidden secrets'.

While researching and writing this book, I discovered few reasons to doubt Shils' thesis, and much to support it.

Secretiveness, this essential trait of British society appears – like so many others – to be rooted very firmly in the class system. And this may explain why the peculiarly uncommunicative nature of the British state does not provoke greater resentment and unease among the British public and media.

The British are, in large part, a deferential people, with a tendency to look up to, and not down upon, governments which remain suffused with the trappings of a monarchical and aristocratic society.

While British society is democratic and pluralistic, it is also hierarchical, with a predilection for ranks and pecking orders. The public appears to desire and respect strong government, both as a means of delivering change and as a way of guaranteeing good order. With few exceptions, people appear to be satisfied that the state keeps secret that which should properly be kept secret, and this has allowed successive governments to keep their secrets, while facing few challenges from the public or the media. Nowhere else, perhaps, could the expression 'a need to know basis' become a euphemism for official secrecy.

State secrecy, as we have seen, took shape and solidified in Britain during the second half of the 19th century, as a political elite whose relationship with its subjects had changed little over the previous 200 years sought to safeguard traditions of gentlemanly discretion, while at the same time managing the growth of government and a rapid expansion of the civil service.

Among the ranks of this new cohort of poorly paid but deferential state servants were a smattering of mavericks, upstarts, and also, perhaps, democrats: men like William Guernsey and Charles Marvin, the mid-19th century leakers of Foreign Office secrets. It was not long before the elite concluded that a code of secrecy, to be effective, must be buttressed by legislation.

The eventual result was Section 2 of the 1911 Official Secrets Act. For the next hundred years, servants of the state were encouraged to understand, as Burke Trend would put it in 1972, that they would 'get much more than a black mark' if they were caught speaking out of turn. They would be vilified, sacked, lose their pensions, face arrest and prosecution and, not infrequently, go to jail.

Section 2 helped to embed an all-embracing culture of secrecy across much of the public sector. When the Liberal MP Clement Freud complained that government gardeners were being instructed to sign the Official Secrets Act, he was not joking.

From time to time there have been challenges to the status quo from politicians in opposition. But while they may speak out in favour of transparency in parliament and campaign on it in elections, once in power, they quickly seem to come to the view that government is not compatible with openness. In recent years, those who govern – while always respecting the electorate's right to kick them out, come election time – have shown no sign that they wish to be troubled by the sort of participatory democracy that greater access to official information might encourage.

The introduction of the Freedom of Information Act in 2000 seemed as though it would mark a turning point in the relationship between the state and the public: it suggested the possibility that whole new areas of participatory and accountable democracy might be opened up in British public life. Members of the public could now use the Act to assert their rights as citizens to know how their country was governed.

And as a consequence, even before the Act came into force, the very New Labour ministers who had promised to be midwives to the Act, who had proclaimed that freedom of information would be their proud legacy, appeared to fear that their unborn child would be a dangerous and subversive insurgent. Attempts to smother it at birth failed and, at the time of writing, 11 years after it came into force, politicians and officials had recently abandoned another attempt to water down its provisions, after failing to find a single news organisation or individual commentator who was prepared to criticise it. Nevertheless, the Act has done nothing to dispel the culture of secrecy in British public life, and government officials are as likely to draw upon it in an attempt to suppress information as they are to set that information free.

In recent years, the technology that supports secrecy has changed: files are no longer stored in manila folders marked 'Top Secret', but in flash memory cells or hosted by a cloud storage service. And it seems that this very technology may pose the biggest challenge to government. In recent years, we have seen unredacted records of British MPs' expenses claims being sold to journalists and millions of GCHQ and NSA files being leaked by Edward Snowden. Is it possible, in an era when millions of documents can be stored and transferred with such ease, that the safeguarding of official secrets has become a near-impossible task? Could it be that digitisation, and the large-scale data dumps that digitisation has enabled, will have a revolutionary impact on the public's access to information and upon political power?

As a writer and journalist, I deal in the recent and, sometimes, not-so-recent past; I generally don't do the future. Were I to make a prediction about the prospects for British state secrecy, however, I would suggest that it will continue along the trajectory that Lord Esher and Colonel Jack Seely did so much to establish more than 100 years ago, when they pushed Section 2 of the Official Secrets Act through Parliament, and along which it has travelled, rarely deflected, ever since.

Leaks from those who serve the UK's secret state are extremely rare, suggesting that the 1989 Official Secrets Act continues to be an effective deterrent, while the 35-year jail sentence that was imposed upon the whistleblower Chelsea Manning in 2013 will doubtless do much to concentrate the minds of their American counterparts.

Despite the way in which technological advances appear to have facilitated these mega-leaks, I believe the political historian Peter Hennessy to have been spot-on: the curtailment of official secrecy in Britain, and not its continuity, would be aberrational.

And I would wager that as you're reading this a team of ingenious government technicians at Hanslope Park – the real-life Qs of the Bond novels – will be working on a technological fix for the data dump problem; devising new and ingenious ways in which the state can continue to secure its secrets.

Notes

Chapter 1: A Short History of a Very British Disease

1. Jeremy Bentham, 'Of Publicity' (Chapter 2 of 'Essay on Political Tactics'), in J. Bowring (Ed.), *The Works of J. Bentham*, 1843, vol. 2, p. 310.
2. Hansard, 14 June 1844.
3. Hansard, 24 June 1844.
4. *The Times*, 17 June 1844.
5. Birkett Report, Cmnd 283, October 1957.
6. Christopher Andrew, *Her Majesty's Secret Service: The Making of the British Intelligence Community*, p. 3.
7. Francis Barrymore Smith, *Radical Artisan, William James Linton 1812–97*, Manchester University Press, 1973, p. 54.
8. David Vincent, *The Culture of Secrecy*, pp. 26–77.
9. Ibid., pp. 44–9.
10. Christopher Moran, *Classified*, p. 31.
11. David Hooper, *Official Secrets*, p. 18.
12. *The Times*, 2 July 1878.
13. Moran, *Classified*, p. 33.
14. Hansard, 10 March 1887.
15. Moran, *Classified*, p. 36.
16. Hansard, 28 March 1889.
17. Hansard, 20 June 1889.
18. Hansard, 11 July 1889.
19. Moran, *Classified*, p. 37.
20. Clive Ponting, *Secrecy in Britain*, pp. 7–8; Hooper, *Official Secrets*, p. 25.

21. *The Times*, 21 August 1908.
22. 'The German Peril', *Quarterly Review*, vol. CCIX, July 1908.
23. Leonard Piper, *Dangerous Waters, The Life and Death of Erskine Childers*, p. 75.
24. Andrew, *Her Majesty's Secret Service*, pp. 54–63.
25. TNA CAB 16/8, Report and Proceedings: Sub-Committee of Imperial Defence: The Question of Foreign Espionage in the United Kingdom.
26. Christopher Andrew, *The Defence of the Realm*, pp. 20–1.
27. Ibid., p. 21.
28. TNA CAB 16/8.
29. Hansard, 25 July 1911.
30. Hansard, 18 August 1911.
31. J. E. B. Seely, *Adventure*, p. 145.

Chapter 2: A Psychological Anchor

1. Nicholas Wilkinson, *Secrecy and the Media*, p. 45.
2. Ibid., p. 49.
3. David Hooper, *Official Secrets*, p. 223.
4. Wilkinson, *Secrecy and the Media*, pp. 493–505.
5. David Williams, *Not in the Public Interest*, p. 34.
6. Imperial War Museum, Art 518.
7. Hansard, 25 June 1920.
8. Hansard, 2 December 1920.
9. Hooper, *Official Secrets*, pp. 246–7.
10. Hansard, 7 December 1938.
11. George Thomson, *The Blue Pencil Admiral*, p. 6.
12. Hooper, *Official Secrets*, p. 249.
13. Ian Cobain, *Cruel Britannia*, p. 14.
14. Hansard, 24 June 1948.
15. Hooper, *Official Secrets*, pp. 76–7.
16. *Isis*, 26 February 1958.
17. *Manchester Guardian*, 19 July 1958.
18. Wilkinson, *Secrecy and the Media*, pp. 513–519.
19. TNA DEFE 53/2.
20. Harold Wilson, *The Labour Government 1964–70*, p. 479.
21. Christopher Moran, *Classified*, p. 142.
22. Wilkinson, *Secrecy and the Media*, p. 330.
23. Pincher, *Dangerous to Know*, pp. 233, 285–6.

24. The Civil Service: Report of the Committee, Cmnd 3638, vol 1, HMSO, June 1968 (The Fulton Report).

25. Moran, *Classified*, p. 181.

26. *Washington Post*, 21 March 1970.

27. TNA HO 292/3, Franks Report, Volume 3.

28. Report of the Departmental Committee on Section 2 of the Official Secrets Act 1911, Cmnd 5104, September 1972.

29. Moran, *Classified*, p. 186.

30. Hansard, 31 January 1973.

31. *Guardian*, 16 October 2013.

32. Hansard, 19 January 1979.

33. Hooper, *Official Secrets*, p. 15.

34. Clive Ponting, *Secrecy in Britain*, p. 64.

35. Hooper, *Official Secrets*, p. 145.

36. *New Statesman and Society*, 10 March 1989.

37. *Guardian*, 26 February 2004.

38. *Daily Mirror*, 22 November 2005.

39. Lucinda Maer and Oonagh Gay, *Official Secrecy*, House of Commons Library, December 2008.

40. Times Newspapers Ltd & Others, 2007 EWCA Crim 1925.

41. Private information.

42. *Guardian*, 8 June 2009.

43. *Guardian*, 24 March 2001.

44. TNA DEFE 53/21.

Chapter 3: Don't Mention the Wars

1. *Manchester Guardian*, 6 December 1945.

2. George Rosie, *The British in Vietnam*, p. 46.

3. Christopher Bayly and Tim Harper, *Forgotten Wars*, pp. 149–53.

4. B. Prasad, et al., *Official History of the Indian Army in the Second World War 1939–45*, p. 199.

5. Imperial War Museum Sound, 7174.

6. *Guardian*, 14 September 2014.

7. Kenneth Matthews, *Memories of a Mountain War*, pp. 71–91.

8. Diary of Germaine Krull.

9. Bayly and Harper, *Forgotten Wars*, pp. 176–81.

10. TNA CAB 121/698.

11. TNA WO 203/2336.

12. Michael Carver, *War Since 1945*, p. 97.

13. Nicholas Wilkinson, *Secrecy and the Media*, p. 519.
14. Carver, *War Since 1945*, p. 95.
15. Harold Wilson, *The Labour Government*, pp. 67–8.
16. John Wingen and Herbert Tillema, 'British Military Intervention After World War II', pp. 293–4.
17. For a fuller list, see: http://www.theguardian.com/uk-news/ng-interactive/2014/feb/11/britain-100-years-of-conflict.
18. Michael Howard, 'The Use and Abuse of Military History'.
19. Ranulph Fiennes, *Where Soldiers Fear to Tread*, p. 13.
20. *Daily Telegraph*, 3 January 1972.
21. *Observer* and *Sunday Times*, 9 January 1972.
22. Walter C. Ladwig, 'Supporting Allies in Counterinsurgency', p. 64.
23. Fred Halliday, *Arabia Without Sultans*, p. 271.
24. Ladwig, 'Supporting Allies in Counterinsurgency', p. 71.
25. Hansard, 25 March 1970.
26. Halliday, *Arabia Without Sultans*, pp. 274–5.
27. Ian Gardiner, *In the Service of the Sultan*, pp. 17-19; Halliday, *Arabia Without Sultans*, p. 313.
28. Halliday, *Arabia Without Sultans*, p. 277.
29. Fiennes, *Where Soldiers Fear to Tread*, p. 19.
30. TNA DEFE 7/2314.
31. David French, *The British Way in Counter-Insurgency*, p. 131.
32. Jeremy Black, *A Brief History of Slavery*, p. 240.
33. Halliday, *Arabia Without Sultans*, p. 278.
34. Abdel Razzaq Takriti, *Monsoon Revolution*, p. 163.
35. Gardiner, *In the Service of the Sultan*, p. 85.
36. Ray Kane, *Coup D'état Oman*, p. 47.
37. Julian Thompson, *The Imperial War Museum Book of Modern Warfare*, p. 256.
38. Captain N. G. R. Hepworth, *Journal of the King's Regiment*, vol. VI, no 6, Winter 1970, quoted in Halliday, *Arabia Without Sultans*, p. 351.
39. *This Week*, Thames TV, 28 December 1972.
40. Halliday, *Arabia Without Sultans*, p. 351.
41. Ian Cobain, *Cruel Britannia*, p. 133.
42. Halliday, *Arabia Without Sultans*, pp. 276, 325.
43. John Akehurst, *We Won a War*, p. xv.
44. Ibid., p. 13.
45. Charles Allen, *The Savage Wars of Peace*, pp. 180–1.

46. Tony Jeapes, *SAS Secret War*, p.11.
47. Gordian Troeller and Marie-Claude Deffarge, 'Secret War No. 11'.
48. Halliday, *Arabia Without Sultans*, p. 327.
49. Allen, *The Savage Wars of Peace*, p. 180.
50. *The Times*, 27 July 1970.
51. *Financial Times*, 28 July 1970.
52. Kane, *Coup D'état Oman*, pp. 93–95.
53. Takriti, *Monsoon Revolution*, p. 181.
54. Stephen Dorril, *MI6*, pp. 729–733.
55. Takriti, *Monsoon Revolution*, p. 181.
56. Ibid., pp. 181–3.
57. *Document*, BBC Radio 4, 23 November 2009.
58. *Daily Express*, 31 July 1970.
59. Ladwig, 'Supporting Allies in Counterinsurgency', p. 72.
60. Pauline Searle, *Dawn Over Oman*, p. 131.
61. Author interview, London, May 2015.
62. Takriti, *Monsoon Revolution*, p. 273.
63. Ladwig, 'Supporting Allies in Counterinsurgency', pp. 76–7.
64. Peter de la Billière, *Looking for Trouble*, pp. 269–70.
65. Tony Geraghty, *Who Dares Wins*, p. 158.
66. Ladwig, 'Supporting Allies in Counterinsurgency', pp. 76–7.
67. Jeapes, *SAS Secret War*, pp. 46–7.
68. Pauline Searle, GB 165-0328, Middle East Centre Archive, St Antony's College, Oxford.
69. TNA FCO 8/2006.
70. Lawrence James, *Imperial Rearguard*, p. 116.
71. Gardiner, *In the Service of the Sultan*, p. 172; Takriti, *Monsoon Revolution*, pp. 307–8.
72. 'UK Armed Forces Operational deaths post World War II', Ministry of Defence, November 2014.
73. Searle, *Dawn Over Oman*, p. 130.
74. TNA PREM 15/537.
75. TNA FCO 46/609/1; *Document*, BBC Radio 4, 23 November 2009.
76. Email exchanges with author, May 2015.
77. See, for example, Robert Elegant, 'How to Lose A War: The Press and Viet Nam'.
78. Jeapes, *SAS Secret War*, p. 11.

79. Phillip Knightley, in David Miller (Ed.), *Tell Me Lies*, pp. 101–02.
80. Phillip Knightley, *The First Casualty*, p. 109.
81. Ibid., p. 435.
82. Hansard, 3 April 1982, 14 April 1982.
83. Justin Lewis et al., *Too Close for Comfort?*; Justin Lewis and Rod Brookes, 'Reporting the War on British Television', in Miller, *Tell Me Lies*.
84. Michael Pfau et al., 'Embedded Reporting During the Invasion and Occupation of Iraq'.
85. Knightley, in Miller, *Tell Me Lies*, p. 100.
86. *Guardian*, 8 April 2002.
87. See, for example, Knightley, in Miller, *Tell Me Lies*, pp. 100–5.
88. *The Defence Manual of Security*, Issue 2, JSP D Def Sy/6/3, MoD October 2001.
89. Jeapes, *SAS Secret War*, p. 11.
90. Alistair Burt, 'Vote that Ties Britain's Hands'.
91. Hansard, 29 August 2013.
92. Hansard, 2 July 2015.
93. *Guardian*, 2 July 2015.
94. Hansard, 20 July 2015.
95. *Daily Telegraph*, 15 January 2016.
96. *Independent*, 20 January 2016.

Chapter 4: Sinning Quietly

1. *The Times*, 8 April 2011.
2. David Anderson, 'Guilty Secrets', p. 150.
3. *Star*, 14 April 2005.
4. Niall Ferguson, *Empire: How Britain Made the Modern World*, p. xiv.
5. *Daily Mail*, 15 January 2005.
6. *The Times*, 5 April 2011.
7. Anderson, 'Guilty Secrets', p. 148.
8. For a summary of Griffith-Jones' concerns, see *Guardian*, 18 April 2012.
9. TNA FCO 141/19891.
10. Hansard, House of Commons, 5 May 2011.
11. Hansard, House of Commons, 6 June 2013.
12. David Anderson, 'Mau Mau in the High Court and the 'Lost' British Empire Archives: Colonial Conspiracy or Bureaucratic Bungle?'

13. Anthony Cary, 'The Migrated Archives: What Went Wrong and What Lessons Should We Draw?'

14. Anthony Badger, 'Historians, a Legacy of Suspicion and the Migrated Archives'.

15. Richard Drayton, 'Britain's Secret Archive of Decolonisation'.

16. TNA FCO 141/19930.

17. *Observer*, 28 December 1947.

18. TNA CO 54/992/3.

19. TNA CO 537/4854.

20. TNA FCO 141/19930.

21. TNA FCO 141/19891.

22. TNA FCO 141/19928.

23. TNA PREM 11/827.

24. TNA FCO 141/19928.

25. TNA FCO 141/6959.

26. Ibid.

27. Ibid.

28. TNA FCO 141/19930.

29. *Guardian*, 18 April 2012.

30. TNA FCO 141/19928.

31. Ibid.

32. TNA FCO 141/19932.

33. TNA FCO 141/19929.

34. TNA FCO 141/19930.

35. TNA FCO 141/19932.

36. FCO 141/19928.

37. Peter Hinchcliffe, John T. Ducker and Maria Holt, *Without Glory in Arabia*, pp. 149, 171–2.

38. Lecture by Professor Tony Badger, Cambridge University, 21 November 2013.

39. Barbara Castle, *Fighting All the Way*, cited by Caroline Elkins in *Imperial Reckoning*, p. 139.

40. National Security Agency, 'Tempest: A Signal Problem'.

41. Peter Wright, *Spycatcher*, p. 112.

Chapter 5: Locks, Keys and Responsible Custodians

1. Government Response to the 30-Year Rule Review, February 2010.

2. Hansard, 21 January 2015.

3. FCO Records: Policy and Practice, London May 2013.

4. *Guardian*, 19 October 2013.

5. Richard Drayton, *Guardian*, 28 October 2013.

6. Philip Murphy, correspondence with author, December 2013.

7. David Williams, *Not in the Public Interest*, pp. 65–6.

8. Hansard, 30 June 1899.

9. TNA CAB 21/1659.

10. TNA CAB 128/31.

11. Review of the 30-Year Rule, January 2009.

12. Author telephone interview, August 2013.

13. Author interview, Hanslope Park, May 2015.

14. Lord Chancellor's Security and Intelligence Instrument, 11 October 2012.

15. Access to Public Records, The National Archives, July 2012.

16. Sir Alex Allan's Records Review, p. 16.

17. Advisory Council Annual Report 2012–13.

18. *International Journal of Cultural Property*, Vol. 8, No. 2, 1992, pp. 448–50 (Oxford University Press).

19. *Daily Mail*, 31 December 2015.

20. Report by the Cabinet Secretary into allegations of UK involvement in the Indian operation at Sri Harmandir Sahib, Amritsar in 1984.

21. Clive Ponting, *Secrecy in Britain*, p. 49.

22. Mike Rossiter, *The Spy Who Changed the World*, pp. 368–71.

23. National Archives Reclosure Panel figures, 2014, available at http://www.nationalarchives.gov.uk/documents/reclosure-panel-2014.pdf.

24. National Archives response to FoI request, February 2014, available at: http://www.nationalarchives.gov.uk/foi/requisitions-government-departments.htm.

25. *Guardian*, 26 April 2013.

26. Tony Badger lecture, Cambridge, November 2013.

27. Richard Drayton, *Britain's Secret Archive of Decolonisation*.

28. *The Times*, 15 April 2011.

29. Email exchanges between author and MoD officials and National Archives staff, August–October 2014.

30. Author telephone interview, August 2013.

31. Email exchange between MoD and author, June 2015.

32. Author interview, London, November 2014.

33. *Guardian*, 28 December 2005.

34. Ponting, *Secrecy in Britain*, p. 49.
35. Tony Blair, speech to the Campaign for Freedom of Information's annual awards ceremony, 25 March 1996.
36. Tony Blair, *A Journey*, p. 516.
37. *Guardian*, 26 October 2001.
38. Andrew Rawnsley, *Servants of the People*, pp. 375–6.
39. Blair, *A Journey*, pp. 126–7.
40. *Sunday Times*, 12 October 2008.
41. Author telephone interview, March 2014.
42. Jack Straw, *Last Man Standing*, pp. 276–87.
43. Cabinet Office newsletter *The Weekly*, 13 September 2004.
44. *Financial Times*, 17 June 2015.
45. Press release, Campaign for Freedom of Information, 25 April 2013.
46. See, for example, Cobain v Information Commissioner and the Crown Prosecution Service EA/2011/0112 & 0113.
47. Hansard, House of Lords, 6 November 2013.
48. Information Commissioner's Decision Notice FS50106800, 20 August 2008; Information Tribunal Appeal Number EA/2008/0078, 20 March 2009.
49. *Financial Times*, 20 September 2011.
50. *Financial Times*, 3 March 2012.
51. *Sun*, 4 September 2015.
52. *Sun*, 18 July 2015.
53. See, for example, Karına Urbach, in *Observer*, 19 July 2015.
54. *Guardian*, 16 October 2012.
55. *Daily Telegraph*, 10 July 2013.
56. *Guardian*, 4 June 2015.
57. Hansard, 23 June 2015.
58. *Guardian*, 9 October 2015.

Chapter 6: The Vault

1. BBC Panorama, *A Licence to Murder*, 19 June 2002.
2. Stevens Inquiry Overview and Recommendations, April 2003.
3. John Stevens, *Not for the Faint-Hearted*, p. 11.
4. BBC Panorama, *A Licence to Murder*, 19 June 2002.
5. Nelson's journal, author's copy.
6. Stevens, *Not for the Faint-Hearted*, p. 190.
7. Report of the Consultative Group on the Past, January 2009.

8. Stevens Enquiry 3, Overview and Recommendations, April 2003.

9. See, for example, Harry McCallion, *Killing Zone*, p. 45.

10. TNA PREM 15/1010.

11. Chris Ryder, *The Ulster Defence Regiment*, pp. 57–59.

12. *Irish News*, 1 July 1991.

13. Paul O'Connor and Alan Brecknell, 'British Counter-Insurgency Practice in Northern Ireland in the 1970s', p. 52.

14. David McKittrick et al., *Lost Lives*, p. 1475.

15. TNA CJ 4/1300.

16. Jeffry Sluka, *Death Squad: The Anthropology of State Terror*, p. 142.

17. Ryder, *The Ulster Defence Regiment*, pp. 181–2.

18. Ibid., p. 184.

19. Anne Cadwallader, *Lethal Allies*, pp. 91–2; Ryder, *The Ulster Defence Regiment*, pp. 182–3.

20. Historical Enquiries Team Report, Bowen, McKenna and McKenna, quoted in Cadwallader, *Lethal Allies*, p. 92.

21. De Silva Review, para 11.43.

22. Historical Enquiries Team Report, quoted in Cadwallader, *Lethal Allies*, pp. 116–17.

23. *Britain's Secret Terror Force*, BBC Panorama, 21 November 2013.

24. Martin Dillon, *The Dirty War*, p. 52.

25. Peter Taylor, *Brits*, p. 129.

26. Frank Kitson, *Bunch of Five*, p. 282.

27. Unpublished manuscript, author's copy.

28. Frank Kitson, *Gangs and Counter-Gangs*.

29. Unpublished manuscript, author's copy.

30. *Britain's Secret Terror Force*, BBC Panorama, 21 November 2013.

31. *Belfast Telegraph*, 3 May 1973.

32. TNA PREM 16/154.

33. McKittrick et al., *Lost Lives*, pp. 814–16.

34. Author interviews with retired RUC officers, Belfast and Antrim, February, August and September 2010.

35. Sir John Hermon, *Holding the Line*, pp. 119–20.

36. ACC J. A. Whiteside to C Department, 23 February 1981: Walker Report – Interchange of Intelligence Between Special Branch and CID.

37. *Sunday Times*, 28 January 2007.

38. De Silva Review, para 4.36.

39. Guidelines on the Use of Terrorist Informers, RUC ACC Wilfred Monaghan, February 1988.

40. Security Service Legal Advisor, 28 April 1989, de Silva para 4.52.

41. De Silva Review, para 4.38.

42. De Silva Review, para 4.78/9; *Collusion*, RTÉ Television, 15 June 2015.

43. See, for example, Rob Lewis, *Fishers of Men*, pp. 227–233.

44. Cory Collusion Report, Finucane, para 1.163.

45. De Silva Review, para 8.173/8.223.

46. *Sunday Times*, 28 January 2007.

47. Alan Simpson, *Duplicity and Deception*, pp. 31 and 35.

48. Johnston Brown, *Into the Dark*, p. 208.

49. De Silva Review para 6.7.

50. De Silva Review, paras 7.267/8.

51. Cory Collusion Report, Finucane, para 1.53.

52. Nelson's journal, author's copy.

53. Ibid.

54. Author interviews, London July 2012.

55. Author interviews, Belfast, July, September 2012.

56. Author interview, Belfast September 2012.

57. Nelson's journal.

58. Author interview, London, July 2012.

59. Relatives for Justice, 1995.

60. Cory Collusion Report, para 1.48.

61. Nelson's journal.

62. Cory Collusion Report, para 1.49.

63. Nelson's journal.

64. De Silva Review, para 7.272.

65. Cory Collusion Report, para 1.50.

66. Cory Collusion Report, para 1.154, De Silva, Vol. 2, pp. 70–74.

67. Cory Collusion Report, paras 1.58/7.99/1.60.

68. De Silva Review, para 7.284.

69. De Silva Executive Summary, para 49.

70. De Silva paras 11.9–11.21.

71. Taylor, *Brits*, p. 289.

72. Stevens, *Not for the Faint-Hearted*, pp. 191.

73. *Independent on Sunday*, 20 October 1991.

74. Cory Collusion Report, para 1.66.

75. De Silva Review, paras 7.135–7.138.

76. Cory Collusion Report, paras 112–116.
77. Cory Collusion Report, para 1.110.
78. Security Service memo, Belfast to London, quoted in de Silva Review, Chapter 15.
79. De Silva Review, paras 14.8–14.14; Cory Collusion Report, paras 1.257/9.
80. Hansard, 17 January 1989.
81. Simpson, *Duplicity and Deception*, p. 29.
82. Cory Collusion Report, para 1.264.
83. De Silva Review, para 117.
84. Stevens Enquiry 3, Overview and Recommendations, para 2.17.
85. De Silva Review, Executive Summary, para 87.
86. De Silva Review, Executive Summary, para 115.
87. Stevens, *Not for the Faint-Hearted*, p. 179.
88. De Silva Review, paras 1001–1004.
89. De Silva Review, paras 21.20–21.31.
90. De Silva Review, para 24.167–70.
91. De Silva Review, Executive Summary, para 106.
92. De Silva Review, Vol II, pp. 236–41.
93. De Silva Review, para 24.165 and Vol II, pp. 249–51.
94. De Silva Review, para 24.175.
95. De Silva Review, para 24.183.
96. *Belfast Telegraph*, 3 September 2003.
97. *Guardian*, 17 April 2003.
98. De Silva Review paras 18.67–69.
99. De Silva Review Executive Summary, paras 95/97; Brown, *Into the Dark*, p. 176.
100. Evidence to Joint Committee on the Draft Detention of Terrorist Suspects (Temporary Extension) Bills, 3 May 2011.
101. *Belfast Telegraph*, 20 April 2012.
102. Northern Ireland Life and Times Survey 2004.
103. Hansard, 12 December 2012.
104. *Irish Times*, 11 May 2015.
105. *Daily Telegraph*, 15 December 2012.
106. *Guardian*, 14 April 2014.
107. Author telephone interview, August 2013.
108. Inspection of the Police Service of Northern Ireland Historical Enquiries Team, HMIC 2013.
109. Press Association, 30 September 2014.

110. *Belfast Telegraph*, 3 June 2014.

111. Ulster TV, 12 September 2011.

112. Det Sgt, Regional Intelligence Unit, to Det Supt., CID South, 7 July 1998.

113. Det Supt (East) to Regional Head, CID South Region, 8 July 1998.

114. Police Authority for Northern Ireland's note of telephone conversation, 7 August 1998.

115. Stevens, *Not for the Faint-Hearted*, p. 200.

116. *Guardian*, 10 April 2007.

117. Email from Metropolitan Police to author, 26 June 2014.

118. Email from Metropolitan Police to author, 28 July 2014.

119. Minutes of the Northern Ireland Policing Board July 2013; *Belfast Telegraph*, 25 November 2014.

120. *Collusion*, RTÉ Television, 15 June 2015.

Chapter 7: Bodyguards of Lies

1. Michael Smith, *The Debs of Bletchley Park*, p. 21.

2. Jean Trumpington, *Coming Up Trumps*, p. 56.

3. Richard J. Aldrich, *GCHQ*, pp. 28–9, 43–4.

4. Aldrich, *GCHQ*, p. 60.

5. Winston Churchill, *The Second World War* Vol. V, p. 338.

6. Michael Howard, *British Intelligence in the Second World War*, Vol. 5, p. 107.

7. TNA HW 14/36.

8. Asa Briggs, *Secret Days*, pp 124–27.

9. Michael Smith, *The Secrets of Station X*, p. 281.

10. TNA CAB 103/288.

11. TNA HW 14/36.

12. Lecture given by Hinsley, Babbage Theatre, Computer Laboratory, University of Cambridge, 19 October 1993.

13. Smith, *The Debs of Bletchley Park*, p. 269.

14. Marion Hill, *Bletchley Park People*, pp. 129–30.

15. Ronald Lewin, *Ultra Goes to War*, p. 64.

16. TNA HW 14/83.

17. TNA HW 62/6.

18. TNA HW 42/15.

19. TNA CAB 103/288.

20. Richard J. Aldrich, *Policing the Past*, p. 928.

21. TNA CAB 81/130.
22. TNA HW 42/15.
23. Hill, *Bletchley Park People*, p. 129.
24. TNA HW 42/15.
25. Thomas Campbell and George C. Herring, *The Diaries of Edward R. Stettinius, Jr.*, p. 40.
26. TNA HW 42/15.
27. Matthew M. Aid, *The Secret Sentry*, p. 11.
28. *Guardian*, 25 June 2010.
29. Peter Freeman, *How GCHQ Came to Cheltenham*, p. 9.
30. Author telephone interview, May 2015.
31. Herbert Butterfield, *History and Human Relations*, pp. 186–199.
32. Władysław Kozaczuk, *Bitwa o Tajemnice: Sluzby wywiadowcze Polski i Rzeszy Niemieckiej 1922–1939*.
33. Gustave Bertrand, *Enigma: Ou la Plus Grande Enigma de la Guerre*.
34. Harold Deutsch, *The Historical Impact of Revealing the Ultra Secret*.
35. Ibid.
36. *Time Out*, 21 May 1976.
37. Ray Wilson and Ian Adams, *Special Branch*, p. 303.
38. Hansard, 2 February 1989.
39. TNA DEFE 47/34.
40. Clive Ponting, *Secrecy in Britain*, pp. 62–63.
41. Christopher Andrew, *The Defence of the Realm*, p. 322; Percy Sillitoe, *Cloak Without Dagger*, p. 177.
42. Andrew, *The Defence of the Realm*, p. 562.
43. Speech by the Director General of the Security Service, Jonathan Evans, at Bristol University, 15 October 2009.
44. Michael Goodman, *The Official History of the Joint Intelligence Committee*, Vol. 1, pp. 263–4.
45. Stella Rimington, *Open Secret*, pp. 163–4.
46. *The Defence Manual of Security*, paras 1013, 1701–13.
47. Wesley K. Wark, *In Never-Never Land?* p. 197.
48. Stephen Lander, *International Intelligence Cooperation: An Inside Perspective*, p. 485.
49. D. J. Cole, *Geoffrey Prime*, p. 112.
50. Ibid., p. 126.
51. Aldrich, *GCHQ*, pp. 371–4.
52. *Everyman*, BBC TV, 15 November 1987.
53. Cole, *Geoffrey Prime*, pp. 159–60.

54. *Sunday Times*, 31 October 1982.

55. Hansard, 11 November 1982.

56. Lander, *International Intelligence Cooperation*, p. 484.

57. Andrew, *The Defence of the Realm*, p. 766.

58. Rimington, *Open Secret* p. 242.

59. Hansard, 6 May 1992.

60. Author telephone interview, January 2012.

61. Gill Bennett, *Declassification and Release Policies of the UK's Intelligence Agencies*, p. 28.

62. Keith Jeffrey, *MI6*, p. xii.

63. *Independent*, 30 July 1998.

64. *Independent*, 24 September 1998.

65. *Daily Telegraph*, 2 October 2001.

66. See https://www.mi5.gov.uk/home/about-us/how-we-operate/managing-information/retention-and-destruction-of-files.html.

67. Bennett, *Declassification and Release Policies of the UK's Intelligence Agencies*, p. 27.

68. *Sunday Times*, 31 October 1982.

69. Hugh Lanning and Richard Norton-Taylor, *A Conflict of Loyalties*, p. 69.

70. Matthew M. Aid and Cees Wiebes, *Secrets of Signals Intelligence During the Cold War and Beyond*, p. 318.

71. *Guardian*, 1 August 2013.

72. James Bamford, *Body of Secrets*, pp. 404, 427–428.

73. European Parliament Report on the Existence of a Global System for the Interception of Private and Commercial Communications, July 2001.

74. Luke Harding, *The Snowden Files*, pp. 88–95.

75. *New York Times*, 16 December 2005.

76. Tweet by Thomas Drake, 9 June 2013.

77. *The Register*, 3 May 2009.

78. JUSTICE, *Freedom from Suspicion*, pp. 136–138.

79. *Guardian*, 1 August 2013.

80. Hansard, 22 June 1967.

81. Reuters, 14 November 2013.

82. Bloomberg News, 10 January 2014.

83. *Guardian*, 28 February 2014.

84. *Guardian*, 1 August 2013.

85. *Guardian*, 17 June 2013.

86. Glenn Greenwald, *No Place to Hide*, pp. 107–17.
87. Hansard, 4 November 2015.
88. *The Intercept*, 25 September 2015.

Chapter 8: Beyond Kafka

1. Geoffrey Robertson and Andrew Nicol, *Media Law*, p. 401.
2. Mike Dodd, 'Open and Shut Justice', published in Judith Townend (Ed.) 'Justice Wide Open' Working Papers, pp. 70–71.
3. Heather Brooke, *The Silent State*, p. 152.
4. Conway v. Rimmer (1968).
5. Hansard, 23 May 1940.
6. TNA ADM 116/4297.
7. John Lukacs, *Five Days in London: May 1940*, p. 27.
8. Joshua Levine, *Operation Fortitude*, p. 59.
9. TNA KV 2/1452.
10. Ibid.
11. Ibid.
12. TNA KV 2/1699.
13. TNA KV 2/107.
14. TNA KV 2/1699.
15. TNA HO 45/25595.
16. Ian Cobain, *Cruel Britannia*, p. 36.
17. TNA CAB 114/51.
18. Nigel West, *MI5*, pp. 257–8.
19. TNA HO 45/25595.
20. Stephen Dorril, *Blackshirt*, p. 337, p. 532.
21. Peter Caterall, *The Macmillan Diaries*, Vol II, p. 380.
22. Tom Bower, *The Perfect English Spy*, p. 268.
23. Nicholas Wilkinson, *Secrecy and the Media*, pp. 253, 518.
24. *Guardian, The Times*, 25 April 1961.
25. Thomas Grant, *Jeremy Hutchinson's Case Histories*, pp. 50–59.
26. Bower, *The Perfect English Spy*.
27. Hansard, 4 May 1961.
28. *New York Times*, 5 May 1961.
29. *Guardian*, 12 May 1961.
30. Kevin Boyle et al., *Law and State*, p. 67.
31. A. W. Brian Simpson, *In The Highest Degree Odious*, pp. 82–91.
32. House of Commons Constitutional Affairs Committee, Seventh Report of Session 2004–05, Vol 1, p. 19.

33. House of Commons Constitutional Affairs Committee: The Operation of the Special Immigration Appeals Commission and the Use of Special Advocates. March 2005, pp. 19–21.

34. Ian Cobain, *When Justice Won't Be Seen To Be Done*.

35. Hansard, 30 October 1997.

36. Guidance issued by Sir James Munby, President of the Family Division, 8 October 2015.

37. Al Rawi and Others v The Security Service and Others, July 2011, para 93.

38. MK and the Secretary of State for the Home Department, Appeal No SC/29/2004, 5 September 2006; *Daily Telegraph*, 12 October 2006.

39. *Guardian*, 16 December 2015.

40. *Guardian*, 22 and 23 January 2015.

41. Cory Collusion Report, p. 109.

42. Peter Cory, letter to Congressman Chris Smith, 15 March 2005, available at: http://www.rwuk.org/new/wp-content/uploads/2013/12/PatrickFinucaneCoryLetter.pdf.

43. *The Times*, 17 January 2009.

44. Ibid.

45. *Guardian*, 9 February 2009.

46. *London Review of Books*, 17 April 2014.

47. *Guardian*, 19 December 2008.

48. Hansard, 7 July 2009.

49. R (on the application of Binyam Mohamed) v Secretary of State for Foreign & Commonwealth Affairs [2010] EWCA Civ 65.

50. *London Review of Books*, 17 April 2014.

51. *Daily Mail*, 18 October 2011.

52. Justice and Security Green Paper, Cm 8194, October 2011.

53. *Mail on Sunday*, 8 January 2012.

54. *Guardian*, 15 October 2015.

55. *Evening Standard*, 26 March 2015.

56. *Guardian*, 12 October 2015.

57. *Guardian*, 9 February 2016.

58. *Guardian*, 14 October 2013.

59. *Guardian*, 6 February 2015.

60. *Guardian*, 5 March 2014.

61. Guardian News and Media Ltd and ors and R and Erol Incedal [2016] EWCA Crim 11.

62. HM Government Response to the Joint Committee on Human Rights, Legislative Scrutiny: Justice and Security Bill Cm 8533 HMSO, London, January 2013.

Bibliography

Books

Aid, Matthew M., *The Secret Sentry* (Bloomsbury Press, New York, 2010)

Aid, Matthew M., and Wiebes, Cees (eds), *Secrets of Signals Intelligence During the Cold War and Beyond* (Routledge, London, 2001)

Aitken, Jonathan, *Officially Secret* (Littlehampton, Worthing, 1971)

Akehurst, John, *We Won A War* (Michael Russell, Salisbury, 1982)

Aldrich, Richard J., *GCHQ* (HarperPress, London, 2011)

Aldrich, Richard J., *The Hidden Hand, Britain, America and Cold War Secret Intelligence* (John Murray, London, 2001)

Allen, Charles, *The Savage Wars of Peace* (Futura, London, 1991)

Andrew, Christopher, *The Defence of the Realm: The Authorized History of MI5* (Allen Lane, London, 2009)

Andrew, Christopher, *Her Majesty's Secret Service: The Making of the British Intelligence Community* (Viking Penguin, New York, 1985)

Ashdown, Paddy, *A Fortunate Life* (Aurum Press, London, 2009)

Asher, Michael, *The Regiment* (Penguin, London, 2008)

Bamford, James, *Body of Secrets* (Arrow Books, London, 2002)

Bamford, James, *The Puzzle Palace: America's National Security Agency and its Special Relationship with Britain's GCHQ* (Sidgwick & Jackson, London, 1983)

Barrymore Smith, Francis, *Radical Artisan, William James Linton 1812–97* (Manchester University Press, Manchester, 1973)

Bates, Stephen, *Asquith* (Haus Publishing, London, 2006)

Bayly, Christopher, and Harper, Tim, *Forgotten Wars: The End of Britain's Asian Empire* (Penguin, London, 2008)

Bell, Duncan (ed.), *Memory, Trauma and World Politics: Reflections of the Relationship Between Past and Present* (Palgrave Macmillan, Basingstoke, 2010)

Birkinshaw, Patrick, *Freedom of Information* (Cambridge University Press, Cambridge, 2010)

Black, Jeremy, *A Brief History of Slavery* (Constable & Robinson, London, 2011)

Blair, Tony, *A Journey* (Arrow, London, 2011)

Bloch, Jonathan, and Fitzgerald, Patrick, *British Intelligence and Covert Action* (Brandon, Dingle, 1983)

Bonner, David, *Executive Measure, Terrorism and National Security* (Ashgate, Aldershot, 2007)

Bower, Tom, *The Perfect English Spy: Sir Dick White and the Secret War 1935–90* (William Heinemann, London, 1995)

Boyle, Kevin, Hadden, Tom, and Hillyard, Paddy, *Law and State: The Case of Northern Ireland* (Martin Robertson, London, 1975)

Brendon, Piers, *The Decline and Fall of the British Empire* (Jonathan Cape, London, 2007)

Briggs, Asa, *Secret Days* (Frontline Books, Barnsley, 2011)

Brooke, Heather, *The Silent State* (William Heinemann, London, 2010)

Brown, Johnston, *Into The Dark: 30 Years in the RUC* (Gill & Macmillan, Dublin, 2006)

Bulloch, John, *MI5* (Corgi, London, 1963)

Burton, Antoinette (ed.), *Archive Stories: Facts, Fictions and the Writing of History* (Duke University Press, Durham, 2005)

Butterfield, Herbert, *History and Human Relations* (Collins, London, 1951)

Cadwallader, Anne, *Lethal Allies: British Collusion in Ireland* (Mercier Press, Cork, 2013)

Callwell, C. E., *Small Wars* (HM Stationery Office, London, 1906)

Campbell, Thomas, and Herring, George C., (eds), *The Diaries of Edward R. Stettinius, Jr.* (New Viewpoints, New York, 1975)

Carruthers, Susan L., *The Media at War* (Palgrave Macmillan, Basingstoke, 2011)

Carruthers, Susan L., *Winning Hearts and Minds: British Governments, the Media and Colonial Counter-Insurgency 1944–1960* (Leicester University Press, London, 1995)

Carver, Michael, *War Since 1945* (Weidenfeld and Nicolson, London, 1980)

Castle, Barbara, *Fighting All the Way* (Macmillan, London, 1993)

Caterall, Peter (ed.), *The Macmillan Diaries, Vol II* (Pan Macmillan, London, 2011)

Childers, Erskine, *The Riddle of the Sands* (Penguin, London, 1995)

Churchill, Winston, *The Second World War, Vol V* (Cassell, London, 1952)

Cobain, Ian, *Cruel Britannia: A Secret History of Torture* (Portobello, London, 2012)

Cohen, Nick, *You Can't Read This Book* (Fourth Estate, London, 2012)

Cole, D. J., *Geoffrey Prime: The Imperfect Spy* (Hale, London, 1998)

Connor, Ken, *Ghost Force, The Secret History of the SAS* (Cassell, London, 1998)

Cook, Judith, *The Price of Freedom* (New English Library, Sevenoaks, 1986)

Copeland, B. Jack and Others, *Colossus, The Secrets of Bletchley Park's Codebreaking Computers* (Oxford University Press, Oxford, 2006)

Craddock, Percy, *In Pursuit of British Interests, Reflections on Foreign Policy under Margaret Thatcher and John Major* (John Murray, London, 1997)

Crowdy, Terry, *Deceiving Hitler* (Osprey, London, 2008)

De La Billière, Peter, *Looking for Trouble* (HarperCollins, London, 1995)

Dewar, Michael, *Brush Fire Wars: Minor Campaigns of the British Armey Since 1945* (Robert Hale, London, 1990)

Dillon, Martin, *The Dirty War* (Arrow, London, 1990)

Dorril, Stephen, *Blackshirt: Sir Oswald Mosley and British Fascism* (Penguin Books, London, 2006)

Dorril, Stephen, *MI6: Fifty Years of Special Operations* (Fourth Estate, London, 2001)

Dorril, Stephen, *The Silent Conspiracy* (Mandarin, London, 1994)

Edwards, Aaron, *Defending the Realm? The Politics of Britain's Small Wars Since 1945* (Manchester University Press, Manchester, 2012)

Elkins, Caroline, *Imperial Reckoning: The Untold Story of Britain's Gulag in Kenya* (Henry Holt and Company, New York, 2005)

Ferguson, Niall, *Empire: How Britain Made the Modern World* (Allen Lane, London, 2003)

Fiennes, Ranulph, *Where Soldiers Fear to Tread* (Hodder and Stoughton, London, 1975)

Freeman, Peter, *How GCHQ Came to Cheltenham* (Government Communications Headquarters, Cheltenham, 2005)

French, David, *The British Way in Counter-Insurgency 1945–1967* (Oxford University Press, Oxford, 2011)

Fry, Helen, *Churchill's German Army* (The History Press, Stroud, 2009)

Fry, Helen, *The M Room* (CreateSpace, Amazon, 2012)

Gannon, Paul, *Colossus: Bletchley Park's Last Secret* (Atlantic Books, London, 2006)

Gardiner, Ian, *In the Service of the Sultan: A First Hand Account of the Dhofar Insurgency* (Pen & Sword, Barnsley, 2006)

Geraghty, Tony, *Who Dares Wins: The Story of the SAS 1950–1980* (Fontana, London, 1980)

Goodman, Michael, *The Official History of the Joint Intelligence Committee: Volume I* (London, Routledge, 2014)

Gordon Walker, Patrick, *The Cabinet* (Jonathan Cape, London, 1970)

Grant, Thomas, *Jeremy Hutchinson's Case Histories* (John Murray, London, 2015)

Greenberg, Joel, *Gordon Welchman: Bletchley Park's Architect of Ultra Intelligence* (Frontline, Barnsley, 2014)

Greenwald, Glenn, *No Place to Hide: Edward Snowden, the NSA and the Surveillance State* (Hamish Hamilton, London, 2014)

Grob-Fitzgibbon, Benjamin, *Imperial Endgame: Britain's Dirty Wars and the End of Empire* (Palgrave Macmillan, London, 2011)

Haines, Joe, *The Politics of Power* (London: Coronet, 1977)

Halliday, Fred, *Arabia Without Sultans* (Penguin, London, 1974)

Harding, Luke, *The Snowden Files* (Guardian/Faber and Faber, London, 2014)

Hart-Davis, Duff, *The War That Never Was* (Arrow Books, London, 2012)

Hennessy, Peter, *Distilling the Frenzy* (Biteback, London, 2013)

Hennessy, Peter, *The Secret State: Preparing for the Worst 1945–2010* (Penguin, London, 2010)

Hennessy, Peter, *Whitehall* (Secker & Warburg, London, 1989)

Hermiston, Roger, *The Greatest Traitor: The Secret Lives of Agent George Blake* (Aurum Press, London, 2013)

Hermon, Sir John, *Holding the Line: An Autobiography* (Gill & Macmillan, Dublin, 1997)

Hill, Marion, *Bletchley Park People: Churchill's Geese That Never Cackled* (The History Press, Stroud, 2012)

Hinchcliffe, Peter, Ducker, John T., and Holt, Maria, *Without Glory in Arabia: The British Retreat from Aden* (I.B. Tauris, London, 2006)

Hinsley, F., et al., *British Intelligence in the Second World War*, Vols. 1–5 (HMSO, London, 1979–90)

Hodges, Andrew, *Alan Turing: The Enigma* (Vintage, London, 2012)

Holroyd, Fred, and Burbridge, Nick, *War Without Honour* (Medium Publishing, Hull, 1989)

Holt, Thaddeus, *The Deceivers: Allied Military Deception in the Second World War* (Phoenix, London, 2005)

Hooper, David, *Official Secrets: the Use and Abuse of the Act* (Secker & Warburg, London, 1987)

Horton, Scott, *The Lords of Secrecy* (Nation Books, New York, 2015)

Howard, Michael, *British Intelligence in the Second World War Volume 5* (HMSO, London, 1989)

Howard, Michael, *War and the Liberal Conscience* (Oxford University Press, Oxford, 1989)

Howarth, Patrick, *Intelligence Chief Extraordinary: The Life of the Ninth Duke of Portland* (Bodley Head, London, 1986)

Hoy, Hugh Cleland, *40 O.B., Or How the War Was Won* (Hutchinson, London, 1932)

Hughes, Geraint, *Harold Wilson's Cold War: The Labour Government and East–West Politics 1964–1970* (Royal Historical Society, Woodbridge, 2009)

Jackson, Robert, *The Malayan Emergency & Indonesian Confrontation* (Pen & Sword, Barnsley, 2011)

James, Lawrence, *Imperial Rearguard: Wars of Empire 1919–85* (Brassey's, London, 1988)

Jeapes, Tony, *SAS Secret War* (HarperCollins, London, 2000)

Jeffrey, Keith, *MI6: The History of the Secret Intelligence Service* (Bloomsbury, London, 2011)

Johnson, John, *The Evolution of British Sigint 1653–1939* (Government Communications Headquarters, Cheltenham, 1998)

Kafka, Franz, *The Trial* (Penguin Books, London, 2000)

Kane, Ray, *Coup D'état Oman* (Smashwords Edition, 2012)

Kitson, Frank, *Bunch of Five* (Faber and Faber, London, 1977)

Kitson, Frank, *Gangs and Counter-Gangs* (Barrie and Rockliff, London, 1960)

Kitson, Frank, *Low Intensity Operations: Subversion, Insurgency, Peacekeeping* (Faber and Faber, London, 1971)

Knightley, Phillip, *The First Casualty* (Pan, London, 1989)

Lanning, Hugh, and Norton-Taylor, Richard, *A Conflict of Loyalties:*

GCHQ 1984–1991 (New Clarion Press, Cheltenham, 1991)

Lapping, Brian, *End of Empire* (Granada, London, 1985)

Lashmar, Paul, and Oliver, James, *Britain's Secret Propaganda War 1948–1977* (Sutton Publishing, Stroud, 1998)

Leigh, David, *The Frontiers of Secrecy: Closed Government in Britain* (Junction Books, London, 1980)

Le Queux, William, *The Invasion of 1910, With a Full Account of the Siege of London* (Eveleigh Nash, London, 1906)

Levine, Joshua, *Operation Fortitude* (HarperCollins, London, 2011)

Lewin, Ronald, *Ultra Goes to War: The Secret Story* (Penguin, London, 2001)

Lewis, Rob, *Fishers of Men* (Hodder and Stoughton, London, 2000)

Lowe, Keith, *Savage Continent: Europe in the Aftermath of World War II* (Penguin, London, 2013)

Lukacs, John, *Five Days in London May 1940* (Yale Nota Bene, Yale, 2001)

McCallion, Harry, *Killing Zone* (Bloomsbury, London, 1996)

McGrattan, Cillian, *Memory, Politics and Identity: Haunted by History* (Palgrave Macmillan, Basingstoke, 2013)

McGuffin, John, *Internment* (Anvil Books, Tralee, 1973)

Mackenzie, Compton, *Greek Memories* (Biteback Publishing, London, 2011)

McKittrick, David, Kelters, Seamus, Feeney, Brian, and Thornton, Chris, *Lost Lives* (Mainstream, Edinburgh, 2000)

MacMillan, Margaret, *The Uses and Abuses of History* (Profile Books, London, 2009)

Marr, Andrew, *The Making of Modern Britain* (Macmillan, London, 2010)

Marr, David G., *Vietnam 1945: The Quest for Power* (University of California Press, Berkeley, 1995)

Masterman, John, *The Double-Cross System in the War of 1939 to 1945* (History Book Club, London, 1972)

Matthews, Kenneth, *Memories of a Mountain War: Greece 1944–1949* (Longman, London, 1972)

Miller, David (ed.), *Tell Me Lies: Propaganda and Media Distortion in the Attack on Iraq* (Pluto, London, 2004)

Mockaitis, Thomas, *British Counterinsurgency in the Post-Imperial Era* (Manchester University Press, Manchester, 1995)

Moran, Christopher, *Classified: Secrecy and the State in Modern Britain* (Cambridge University Press, Cambridge, 2013)

Moynihan, Daniel Patrick, *Secrecy* (Yale University Press, New Haven, 1998)

Murray, Raymond, *The SAS in Ireland* (Mercier, Dublin, 1990)

Neville, Peter, *Britain in Vietnam: Prelude to Disaster, 1945–46* (Routledge, London, 2007)

Newsinger, John, *The Blood Never Dried: A People's History of the British Empire* (Bookmarks, London, 2006)

Omand, David, *Securing the State* (Hurst, London, 2010)

Peirce, Gareth, *Dispatches from the Dark Side* (Verso, London, 2010)

Pincher, Chapman, *Dangerous to Know: A Life* (Biteback, London, 2014)

Piper, Leonard, *Dangerous Waters: The Tragedy of Erskine Childers* (Hambledon, London, 2003)

Pocock, Tom, *Fighting General* (Collins, London, 1973)

Ponting, Clive, *Secrecy in Britain* (Basil Blackwell, Oxford, 1990)

Prasad, B., Bhargava, K. D., and Khera, P. N. (eds), *Official History of the Indian Army in the Second World War 1939–45* (Orient Longman, Calcutta, 1958)

Punch, Maurice, *State Violence, Collusion and the Troubles* (Pluto Press, London, 2012)

Ratcliffe, Peter, *Eye of the Storm* (Michael O'Mara Books, London, 2001)

Rawnsley, Andrew, *Servants of the People: The Inside Story of New Labour* (Hamish Hamilton, London, 2000)

Reynolds, David, *Britannia Overruled: British Policy and World Power in the 20th Century* (Longman, London, 1991)

Richter, Heinz, *British Intervention in Greece: From Varkiza to Civil War* (Merlin, London, 1985)

Rimington, Stella, *Open Secret: The Autobiography of the Former Director-General of MI5* (Arrow, London, 2002)

Roberts, Alasdair, *Blacked Out: Government Secrecy in the Information Age* (Cambridge University Press, New York, 2006)

Robertson, Geoffrey, *The Justice Game* (Vintage, 1999, London)

Robertson, Geoffrey, and Nicol, Andrew, *Media Law* (Penguin Books, London, 2002)

Robertson, K. G., *Public Secrets: A Study in the Development of Government Secrecy* (Macmillan, London, 1982)

Rolston, Bill, *Turning the Page Without Closing the Book: The Right to Truth in the Irish Context* (Irish Reporter Publications, Dublin, 1996)

Rosie, George, *The British in Vietnam* (Panther, London, 1970)

Rossiter, Mike, *The Spy Who Changed the World* (Headline, London, 2014)

Rowe, Dorothy, *Why We Lie* (Fourth Estate, London, 2010)

Ryder, Chris, *The Ulster Defence Regiment: An Instrument of Peace?* (Methuen, London, 1992)

Searle, Pauline, *Dawn Over Oman* (George Allen and Unwin, London, 1979)

Seeley, J. E. B., *Adventure* (Heinemann, London, 1930)

Shils, Edward A., *The Torment of Secrecy* (Elephant Paperbacks, Chicago, 1996)

Sillitoe, Percy, *Cloak Without Dagger* (Pan, London, 1956)

Simpson, Alan, *Duplicity and Deception: Policing the Twilight Zone of the Troubles* (Brandon, Dingle, 2010)

Simpson, A. W. Brian, *In The Highest Degree Odious: Detention Without Trial in Wartime Britain* (Oxford University Press, Oxford, 1992)

Simpson, Kirk, *Truth Recovery in Northern Ireland: Critically Interpreting the Past* (Manchester University Press, Manchester, 2013)

Sluka, Jeffrey (ed.), *Death Squad: The Anthropology of State Terror* (University of Pennsylvania Press, Philadelphia, 2000)

Smith, Michael, *The Debs of Bletchley Park* (Aurum, London, 2015)

Smith, Michael, *The Secrets of Station X* (Biteback, London, 2011)

Snow, Edgar, *The Other Side of the River* (Gollancz, London, 1963)

Stevens, John, *Not for the Faint-Hearted* (Phoenix, London, 2006)

Straw, Jack, *Last Man Standing: Memoirs of a Political Survivor* (Pan Books, London, 2013)

Takriti, Abdel Razzaq, *Monsoon Revolution, Republicans, Sultans and Empires in Oman 1965–1976* (Oxford University Press, Oxford, 2013)

Taylor, Peter, *Brits: The War Against the IRA* (Bloomsbury, London, 2001)

Thompson, Julian, *The Imperial War Museum Book of Modern Warfare* (Sidgwick and Jackson, Basingstoke, 2002)

Thomson, George, *The Blue Pencil Admiral: The Inside Story of Press Censorship* (Sampson Low, Marston & Co, London, 1947)

Thorne, Christopher, *Allies of a Kind* (Oxford University Press, Oxford, 1978)

Thurlow, Richard, *The Secret State: British Internal Security in the 20th Century* (Blackwell, Oxford, 1994)

Tonge, Jonathan, *Northern Ireland* (Polity, Cambridge, 2006)

Towle, Philip, *Going to War: British Debates from Wilberforce to Blair* (Palgrave Macmillan, London, 2009)

Townend, Judith (ed.), *Justice Wide Open: Working Papers* (City University London, 2012)

Trumpington, Jean, *Coming Up Trumps: A Memoir* (Macmillan, London, 2014)

Unwin, Margaret, *Counter-Gangs: A History of Undercover Military Units in Northern Ireland 1971–1976* (Spinwatch, Glasgow, 2012)

Van der Bijl, *Confrontation: The War With Indonesia, 1962–1966* (Pen & Sword, Barnsley, 2007)

Vincent, David, *The Culture of Secrecy: Britain 1832–1998* (Oxford University Press, Oxford, 1998)

Vinen, Richard, *National Service: Conscription in Britain 1945–1963* (Allen Lane, London, 2014)

Welchman, Gordon, *The Hut Six Story: Breaking the Enigma Codes* (Penguin, London, 1982)

West, Nigel, *The A to Z of British Intelligence* (Scarecrow Press, Lanham, 2009)

West, Nigel, *A Matter of Trust: MI5 1945–72* (Weidenfeld and Nicolson, London, 1982)

West, Nigel, *MI5: The True Story of the Most Secret Counterespionage Organization in the World* (Military Heritage Press, New York, 1981)

Wilkinson, Nicholas, *Secrecy and the Media: The Official History of the United Kingdom's D-Notice System* (Routledge, Abingdon, 2009)

Williams, David, *Not in the Public Interest: The Problem of Security in Democracy* (Hutchinson, London, 1965)

Wilson, Des (ed.), *The Secrets File* (Heinemann, London, 1984)

Wilson, Harold, *The Labour Government 1964–70* (Pelican, London, 1974)

Winter, Jay, *Remembering War* (Yale University Press, New Haven, 2006)

Winterbotham, F. W., *The Ultra Secret* (Futura, London, 1974)

Winterbotham, F. W., *The Ultra Spy: An Autobiography* (Papermac, London, 1991)

Wright, Peter, *Spycatcher: The Candid Autobiography of a Senior Intelligence Officer* (Viking, New York, 1987)

Yardley, Herbert O., *The American Black Chamber* (Ballantine Books, New York, 1981)

Articles

Aiken, N. T., 'Learning to Live Together: Transitional Justice and Intergroup Reconciliation in Northern Ireland', *International Journal of Transitional Justice*, Vol. 4, No. 2, 2010, 166–88

Aldrich, Richard J., 'Never-Never Land and Wonderland? British and American Policy on Intelligence Archives', *Contemporary Record*, Vol. 8, No. 1, 1994, 133–52

Aldrich, Richard J., 'Policing the Past: Official History, Secrecy and British Intelligence Since 1945', *English Historical Review*, Vol. CXIX, No. 483

Aldrich, Richard J., 'The Waldegrave Initiative and Secret Service Archives: New Materials and New Policies', *Intelligence and National Security*, Vol 10, No. 1, 1995

Anderson, David, 'Guilty Secrets: Deceit, Denial and the Discovery of Kenya's "Migrated Archive"', *History Workshop Journal*, No. 80, 2015

Anderson, David, 'Mau Mau in the High Court and the 'Lost' British Empire Archives: Colonial Conspiracy or Bureaucratic Bungle?' *Journal of Imperial and Commonwealth History*, 39, 2011

Anonymous, 'Tempest: A Signal Problem', *Cryptological Spectrum*, Vol. 2, No. 3, National Security Agency, Maryland, USA, 1972

Badger, Anthony, 'Historians, a Legacy of Suspicion and the Migrated Archives', *Small Wars & Insurgencies*, Vol. 23, Nos 4–5, 2012

Banton, Mandy, 'History Concealed; Justice Denied? (Mis)management of the Records of Britain's Colonial Dependencies'. Paper presented at the Institute of Commonwealth Studies, London, 29 May 2014

Bell, C., 'Dealing with the Past in Northern Ireland', *Fordham International Law Journal*, Vol. 26, No. 4, 2003, 1095–1147

Bennett, Gill, 'Declassification and Release Policies of the UK's Intelligence Agencies', *Intelligence and National Security*, Vol. 17, No. 1, 2002, 21–32

Burt, Alistair, 'Vote that Ties Britain's Hands', *The World Today*, Vol. 70, No. 1, February 2014, Royal Institute of International Affairs

Campbell, Duncan, 'Official Secrecy and British Libertarianism', *Socialist Register*, Vol. 16, 1979

Campbell, Duncan, 'Somebody's Listening', *New Statesman*, 12 August 1988

Campbell, Duncan, and Hosenball, Mark, 'The Eavesdroppers', *Time Out*, 21 May 1976

Carruthers, Susan L., 'No One's Looking: The Disappearing Audience for War', *Media, War & Conflict*, Vol. 1, No. 70, 2008

Cobain, Ian, 'When Justice Won't be Seen to be Done', *British Journalism Review*, July 2012

Crossman, Richard, 'The Real English Disease', *New Statesman*, 24 September 1971

Deutsch, Harold, 'The Historical Impact of Revealing the Ultra Secret', *Journal of the US Army War College*, Vol. VII, No. 3, 1977

Drayton, Richard, 'Britain's Secret Archive of Decolonisation', History Workshop Online, April 2012, available at: http://www.historyworkshop.org.uk/britains-secret-archive-of-decolonisation/

Elegant, Robert, 'How to Lose A War: The Press and Viet Nam', *Encounter*, August 1981, available at: http://academics.wellesley.edu/Polisci/wj/Vietnam/Readings/elegant.htm

Hampshire, Edward, 'Apply the Flame More Searingly: The Destruction and Migration of the Archives of British Colonial Administration: A Southeast Asia Case Study', *Journal of Imperial and Commonwealth History*, Vol. 41, No. 2, May 2013, 334–52

Hegarty, A., 'The Government of Memory: Public Inquiries and the Limits of Justice in Northern Ireland', *Fordham International Law Journal*, Vol. 26, No. 4, 2003, 1148–92

Howard, Michael, 'The Use and Abuse of Military History', *RUSI Journal*, February 1993

Jamieson, Ruth, and McEvoy, Kieran, 'State Crime by Proxy and Juridical Othering', *British Journal of Criminology*, Vol. 45, No. 4, July 2005, 504–27

Johnson, Thomas J., and Fahmy, Shahira, 'Embeds' Perceptions of Censorship: Can You Criticize a Soldier Then Have Breakfast With Him in the Morning?' *Mass Communication and Society*, Vol. 12, No. 1, 52–77

Knightley, Phillip, 'There's More to This', *British Journalism Review*, Vol. 25, No. 3, September 2014

Ladwig, Walter C. (2008) 'Supporting Allies in Counterinsurgency: Britain and the Dhofar Rebellion', *Small Wars & Insurgencies*, Vol. 19, No. 1, 62–88

Lander, Stephen, 'International Intelligence Cooperation: An Inside

Perspective', *Cambridge Review of International Affairs*, Vol. 17, No. 3, 2004, 481–93

Lewis, Justin, et al., 'Too Close for Comfort? The Role of Embedded Reporting during the 2003 Iraq War: Summary Report', Cardiff School of Journalism, 2004

McGovern, Mark, 'Inquiring into Collusion? Collusion, the State and the Management of Truth Recovery in Northern Ireland', *State Crime*, Vol. 2, No. 1, 4–29

McNamara, L., and Lock, D., 'Closed Material Procedures Under the Justice and Security Act 2013: A Review of the First Report by the Secretary of State', Bingham Centre Working Paper 2014/03, Bingham Centre for the Rule of Law, BIICL, London, August 2014

Melvern, Linda, Hosenball, Mark, Knightley, Phillip, and Anning, Nick, 'Exit Smiley, Enter IBM', *Sunday Times*, 31 October 1982

O'Connor, Paul, and Brecknell, Alan, 'British Counter-Insurgency Practice in Northern Ireland in the 1970s – A Legitimate Response or State Terror?' In Scott Poynting and David Whyte (eds), *Counter-Terrorism and State Political Violence: The 'War on Terror' as Terror*, Routledge, New York, 2012

Pfau, Michael, et al., 'Embedded Reporting during the Invasion and Occupation of Iraq: How Embedding of Journalists Affects Television News Reports', *Journal of Broadcasting & Electronic Media*, Vol. 49, No. 4, 468–87

Phillips, Nicholas, 'Closed Material', *London Review of Books*, Vol. 36, No. 8, 17 April 2014

Porter, Bernard, 'Boarder or Day Boy', *London Review of Books*, Vol. 21, No. 14, 15 July 1999

Purnell, Nicholas, 'Closed Material Procedures, Rudi Dutschke and King's', *King's Review*, London, 2013

Purvis, Stewart, 'What are they so anxious to hide?' *British Journalism Review*, June 2014

Salisbury, Harrison, 'Big Brother is Listening to You', *The Progressive*, November 1980

Shepherd, Elizabeth, 'Freedom of Information, Right to Access Information, Open Data: Who is at the Table?' *The Round Table*, Vol. 104, No. 6, December 2015

Sloan, Lawrence D., 'ECHELON and the Legal restraints on Signals

Intelligence: A Need for Reevaluation', *Duke Law Journal*, Vol. 50, No. 5, March 2001

Spencer, M., and Spencer, J., 'Coping with Conway v. Rimmer [1968] AC 910: How Civil Servants Control Access to Justice', *Journal of Law and Society*, 37, 2010, 387–411

Tordella, Louis, 'The Ultra Secret by F. W. Winterbotham – Review', *Centre for the Study of Intelligence*, Vol. 19, No. 3, Central Intelligence Agency, Declassified July 1996

Troeller, Gordian, and Deffarge, Marie-Claude, 'Secret War No. 11', *Atlas Magazine*, Vol. 18, No. 5, November 1969

Walsh, Patrick F., and Miller, Seumas (2015) 'Rethinking "Five Eyes" Security Intelligence Collection Policies and Practice Post Snowden', *Intelligence and National Security*

Wark, Wesley K., 'In Never-Never Land? The British Archives on Intelligence', *The Historical Journal*, Vol. 35, 1992, 195–203

Wingen, John, and Tillema, Herbert, 'British Military Intervention After World War II: Militance in a Second-Rank Power', *Journal of Peace Research*, Vol. XVII, No. 4, 1980

Unpublished Diaries

Krull, Germaine, *Diary of Saigon Following the Allied Occupation, September 1945*, available at: http://www.vietnam.ttu.edu/virtualarchive/items.php?item=2410207001

Nelson, Brian, personal journal, 1991–2, author's copy

Reports and Manuals

30 Year Rule Review, HMSO, January 2009

Allan, Sir Alex, 'Records Review', Cabinet Office, November 2014

Amnesty International, Northern Ireland, 'Time to Deal with the Past', September 2013

'An Agreement among the Parties of the Northern Ireland Executive on Parades, Select Commemorations, and Related Protests; Flags and Emblems; and Contending with the Past' (Final Haass Proposal), 31 December 2013

Cary, Anthony, 'The Migrated Archives: What Went Wrong and What Lessons Should We Draw?' FCO, February 2011

Consultative Group on the Past, 'Report of the Consultative Group of the Past', Belfast, Consultative Group on the Past, 2009

Cory, Peter, 'Collusion Report – Pat Finucane', HMSO, London, 2004

Departmental Committee on Section 2 of the Official Secrets Act 1911 (Franks Report), HMSO, London, 1972

De Silva, Desmond, 'The Report of the Patrick Finucane Review', HMSO, London, December 2012

Government Response to the 30 Year Rule Review, Cm 7882, HMSO, February 2010

Heywood, Sir Jeremy, 'Allegations of UK Involvement in the Indian Operation at Sri Harmandir Sahib, Amritsar 1984', Cabinet Office, February 2014

House of Commons Constitutional Affairs Committee, 'The Operation of the Special Immigration Appeals Commission (SIAC) and the Use of Special Advocates', Seventh Report of Session 2004–05, Vol. 1

House of Commons Northern Ireland Affairs Committee, 'Ways of Dealing with Northern Ireland's Past: Interim Report – Victims and Survivors', Government's Response to the Committee's Tenth Report of Session 2004–2005, HMSO, London, 2005

House of Lords Select Committee on the Inquiries Act, 'The Inquiries Act 2005: Post-Legislative Scrutiny', HMSO, London, 2014

Inspection of the Police Service of Northern Ireland Historical Enquiries Team, HMIC 2013

Intelligence and Security Committee Annual Report 2006-2007, Cm 7299, HMSO, London, 2008

JUSTICE, 'Freedom from Suspicion: Surveillance Reform for a Digital Age', October 2011

Maer, Lucinda, and Gay, Oonagh, 'Official Secrecy', House of Commons Library, 30 December 2008

Maer, Lucinda, 'Freedom of Information and the Royal Family', House of Commons Library Briefing Paper, 13 May 2015

'Modern Public Records: Selection and Access' (The Wilson Report), Cmd. 8204, HMSO, London, 1981

Relatives for Justice (1995) 'Collusion 1990–1994: Loyalist Paramilitary Murders in the North of Ireland', Derry, Relatives for Justice

Research Paper 96/16 25 January 1996, House of Commons Library

Schmid, Gerhard, 'Report on the Existence of a Global System for the Interception of Private and Commercial Communications (ECHELON Interception System)', European Parliament, July 2001

Summary of the Report of the Deputy Chief Constable of Cambridgeshire John Stevens, into Allegations of Collusion between Members of the Security Forces and Loyalist Paramilitaries (Stevens 1), Cambridgeshire Constabulary, 17 May 1990

'The Apparatus of Impunity? Human Rights Violations and the Northern Ireland Conflict', Committee on the Administration of Justice, January 2015

The Defence Manual of Security, Volumes 1, 2 and 3, No. 2, Ministry of Defence, London, October 2001

Watson, Fiona M., 'The Scott Inquiry' Approaching Publication Research Paper 96/16 25 January 1996, House of Commons Library

Acknowledgements

I owe an enormous debt to a great many people for the assistance I have received while researching and writing this book. Some, due to the nature of some of the subject matter, would doubtless wish to remain unnamed.

I am grateful to Kate Shaw of the Viney Agency, who saw that the themes of concealment and denial that emerged in my first book, *Cruel Britannia*, could be explored more broadly in a study of British official secrecy.

I am once more indebted to Laura Barber, my editor at Portobello Books, for her skill and good sense, and for her complete dedication to this book. My thanks go also to Ka Bradley, Iain Chapple, Pru Rowlandson and all the other members of the Portobello team.

I am grateful for the assistance of Martin Soames, and for the good advice that he offered after reading the manuscript.

Very special thanks go to a great many librarians and archivists, including those at the National Archives, the British Library, the Imperial War Museum, the Linen Hall Library, the Public Record Office of Northern Ireland, the House of Commons Library and the *Guardian*. Thanks go also to the staff at Bletchley Park, David Stanley and John Pether at the National Museum of Computing, and Debbie Usher and Kaya Wawrzak at the Middle East Centre, St Antony's College, Oxford.

I would like to thank Peter Riddell for the advice that he offered after reading the sections of Chapter 1 that concern the Privy Council and the development of ministerial and collective responsibility, and Anne Cadwallader and Paul O'Connor for their advice on the passages in Chapter 6 that concern the Historical Enquiries Team and the Ulster Defence Regiment.

Some people deserve particular thanks for the various ways in which they have assisted me. They are Maurice Frankel for sharing his understanding of New Labour's early antipathy to its own Freedom of Information Act; Ben Jaffey for his assistance in helping me understand aspects of the Investigatory Powers Tribunal; Joshua Levine for pointing me in the right direction when I was researching the Treachery Act trials; Barry McCaffrey for being so generous with both his time and his knowledge; Tommy Norton for helping me to spot one or two matters that had eluded me; Richard Norton-Taylor for nurturing my trouble-making tendencies; Mike Rossiter for alerting me to the disappearance of historical documentation concerning Klaus Fuchs; William St Clair for helping me to navigate some of the murkier passages of the Public Records Acts; and Nick Wilkinson for his generous advice when I was researching the D-Notice system.

Anthony Hudson, Zoe Norden and Ben Silverstone deserve thanks not only from me, but from the wider public for their efforts to bring into the public domain some of the hidden aspects of the Erol Incedal case.

To Abdel Razzaq Takriti, historian of our war in Dhofar, and to Ian Gardiner and Steve Pratt, who fought and lost friends there, I offer my heartfelt thanks.

So many other people offered assistance, information and advice while I was researching this book, and I am grateful to them all: Matthew Aid, Richard Aldrich, Tayab Ali, Peter Allen, Prof David Anderson, David Anderson QC, Tony Badger, Mandy Banton, Stephen Bates, David Benest, Huw Bennett, Douglas

Bernhardt, Raju Bhatt, Jonathan Bloch, David Bonner, Owen Bowcott, Alan Brecknell, Heather Brooke, David Brown, both Duncan Campbells, Dominic Casciani, Nick Cohen, Patricia Coyle, Kat Craig, Simon Creighton, Cori Crider, Michael Culbert, Jonathan Dingle, Liam Diver, Stephen Dorril, Richard Drayton, Aaron Edwards, Caroline Elkins, Katie Engelhart, Rob Evans, Terry Fairfield, Nick Fielding, John Gearson, Rosa Gilbert, Harry Gow, Ben Griffin, Clara Gutteridge, Luke Harding, Anna Hartt, Paddy Hillyard, Daniel Holder, Alexander Horne, Scott Horton, Alison Houston, John Jackson, Nigel Jones, Maeve Kennedy, Paul Lashmar, Dan Leader, Noel Little, David Lowry, Margaret MacMillan, Sapna Malik, Charlotte McDonald-Gibson, Kieran McEvoy, Gemma McKeown, Lawrence McNamara, Allison Morris, Andrée Murphy, Niall Murphy, Philip Murphy, Raymond Murray, Richard Nelsson, Pádraig Ó Muirigh, Hugh Orde, Aidan O'Toole, Gareth Peirce, Simon Prince, Emma Rogan, David Rose, Alice Ross, Alan Simpson, Rebecca Simpson, Paul Stevenson, Katy Stoddard, John Teggart, Mark Thompson, Lexy Topping, Alan Travis, Margaret Urwin, Susan Williams, Kevin Winters and Paul Woolwich. I apologise to anyone whom I have inadvertently omitted from this list.

Once again, I would like to thank my wife Jackie and children Max and Kate for their patience.

Finally, I believe I should acknowledge a debt of gratitude to all those politicians, civil servants, intelligence officers, Whitehall 'information officers', government lawyers, 'strategic communications consultants' and assorted desk wallahs who have attempted, over several decades, to frustrate my attempts and those of my colleagues to keep the public informed: your efforts have always inspired me to try harder.

Index

Keep in touch with
Portobello Books:

f t

Visit portobellobooks.com to discover more.

CRUEL BRITANNIA

A Secret History of Torture

WINNER OF THE PADDY POWER TOTAL POLITICS DEBUT BOOK OF THE YEAR AWARD

'A fine study of the role Britain has played in the business of torture'
Sunday Times 'Must Read'

'In one of the most shocking and persuasive books of the year,
Ian Cobain details not just British complicity in torture but the
longstanding practice of the thing itself, and the lies British politicians
have always told, and are still telling, to cover it up' David Hare

'Ian Cobain's particularly fine book [shows] . . . what's been done
under the aegis of the British state [and] will shock anyone who
cherishes civilised values' *Metro*

'*Cruel Britannia* makes it clear that a culture of secrecy doesn't just serve
to protect the elite but is also the soil in which the worst aspects of
humanity can take root and grow. This is a shocking book that deserves
a wide readership . . . to ignore its findings would be to grant impunity
to actions that reveal the worst of human behaviour' *New Statesman*

'Utterly gripping . . . I will not forget what I have learnt from this
book, and I will be telling others about it for years to come' PJ Harvey

'A dramatic challenge to official dishonesty and public complacency,
past and present' *Independent*

'A genuine contribution to history' *Daily Telegraph*

'Absorbing and devastating' *Observer*